MY LIFE AND TIMES
OCTAVE FOUR:
1907-1915

A

BY COMPTON MACKENZIE

Novels and Romances

SINISTER STREET
SYLVIA SCARLET
GUY AND PAULINE
CARNIVAL
FIGURE OF EIGHT
CORAL
THE VANITY GIRL
ROGUES AND VAGABONDS
THE ALTAR STEPS
THE PARSON'S PROGRESS
THE HEAVENLY LADDER
HUNTING THE FAIRIES
WHISKY GALORE
KEEP THE HOME GUARD TURNING
THE MONARCH OF THE GLEN
THE RIVAL MONSTER
THE RED TAPEWORM
ROCKETS GALORE
THE LUNATIC REPUBLIC
POOR RELATIONS
APRIL FOOLS
RICH RELATIVES
BUTTERCUPS AND DAISIES
WATER ON THE BRAIN
VESTAL FIRE
EXTRAORDINARY WOMEN
THIN ICE
EXTREMES MEET
THE THREE COURIERS
OUR STREET
THE DARKENING GREEN
THE PASSIONATE ELOPEMENT
FAIRY GOLD
THE SEVEN AGES OF WOMAN
PARADISE FOR SALE
THE FOUR WINDS OF LOVE:
    THE EAST WIND
    THE SOUTH WIND
    THE WEST WIND
    THE NORTH WIND
MEZZOTINT

Play

THE LOST CAUSE

Verse

POEMS 1907
KENSINGTON RHYMES

History and Biography

EASTERN EPIC. VOL. I
ALL OVER THE PLACE
GALLIPOLI MEMORIES
ATHENIAN MEMORIES
GREEK MEMORIES
AEGEAN MEMORIES
WIND OF FREEDOM
MR ROOSEVELT
DR BENES
PRINCE CHARLIE
PRINCE CHARLIE AND HIS LADIES
CATHOLICISM AND SCOTLAND
MARATHON AND SALAMIS
PERICLES
THE WINDSOR TAPESTRY
THE VITAL FLAME
I TOOK A JOURNEY
COALPORT
REALMS OF SILVER
THE QUEEN'S HOUSE
MY RECORD OF MUSIC
SUBLIME TOBACCO
GREECE IN MY LIFE
CATS' COMPANY
CATMINT

Essays and Criticism

ECHOES
A MUSICAL CHAIR
UNCONSIDERED TRIFLES
REAPED AND BOUND
LITERATURE IN MY TIME
ON MORAL COURAGE

Children's Stories

LITTLE CAT LOST
SANTA CLAUS IN SUMMER
TOLD
MABEL IN QUEER STREET
THE UNPLEASANT VISITORS
THE CONCEITED DOLL
THE ENCHANTED BLANKET
THE DINING-ROOM BATTLE
THE ADVENTURES OF TWO CHAIRS
THE ENCHANTED ISLAND
THE NAUGHTYMOBILE
THE FAIRY IN THE WINDOW BOX
THE STAIRS THAT KEPT ON GOING
    DOWN

Autobiography

MY LIFE AND TIMES: OCTAVE ONE
MY LIFE AND TIMES: OCTAVE TWO
MY LIFE AND TIMES: OCTAVE THREE

MY LIFE
AND TIMES

OCTAVE FOUR
1907-1915

Compton Mackenzie

1965
CHATTO & WINDUS
LONDON

Published by
Chatto & Windus Ltd
42 William IV Street
London, W.C. 2

*

Clarke, Irwin & Co. Ltd
Toronto

Printed in Great Britain by
T. & A. Constable Ltd
Hopetoun Street, Edinburgh

To an Octet
of octogenarian friends

CHRISTOPHER STONE,
MARTIN SECKER,
JOHN MAVROGORDATO
HARRY PIRIE-GORDON,
ORLO WILLIAMS,
GEORGE CHAMBERS,
FRANK SWINNERTON,
and ARTHUR RANSOME

ACKNOWLEDGMENTS

My grateful thanks for permission to quote unpublished material are due to the following: Mr John James of Cambridge, Massachusetts, for letters from Henry James; the Hon. Robert Gathorne-Hardy, for letters from Logan Pearsall Smith; Miss F. Quiller-Couch, for letters from Sir Arthur Quiller-Couch; Miss Imogen Holst, for a letter from Gustav Holst; Miss Daphne du Maurier, for a letter from Gerald du Maurier; Mr Julian Trevelyan, for a letter from R. C. Trevelyan; Messrs Kneale & Co. (notaries) and the literary heirs for a letter from Hall Caine; David Higham Associates, for a letter and telegrams from Sir Edward Marsh; William Heinemann Ltd, for a letter from William Heinemann, and to his estate for a letter from Sir Max Beerbohm. I must also thank the executors of Sir Edmund Gosse and William Heinemann Ltd for permission to quote a letter previously published in *The Life and Letters of Sir Edmund Gosse*.

I would like to offer my apologies to those literary heirs whom I have been unable to trace. I hope they will accept this general acknowledgment for material I have quoted.

Finally I have to thank Mr J. H. Martin for rescuing the photograph of Hamlet at Fowey and Mr J. Patterson for helping me check my reminiscence of General Sickles.

C.M.

CONTENTS

*

PLATES

*

I ENDED my previous Octave by sitting down in Cury Vicarage to start the ideal performance of my play *The Gentleman in Grey* by turning it into a novel called *Curtain Wells*. Almost exactly three years later, three months before it was to be published by Martin Secker, the title was changed to *The Passionate Elopement*.

By what I accepted at the time as a gift from Thalia, the Muse of Comedy, to whom throughout my life I have accorded greater reverence than to any of her eight sisters, Sandys Wason put into my hands a large album filled with cuttings from eighteenth-century journals and magazines; this was the commonplace book of one of his ancestors, and a treasury of information. I recapture now as I record it the thrill with which I found a tailor's bill from about 1750 and read in faded ink the account for a suit of figured Manchester velvet costing forty guineas. Nor was this the sum of the Muse's benevolence; among a few odd volumes in a Helston junk-shop I found, two or three days later, a copy of Christopher Anstey's *New Bath Guide*, a delicious light satire in verse which struck for me the very note I wanted for Beau Ripple, as much the autocrat of Curtain Wells as Beau Nash had been of Bath. Devoted as I was in youth to *Roderick Random* and *Peregrine Pickle*, I had never read *Humphrey Clinker* and not until many years later was I to realize how much Smollett owed to the *New Bath Guide*; I confess to a faint gratification at finding myself a fellow-debtor with Tobias Smollett.

Every afternoon at five o'clock I lighted those two candles with red shades and wrote away with a copying-ink pencil until dinner-time, which occasionally might be at eight but more usually was much later to accommodate Wason's genius as a cook. By the middle of January 1908 I had written about a quarter of the longish novel that *Curtain Wells* was to be. That is enough for the present about that first novel of mine; I have disliked talking about books I have written or am planning to write ever since that first novel was published on my twenty-eighth birthday in January 1911. The least agreeable prospect in the Octaves that remain to be written is that of talking about what will be over a hundred books when *My Life and Times* is complete.

By the time Faith and I arrived as paying guests at Cury Vicarage dear Wason had managed to empty the church of any congregation it ever had by what in those days was called ritualism. The Methodist farmers of the parish liked to have their children baptized in the church and looked forward to being married there and buried in the church- yard; except for the harvest festival they never attended a service. Wason had enraged them by appointing as his warden a farm-labourer called Martin who with his wife and two small children were his only supporters in Cury Churchtown, a small straggling village, the princi- pal feature of which was the rural sorting office at Cury Cross Lanes. As well as being his churchwarden, Martin served Wason at the altar and swung a thurible when called upon.

Gunwalloe, the other village of Wason's living, was incomparably more attractive both as a village and for the people who lived in it. The church is the only one I have seen where the churchyard wall is washed by the sea at high tide. It was sheltered from the full fury of the south-west gales by a rocky headland known as the Castle, to which was tacked the ancient tower separated from the church itself. Legend said the reason for this separation was that two Breton princesses who had been saved from a shipwreck each wanted to express her own gratitude to God—one by building a church, the other by building a tower. On the south side of Gunwalloe cove the cliffs on which the Poldhu wireless station had been built rose up about two hundred feet. There, too, was a large hotel, full of visitors in summer who came mostly to enjoy the golf on the towans, as the sweep of sand-dunes rising up to Cury were called. Beyond Gunwalloe church the road climbed to the summit of the Helzephron cliffs, whence it ran gradu- ally down to the village, a mile and a half north. Gunwalloe village was compact and picturesque; I at once put an eye on a four-roomed thatched cottage in a state of disrepair and resolved to ask the land- lord's agent what chance there was of putting it in order and giving me a lease.

At the same time I had cast an eye on a small house at the southern edge of the Helzephron cliffs. This belonged to a Captain Sich who had a passion for golf and gardening. Sich was a member of the brewing family in Chiswick and the chief figure of the Cury golf club, over the pavilion of which he could be said to preside. He had been warden to the previous vicar but had resigned his office in protest against Wason's ritualistic excesses. He was probably more worried about the effect of incense upon the golfing visitors in the summer than upon the parish- ioners of Cury. He was a short, sallow man with a carefully tended dark moustache, married to a plump and discontented blonde who always made the most of the slightest headache to persuade him to give up that house he had built on the edge of Helzephron cove. I felt that Mrs Sich might in the end be successful and was more than anxious to acquire that cottage in Gunwalloe so that if Sich's house came into the market a couple of years hence I should be the first in the field either as a purchaser or a tenant. My sanguine temperament was as incurable in 1907 as it remains to-day.

It seemed to me the perfect house, built on one floor round a square patio. Two sides provided the living accommodation; the other two sides were respectively a heated and an unheated greenhouse with blank walls behind, built to exclude the wind. The great attraction, however, of Sich's house was the extraordinary garden he had made for himself down the fall of the 300-feet high Helzephron cliffs in the teeth of the gales sweeping into Mount's Bay from the Atlantic. Artificial shelter was afforded by hurdles and lathing into which had been woven dozens and dozens of the straw covers made for wine-bottles. As the member of a brewing family Sich may have been able to obtain these straw covers more easily than most people; they were certainly better able to resist the wear and tear of the wind than loose straw would have been. The tops of those shelters, each of which was about the size of an ordinary room, were covered with glass; how those glass roofs were held in place I have forgotten.

In this queer jumble of what from the outside looked like a rubbish chute poured over the edge grew some astonishing plants to see in flower, even on a Cornish cliff. Among others I remember a prodigally blooming pink *Justicia carnea* (I believe it is called *Jacobinia* nowadays) from Brazil and a *Hoya carnosa* apparently as much at home as in its native Queensland. Sich used to travel all round the world, bringing back unusual plants, the names of which he never could remember accurately; being at this date a novice of sub-tropical gardening, I shall not risk mentioning any more of Sich's astonishing collection.

Beyond the Helzephron cliffs the road ran down almost to sea-level past the Helzephron Inn kept by a retired petty officer with a full white beard, a limp and a very bad temper, named Ransome. The Helzephron Inn reminded me of the *Admiral Benbow* immortalized by R.L.S. Ransome was the verger of Gunwalloe church, which he regarded as his private property. Wason had made an enemy of him by putting in a stone altar designed by Comper and substituting chairs for the old box-pews. The previous incumbent had used Ransome as a clerk and he much resented being deprived of his part in the services and what he considered Wason's profanation of morning prayer by concentrating on the Communion service. Wason's hastily mumbled

Matins half an hour before the Communion service began upset Sich, who felt the golfing visitors would be offended.

"They're used to Matins and the first part of the Communion service with the sermon. A few, of course, will stay on for the second service, which is what they're used to doing at home," Sich would protest.

Wason refused to compromise.

For my part Ransome was the very landlord I would have wished for the Helzephron Inn; when he was in the right mood he could discourse eloquently about the Royal Navy of his youth and recall vividly various naval occasions. He seemed to me like a character in Q's romance *Dead Man's Rock*. I suppose no young people read *Dead Man's Rock* to-day. I was lucky enough to be born in time to be spellbound by it, just as I was lucky enough to be born in time to be spellbound by the long tale of wrecks along that west coast of the Meneage, as the Lizard peninsula is called.

Beyond the coastguard's station at Gunwalloe stretched the long beach that ended at Porthleven. "On one side lay the Ocean, and on one/Lay a great water"; on one side was the great water of the Looe Pool, on the other side was the expanse of Mount's Bay opening to the Atlantic beyond. It was from the Looe Pool that Arthur received Excalibur; nothing in all Cornwall could offer so much romantic beauty as the wooded slopes around it and above it. A hundred yards out in Mount's Bay one could look into its depth at a low spring tide and see the *Primrose*, sloop of war, sunk a century before. She would sometimes swing over in the undertow and one could see her guns swing with her from starboard to port or from port to starboard. If a south-east gale was followed almost at once by a south-west gale there was always a chance of picking up on that long stretch of beach a doubloon from the wreck of an Armada ship. Even in those days they were worth £8, 10s. solely for that square of gold. One of those doubloons used to turn up about every other year.

In 1906 the great liner *Suevic* was wrecked at the Lizard and people were still talking about the riches with which her cargo rewarded those who had tramped from all over Cornwall to see what they could get hold of. The *Suevic* had the same attraction as thirty-five years later the *Politician* with her golden cargo of whisky would have for the Western Isles. Wool had been part of the *Suevic's* cargo and I was told tales of how by muffling the wheels of the waggons many a bale had avoided the attentions of the excisemen and been safely stored away in Helston cellars. I decided it was time that I had a try at the fruit of a wreck.

During the Peninsular War the *Susan and Rebecca*, a transport bringing home troopers of the 4th Light Dragoons, had been wrecked in Helzephron cove; owing to the men's putting the gold they brought back with them from Spain in their helmets many were drowned, and their bodies had been hauled up the cliff and buried at the top of it; the mounds were still visible. Two of the village lads approached me to find out if I would stand by while they dug down to find if the gold was still in what by now would have been the helmets of skeletons. I was compliant, and on a night at November's end I met the two lads by the graves. They had brought with them a couple of long-handled Cornish spades, which in 1907 were used throughout the Duchy. I have not revisited Cornwall during the last fifty years and do not know if the short-handled spade of the rest of Great Britain has displaced the Cornish spade; I hope not.

It was a windless night and quite dark when we met for our macabre task, but as the waning moon rose above the great sweep of Goonhilly Down a little breeze began to whisper among the clumps of that tall Cornish heather (*Erica vagans*) which grows in Britain only on the magnesian soil of the Lizard peninsula. The coincidence of that moonrise with the whispering breeze was fatal to the courage of the two diggers. They believed they were surrounded by the ghosts of those dead Light Dragoons and, throwing down the long-handled spades, they fled to the safety of their village. And that was the last attempt to disturb those skeletons.

The decision I had made after the publication of that volume of poems to turn to prose was not changed by the various laudatory reviews I was given. That valuable slating in *Country Life* which I quoted in my last Octave remained the most influential.

The following letter from Logan Pearsall Smith reinforced that decision, although it was the last thing that Logan intended:

Court Place
Iffley
Oxford

Nov. 23, 1907.
My dear Monty,
    Bob Trevelyan asked me to send you the enclosed.
    How are you getting on? I haven't heard from you or of you for some time. I don't know whether I wrote to say how much I like the look of your "Poems" in print. You have a genuine and rich gift, and I hope you are cultivating it. I quite often hear people in Oxford say they have your book, and read and re-read it.
    Wotton is out and is being far more favourably received and reviewed than I

had ever expected, or than I secretly think it deserves. There is a review by H. A. L. Fisher in to-day's "Nation" and another in to-day's "Spectator" that really make me blush.

The next allusion is to Christopher Stone's novel *Scars* which had just been published by Heinemann. It was the best novel he ever wrote. Desmond MacCarthy, its godfather, confidently predicted a future for Christopher as a novelist.

What do you think of "Scars"? It is very different from what I expected and much better. I think it shows real objective power, but of course it is too hasty. The thing to do is to give years of patient labour and meditation to a book and to put all one's best and only one's best into it, and then you get your reward, and more than your reward. "Success" as Trollope says somewhere "is a necessary evil, lucky the man to whom it comes late in life."

Let me have your news.

Yours ever

Logan Pearsall Smith

The enclosure from R. C. Trevelyan was a letter to Logan about my poems, the first part of which, largely complimentary, I quoted in Octave One. It continued thus:

"The Hill of Death" does not seem to me quite to come off and I can't quite say why. I suppose the short poems and sonnets are the most successful, for on that scale he has a good deal of feeling for form; but they interest me less than the long ones. I always find love-poems difficult to appreciate unless they are by great masters, and not always then, and C.M. is not a great master yet; though I hope he will be some day. On the whole what seems to me most unsatisfactory is not so much his form or the style as his subject matter, which is, I suppose, very modern and interesting, but somehow seems a little thin as a rule. I think it is a great pity that young poets don't exercise themselves upon classical subjects, at least to some extent; not because such subjects are necessarily better than others, but because when we are young we simply cannot possibly have enough good material for poetry of our own, and it is wiser to take some at least from those who came before us. All the great masters, except Wordsworth, and in part Shelley did so: Keats, Shakespeare, Milton, Chaucer and old Mat. all learnt their trade by practising upon old Classical myths and ideas. Even Browning, except in Pauline, took his material from elsewhere and did not spin it out of himself. Wordsworth no doubt did, but then he had, as they say, a message to deliver to the world; in fact he had rather too much than too little material. But C.M., so far as I can see, has no message for the world (not that he's any the worse for that), and at present is interesting only as an artist, and the fatal thing for an artist is to have a lot of materials.

However these random considerations and doubts don't amount to much, I dare
say. He certainly ought to do something really good some day, if he is wise.
Kindest remembrances from us both.

Yours ever,

R. C. Trevelyan

I was naturally grateful to Trevelyan for bothering to pay so much
attention to my poems and wrote to him accordingly; within a day or
two he replied and I have no doubt that it was getting letters like his
and others I shall quote which implanted in me a resolve always,
within physical possibility, to pay attention to the work of men younger
than myself.

The Shiffields
Holmbury St Mary
Dorking
12 *Dec.* 1907

Dear Mackenzie,
   I had not intended Logan to send you my letter; otherwise I should have been
less off-hand in some of my criticisms. However I am not sorry he did so, as the
result has been your letter, which interested me a great deal. I think I understand,
more or less, some of your difficulties, and sympathise with much of what you say.
Advice is always dangerous; but if I were to venture on any, it would be not to
worry too much about what even the most intelligent critics say (I include myself
among them) with regard to choice of subject matter etc., and (though perhaps
their criticism is likely to be more helpful) with regard to style, diction and so on.
It is clear that potentially all kinds of subject matter are good, whether modern
or Classical, subjective or objective . . . the only important problem is how to
make the most of your material, whatever it is, and to find the form and style that
will express it most effectively. Only of course some subject matter on the whole
suits one person better than another; and it may well be for instance, that Classi-
cal subjects are not the ideal material for you. But then I am sure that no artist
was ever the worse for making experiments in directions not quite natural to him,
even if unsuccessful in them. One learns no end of things by taking a subject that
requires a treatment not natural to one, or with which one is not bitterly familiar,
and I am sure most artists suffer from not boldly enough experimenting in all
directions. The chief advantage of Classical subjects is that one has ready to hand
an almost endless variety of dramatic or narrative themes for experimenting upon
in almost any form or mood you choose, Miltonic, Aristophanic, Keatsian, or for
aught I know Tolstoian and Shawesque; and the more wide the range of such
experiments have been the more completely one will be able to express one's own
personality (whatever that means) in the end. One's own personality certainly
does mean something, but after all it can only reveal itself by the way it treats

B

other things different to itself, and the more various those are, the more fully will it do so. But I don't know why I should preach like this, as I don't practise it myself much, and any truth there is in what I say you must know already. Anyhow I certainly do not wish to discourage you from treating either modern or subjective subjects (to use two vague and tiresome phrases), for you certainly have shown that you can do so with a good deal of success already. I did not care for everything in the Chelsea bridge poem, but much of it was very interesting, and you use the terza rima form admirably, it seems to me; and the last unrhymed line I found very effective. I do not see at all why you should not write very good blank-verse. Rhymed verse in more or less strict form is, I believe, far the best training for writing blank-verse (you have a truly vital sense of movement, which is absolutely essential in blank-verse) can, I am sure, be best learnt by writing in strict rhyming forms; and I should say you had learnt that already. No doubt you would find it difficult at first, but I am sure you would succeed in the end, so long as you were determined not to fall into tricks and easy formulas like Swinburne for example. Of course blank-verse does not suit all poetical material equally well; but then some of the finest poetical ideas can hardly be expressed as well in any other way, and a really fine dramatic subject of the right kind would almost compel you of itself to write fine blank-verse. After all no verse is exactly good in itself, but only because it expresses its content in the best way possible. But this is so large a subject, that one cannot discuss it in a letter. I hope some day we can meet again and could then talk over some of these things. I should like to persuade you to come and see me here for a few days if possible, and my wife and I will be very glad if you would propose yourself whenever you liked. . . . I should be very glad if I could get you to criticize as severely as you like some of my unpublished work—for I hardly ever get any criticism from others who are also writing poetry, and that is just the most useful kind.

What you say about the indifference and real ignorance of cultured people with regard to poetry is true enough: but I don't think one ought to bother too much about that. Good work almost always gets recognized in the end, and sooner than one sometimes thinks, I imagine. Still no doubt the most original work, even if partially successful, is never really understood for a long time, and then only by a few. I don't think we ought to let that disconcert us, though it is sometimes trying; and certainly it ought not to be allowed to affect one's work, either by playing down to the public's level, or in disgust playing out of sight and hearing of them. "Art for art's sake" is not a bad motto, though it has been vilely misapplied and abused. If you would care to come, do let me know. I shall be at Oxford next Sunday and hope to see Logan. I thought his book very good, though I have not finished it yet.

Yours sincerely,

R. C. Trevelyan

I read through that long letter and marvel how even so lovable a man as Robert Calverley Trevelyan could have been bothered to give himself so much trouble over the work of a man eleven years younger than himself. The poem about Chelsea Bridge, which is 167 lines long, may be read in an appendix; in due course Henry James would consider it the most promising poem in that volume of mine and Quiller-Couch would condemn it as one of which he disapproved.

Money was so short at this time that I could not afford the railway fare from Cornwall to Surrey. Later on when I had surrendered to prose I felt that Trevelyan, who throughout a long life never gave up writing poetry, would not be interested in work of mine and would not suppose I could be usefully interested in work of his own. He was overshadowed by his younger brother, George Macaulay Trevelyan, but he left behind him a fine body of verse including some admirable translations from the Greek tragic poets and Lucretius.

When Trevelyan wrote to me at Cury I was still not sure whether the writing of that first novel of mine was going to be an achievement or an unprofitable diversion from play-writing. Soon after I received that letter I had an experience which sent my mind back to the drama. I was walking back from Gunwalloe on the edge of a gusty twilight when I met a farmer I knew. He was a tall gaunt dark man, a prominent figure in the Methodist congregation but not a local preacher.

"You've been away quite a while," I said.

"Ess, ess, I was up along to London. I got myself married there."

"You did, did you? I thought it was the show at the Agricultural Hall you went up to see. Congratulations."

"I came home along yesterday. Did you ever hear tell of a place they do call the Leicester Lounge?"

"I used to know it well once upon a time."

I did not add that it was hardly the resort in which I should expect to find a teetotaller and pillar of Gunwalloe's Methodist congregation. I could not imagine anybody more out of place than he would have seemed among the ladies of the town who sat at every table.

"I married one of the barmaids to the Leicester Lounge. It was quick work by special licence at a registry office as they do call it. Would 'ee like to meet my missus and have a cup of tay with us?"

I accepted his invitation with alacrity, so curious was I to see this barmaid who had been persuaded to exchange the noise and glitter of the Leicester Lounge for the quiet of a small Cornish farm five miles from a railway station.

We turned off from the road and walked along the rough track that led to the farm-house in the middle of the fifty windswept acres cultivated by this farmer whose name I have forgotten. It was dark when we reached the small farm-house.

"How are 'ee sitting without a lamp, my handsome?" her husband exclaimed in a tone that was meant to be jovial but only succeeded in sounding gruff.

"I was waiting for you to light the lamp," a sad Cockney voice replied.

The farmer struck a match and lighted a paraffin lamp without a shade.

"This is Mr Mackenzie who used to know the Leicester Lounge. Maybe he's seen you there."

She rose and offered me a limp hand.

"Pleased to meet you," she murmured, and quickly sat down again at the table, plucking at the cloth with her fingers.

"Well, aren't 'ee going to offer Mr Mackenzie a cup of tay, Dolly? I showed 'ee where we do keep the clomb."

She rose again and moved in an uncertain way toward the cupboard where the crockery was.

"And what have 'ee been doing to the slab? There's hardly enough fire to boil the kettle."

He went across to put more coal on the feeble embers in the range.

I looked at that plumpish woman with a full head of peroxide curls and asked myself what on earth could have persuaded her to marry this gaunt farmer and leave London. I tried hard to make her talk; she answered in monosyllables. Her eyes were blank, neither sad nor puzzled, merely blank. She seemed utterly lost in this kitchen, and as the rising wind began to moan round the farm-house the blankness of her eyes was lighted for a moment by fear.

On my way back to the Vicarage at Cury I began to weave a story round that lost plumpish woman somewhere in her late twenties with that full head of peroxide curls. I decided she must have had an unhappy love-affair and that in her desire to cut herself utterly off from the past she must have accepted that Cornish farmer's offer of marriage. By now she must be repenting of what she had done. She must be realizing that she could never adapt herself to this strange new life. What a play her story would make! But it would have to wait until I was more familiar with the Cornish dialect; the Cockney thanks to my dramatization of *Kipps* would be easy. I might make Hampshire the rural setting; no, Hampshire was not far enough away from London.

A week later that lost peroxided London nymph fled back to London to escape the teetotal satyr who had carried her away. My meeting with her that evening remained in my mind; over three years hence I would build upon that inexplicable marriage my novel *Carnival*.

Early in that December I met for the first time an outstanding personality. This was Bernard Walke. I was delighted to find somebody with every one of whose ideas I was myself in sympathy and who himself was in equal sympathy with all of mine. He came for the night with Wason from Truro where they had been taking part in an Advent retreat.

"I hope you won't do what X—did to me last year, Walke," Wason said to him.

"What was that?"

"Why, I spent a night with him at — and after I'd been in bed for about an hour there was a knock at the door and X— entered fussily in his nightgown, with a candlestick. 'Get up, get up, Wason,' he said. I thought the house must be on fire, and jumped out of bed. 'It's twelve o'clock,' said X—. 'Time to change beds.' And before I could say a word he had jumped into my bed and blown out the candle."

"What on earth did you do?" we asked.

"There was nothing to do except find my way somehow in the dark to X—'s bedroom and get into X—'s bed," Wason told us.

Walke laughed.

"Our brethren think you and I are lunatics," he said. "I'm glad to hear of one of them who is madder than either of us."

Somehow that evening the conversation turned to capital punishment and I was glad to hear Walke was as much against it as myself.

"Look," he said suddenly. "Come back with me to-morrow to Polruan and I'll arrange for you to give a talk about capital punishment to my chaps in our mission hall. I'll try and get old Trusted to take the chair."

Trusted was the vicar of Lanteglos of which parish Polruan was a mission. Trusted was a rich elderly bachelor entirely preoccupied with the restoration of Lanteglos church, on which he had spent and was still spending a great deal of money. His pastoral duties in that small village in the depth of the country were not arduous enough to interrupt his preoccupation with his lovely old church: the life of his parish was concentrated in Polruan, which on the whole he left in Bernard Walke's care without interference, although occasionally sending him a reproachful note about what he considered an excessive display of Anglo-Catholicism.

That first crossing of the ferry from Fowey to Polruan made a deep

impression on me which I tried to preserve in a poem I scribbled that
night in Walke's house.

> Voices over the water,
> Starshine over the sea,
> Oars that dip to the water
> As the ferry-boat ferries me
> Over the shining water
> Into the shining town.
> Huddled we sit in the ferry-boat,
> Each one wearing a crown,
> Wearing a crown of starshine
> To circle a beating heart,
> Hearts that beat as the ferry-boat
> Ferries us far apart.
> Each one loves his neighbour,
> Fain would clasp his hand,
> Dreads the moment of parting
> And the looming shadow of land.
> Voices over the water,
> Starshine over the sea,
> A star in every window-pane
> And a star in the heart of me.

To-day the emotion roused by the rhythmic sound of oars will sound
very sentimental to those who cross the ferry between Fowey and Polruan by motor-boat.

Bernard Walke's small house in the middle of Polruan was a most
uncomfortable lodging. His stipend as curate-in-charge of the mission
was £150 a year, of which he did not feel justified in spending a penny
more than £50 on himself, his household or his comforts. The rest of it
was almost all given away to relieve the needs of his many poor parishioners. When I look back to that Francis of Assisi attitude of his
toward his people I feel ashamed to mention that the bed in which I
slept had broken springs, that the mattress was leaking wool, that the
plug in the water-closet seldom worked, that there was not so much as
a mat on any floor, that the elderly woman who looked after his domestic affairs was so rheumatic that she could never get down to scrubbing the bare floors or reach up to brush away the cobwebs in the
corners of every room, that the food she prepared was almost uneatable
and that except for an hour or two in the middle of the night there
was continuous noise inside and outside the house. The discomfort did

not seem to matter in that flow of fellowship which made the abode of that bedraggled and drafty interior warm and comfortable. I have written in previous Octaves of Robert Dolling; Bernard Walke had the same gift of love for the poor, the same burning devotion to the example of Jesus Christ.

In an old notebook are some notes for the talk I was giving to Walke's club on capital punishment, and I find I was using every argument that is being used to-day, when the abolition of capital punishment has many more supporters than it had in 1907. There is one argument that I have not heard used except by myself, which for me is one of the most powerful. In 1907 I put it forward without the weight of evidence with which I can reinforce it to-day. Among the most precious volumes in my library are all the Old Bailey session-papers which provided our predecessors with the weekly reading they would later on obtain from the *News of the World*. Bound volumes of those session-papers are very scarce and it has taken me years to complete my records of the eighteenth century and earliest years of the nineteenth century. When the penal laws were at their fiercest it was death for larceny over thirty-nine shillings and for breaking and entering or for hold-ups by footpads or highwaymen over five shillings. Therefore it was clearly to the interest of the footpad or highwayman to kill the man he robbed because it was the victim who could provide almost the only incriminating evidence against him. Nevertheless, throughout a century and a quarter there are scarcely any murders by footpads or highwaymen even although so many of them might have escaped Tyburn if instead of saying "your money or your life" they had taken the life first and the money afterwards. That being an easily established fact, how can it be argued that capital punishment is a deterrent? The highwayman who was a killer killed; the great majority of highwaymen were not killers, even when it was much to their advantage to kill. In 1907 I was only familiar with the Newgate Calendar but I was already asking myself why so few highwaymen were murderers.

Bernard Walke was enthusiastic about my idea of becoming a lay-reader, and when I got back to Cury I made a formal application.

On December 21st I was writing to my father-in-law:

There is a most intolerable lot of red tape about Lay Readerships, and you are supposed to take an elementary exam. in Maclear's text-books of Scripture. I have not seen them since the Fourth Form at school. I have written to say that a second in History and the passing of Divinity Moderations ought to be enough. . . . I've written 100 pages of my novel. At the present rate of progress it will be a 400-

page book at least. I've also started a book of fairy-stories in the Hans Andersen school of fairy thought. . . .

As for Blake I think him in some ways our greatest poet. How the 18th century produced him I cannot pretend to guess. He belongs to an age in advance even of our own.

Just after Christmas I was invited to lunch by the Bishop of Truro, at Lis Escop, the episcopal "palace". Dr C. W. Stubbs had succeeded the saintly Bishop Wilkinson in 1906; he had been Dean of Ely. Mrs Stubbs bemoaned the move; Lis Escop was so new after the Deanery.

"And our lovely garden there. Oh dear, this is such a sad come down," she sighed.

Full of ambition to go in for sub-tropical gardening after I had seen Sich's collection, I tried to paint the possibilities of the Lis Escop garden for Mrs Stubbs; she refused to be consoled for the loss of the Deanery garden in Ely.

The Bishop was friendly and agreed to my being licensed as a lay-reader. He was doubtful whether it would be possible to give me a special licence to preach in church because the Chancellor of the diocese disapproved of such a licence; the eloquence must be confined to mission halls. However, presently I was given that special licence.

In the first week of January 1908 I was formally "ordained" as a lay-reader in the cathedral of Truro; I have completely forgotten any detail of the ceremony, by which I could not have been much impressed.

To my mother I wrote:

I am starting a Sunday school run on my own lines—almost as much like an ordinary Sunday school as a pig to a pea.

TWENTY-FIVE YEARS OLD: 1908

I STARTED my Sunday school with three children; on January 27th I was writing to my father-in-law:

I had 9 children last Sunday. So the percentage is going up. My Sunday school is rather a secular affair in some ways, but I don't think small children can have too much high theology at a stretch. I asked one of the Methodist children in the village to show me one of the questions she had been asked in her Sunday school.

It happened to be "What is God?" And the approved answer was to be, "God is a Spirit Who always has been and always will be."

So far as I can see, such a definition to the mind of a little girl of six could only connote a sort of immortal whisky. Could anything be more intolerably remote from anything in the nature of real instruction?

Did you see Bishop Mitchinson's letter in Saturday's "Times" in favour of secular education? Very sound, I thought. Certainly anything would be better than the pretentious jargon quoted above. . . . Have you read "Lord of the World" by Hugh Benson? It is grossly sensational, but is a clever bit of propaganda in its assumption that Humanitarianism and Catholicism will struggle for the supremacy of thought with more than rhetorical weapons a hundred years hence. Christianity of the professional type seems bent on destroying itself just now.

But I have great hopes from the Modernists and the Christian Socialists. Christianity should mean Humanitarianism pace Hugh Benson.

Those first three scholars of mine were Lily and Nellie Francis, the daughters of the coastguard, and Leslie Williams, the only child of Mr and Mrs Williams who kept the village shop.

Leslie was lame, a boy of temperament and originality, eleven years old. His parents, much as they sometimes deplored what was considered Wason's eccentricity, religious and social, were passionately loyal to him, and never criticized him, except to me in the hope of my being able to persuade him to humour his conservative parishioners. In front of John Williams' shop was a sizable vegetable garden entered by a wicket-gate the latch of which was broken, so that John always had to untie the string with which it was tied before it could be opened for a visitor.

"You ought to get this gate mended, John," I said to him one day.

"Dash it, old Bray has been going to mend that gate for nine years and he's never done it yet," said John, shaking his head. Old Bray was the village carpenter. Much of my life has been spent with people devoted to *mañana*—in Capri, in Greece, in the Hebrides, and one of the pleasures of my old age has been to find in south-west France a countryside where to-morrow rules again. Yet that nine-years-old to-morrow of old Bray remains a record.

John Williams' wife, thin, dark, was passionately unable to believe that anybody else in Gunwalloe or Cury was capable of being as disinterested in their support of the Vicar as herself and John. Luckily she gave me her complete confidence; therefore I was often able to smooth out some of the jealousies that were inevitable in that remote and isolated community. Mrs Williams' particular resentment was Miss Freeman, the sister of John Freeman, a burly bearded farmer of simple integrity whom Wason had made his churchwarden. Miss Freeman was always well-dressed and, as it seemed to some of her neighbours, too excessively "ladylike". She had been a school teacher before she came to keep house for her brother when he was widowed. She never missed a parish gathering or a treat, at which her vein of quiet reserve made the other women accuse her of giving herself airs. No doubt she was entitled to remain aloof from minor squabbles, but I used to wish she would not always speak with such obviously patient charity about the weaknesses of others. Indeed, when I went to tea with her in that immaculate farmhouse I ventured once or twice to imply a faint criticism of her attitude; that patiently charitable smile and that scrupulously neat head of grey hair would be turned on me, and I would sympathize with Mrs Williams.

My other two scholars, Lily and Nellie Francis, were then aged eight and six, both with very pink cheeks and very blue eyes. Their father the coastguard, whose job it was to patrol between Porthleven and Gunwalloe church cove, was a delightful man with an equally delightful wife. Mrs Francis produced an infant son in that spring of 1908.

In 1949 she must have written to me after some broadcast and I received from her the following letter from Swansea after my acknowledgment of her card:

It was nice to hear from you, I was quite excited. . . . Well, I must tell you some of my life. We started here in Wales. I nursed in this district for 36 years, when I retired. I got on very well and brought nearly 3000 babies into the world with very little loss of life.

I did a bit of nursing through the war in the hospital. Unfortunately I lost my husband in 1927. We did miss him.

Lily has not married but she has a good job, travelling supervisor for the G.P.O. She is often away for days at a time.

Jack is married, he has one daughter. We had him away in Denbigh Sanatorium for 4 years, but he is strong now. Nellie is married. She has a boy and a girl. She is very comfortably off. Also, there is Sybil, born here in Wales. She also is married with two girls and is very comfortable.

So in my old age, I can always thank God that we met you in Cornwall. Without your help I don't really know what we should have done. Lily and Nellie remember you.

I went over to Jersey after the liberation because my sister was there all through the occupation of the Germans. She wanted me to go over and stay with her for the duration but I tried too late and I could not get permission to go but I got a permit as soon as the war was over. She had a rotten time with the Germans. I stayed with her until she died. The Germans sent her solicitor to the camps and murdered him. So I had an awful time there, fighting for her and her property. She lived on for nearly 12 months after I won the case but she was too weak for me to bring her back. So now I am quite settled. You would like it here in Wales.

I am afraid I am writing too much. Yet I don't feel I have told you half enough.

The children were very excited about your letter.

Thanking you for all past kindnesses,
        from
        Yours very sincerely,
            L. Francis

P.S. Do you remember a bottle washed ashore from a ship? A boy brought it and my own brother was one who had helped to put the message in the bottle.

In 1909 it was decided to abolish the coastguard station in Gunwalloe and let the two cottages at once. As I remember, I wrote one or two strong letters to the authorities and managed to get the immediate departure of the Francis family postponed until they could move directly to George Francis' next job. I have included the story about her sister in Jersey because for me a simple unadorned tale like that of what a German occupation meant in the last war is more impressive than any amount of piled-up horrors. I have to be thankful that Providence ruled I should leave the Channel Islands before that unimaginable occupation of the future. I had forgotten the strange coincidence of that bottle's being washed ashore and brought to the home of the sister of one of those who had put their names inside it.

I have not yet mentioned the indomitable Miss Gleig. She was a granddaughter of the Reverend George Robert Gleig who fought as an Ensign in the 85th regiment at Waterloo, after which he took holy orders, and in time became Chaplain-General to the Forces. He wrote many successful books, including a popular life of the Duke of Wellington, whom he had known, and he lived to be ninety-six years old. Miss Gleig had met Wason in one of his curacies and had made up her mind he must be protected maternally by herself. So when he obtained the living of Cury *cum* Gunwalloe she had followed him to Cornwall.

Wason had stipulated that Miss Gleig must not live in Cury but find rooms in Gunwalloe. Here she lived in a semi-detached little villa which was sadly out of keeping with the thatched cottages on either side of it. Her devoted companion was a collie called Rover, and with him in any weather between six o'clock in the morning and nine o'clock at night she was liable to turn up on her bicycle at the Vicarage. She was about forty-five years old with a weather-beaten complexion, a gaunt clumsy figure and inexhaustible vitality. Wason used to get rather bored by her turning up on stormy evenings with a local problem she was inviting him to solve.

"She must be frightened off calling on us at night," he declared.

"You'll never frighten Miss Gleig," I assured him. "She's as indomitable as that grandfather of hers must have been."

Leonard Dunstan, the son of a Helston tailor, used to come to Cury every week and play the harmonium at the service attended by a congregation of never more than six people.

"You must dress up as a ghost, Leonard," said Wason, "and frighten her when she's wheeling her bicycle up the drive."

So one evening Leonard Dunstan was draped in a sheet and his face made phosphorescent. He stood in the shrubbery beside the drive and made what he thought were suitably ghostly gestures at Miss Gleig.

Rover's tail went between his legs but Miss Gleig peered into the gloom with her short-sighted eyes.

"I can't just see who it is," she said. "But whoever it is is going to catch a bad cold."

And on she went to lean her bicycle against the side of the Vicarage and knock at the door.

One afternoon I had just arrived in Gunwalloe when from the steps of the villa in which she lived Miss Gleig called out to ask me if I would come in and advise her what she was to do.

"I'm in despair," she moaned. "Mr Y— is coming along to shoot Rover. What am I to do?"

I went in and found poor Miss Gleig in almost a frenzy of nerves, her weather-beaten face twitching with apprehension.

"Mr Y— says Rover has killed one of his sheep and I offered to pay for it, but he won't listen. He says Rover must be shot and he's coming along presently to shoot him."

Y— whose name I have forgotten was a red-headed, foxy-faced, swaggering farmer who had recently got a half-witted servant girl of his in the family way and allowed his wife to turn her out of the house. I told Miss Gleig I would wait and talk to Mr Y—.

In due course Y— arrived with a gun under his arm.

"Oh, Mr Y—, Mr Y—," Miss Gleig wailed. "Please, please don't shoot Rover!"

I cut in.

"I'll talk to Mr Y—." I turned to him. "You say Miss Gleig's dog killed one of your sheep. What witness have you got?"

"I saw the dog chasing it," Y— declared.

"Yes, but you have quite a reputation as a liar, haven't you, Mr Y—?"

"What do 'ee mean?"

"I mean exactly what I say. You collected a lot of louts to stone Mr Wason last year and you lied yourself out of that, didn't you? And now you've got that wretched half-witted girl of yours in the family way and tried to lie your way out of that. You're a blackguard, Mr Y—, in spite of your red hair, and if you dare to shoot Rover or try to extract money out of Miss Gleig under false pretences I'll make your name stink all over Cornwall. Hasn't your own minister made you resign whatever job you held in the chapel? Now get out with that gun of yours."

I was glad when Mr Y— did get out; if he had refused I should have looked rather foolish.

When he was gone I told Miss Gleig that whether Rover was guilty or not she must never let him out alone in future.

The next recruits to the Sunday school were from the Bolitho family. Bolitho himself was a depressed carroty little labourer on whatever farm in turn called for his services. His wife, fair, voluble, spectacled and feckless, had borne him a large family in fifteen years, of whom seven had survived. They lived in a half-furnished four-roomed cottage, the thatched roof and the walls of which were in a state of leaky disrepair owing to the fact that it had been leased for a term of three lives by which it was held, the last of which was that of an old woman in Helston verging on eighty. When she died, the cottage would revert to the Penrose estate. Meanwhile, the present owner, one of the local farmers, did not see his way to repair it for the benefit of a man he esteemed less than a distant savage.

Bolitho earned thirteen shillings and sixpence a week; in August his

two eldest sons, Charlie and Ernie, aged fourteen and thirteen, sometimes earned between them as caddies on the links as much as ten
shillings in the week, but for the rest of the year no more than an odd
shilling occasionally. In spite of their poverty and the miserable cottage
from which they were liable to be evicted as soon as the old woman in
Helston died they were, except for Bolitho himself, a cheerful family.
The children, most of them orange-headed like their father and sub-
sisting almost entirely on bread and a jam made from a certain kind of
seaweed, were in spite of that the jolliest children in Gunwalloe.

Beatrice, the eldest of my first scholars, was the same age as Leslie
Williams. Her sister Bessie, aged nine, was in her own words to me on
one occasion as happy as a piece of gold. She had a much more force-
ful personality than her elder sister, Beattie; indeed, she dominated all
the other children in that small parish-hall where the Sunday school
was held. Her younger brother Alec, aged eight, would sometimes try
to rebel; Bessie always won any verbal contest.

My greatest pleasure in that Sunday school was the company of
these children on walks with them either inland or along the cliffs or
by the shore. I made a great point of trying to inculcate kindness to
beasts, birds and even insects. If birds-nesting was done it was to be
done with consideration. If the lovely nest of a copperfinch, as the
chaffinch was called, was found, never more than two eggs were to be
taken. A horrible habit prevailed in those days of baiting fishhooks to
catch curlews and plovers, and my children were sworn in to denounce
to me anybody they knew who did this. I was able to convince them
that dragon-flies, which they called horse-stingers, were harmless to
human beings or horses. I had to agree that apple-bees, as they called
wasps, did have to be obliterated occasionally, but pleaded for moths
that came fluttering into a lighted room. I pleaded for eeriwigs, too,
because they were such good mothers, and even for wood-lice or
gramma-sows because they were harmless.

"You call moths piskies, suppose they really are fairies, you don't
want to hurt fairies?"

This might lead to a tale of how somebody or other had been pisky-
led when he was on his way home from Helston one evening and found
himself waking up on Goonhilly Down instead of in his own bed. It
was not for me to spoil the magic by saying that whoever it was had
probably drunk more beer than was good for him in Helston and
wanted to find an excuse for sleeping it off before he encountered his
wife. Merrymaids produced so many tales that I began to wonder if
mermaids really might exist after all.

I apologize for quoting from the volume of reminiscences called
As Much As I Dare[1] in which Faith wrote:
"Like the Pied Piper he would set out for a walk, and soon he would
be surrounded by village children. From the cottages they would come
running, fighting for his hand as he led them to the cliffs or the sea-
shore. His exciting attitude to such commonplaces as flowers and birds,
and his story-telling gifts gave an enchantment to the lives of those
children. They lived in a new world, and it was not surprising that
they all wanted to come to his Sunday school."

I recall from one of those walks asking Alec Bolitho why he was
looking so sad, and Alec's reply:
"How do 'ee belong to take the maids' hands when we do go for a
walk? How don't 'ee ever take boy Charlie's hand and mine?"

Boy Charlie was Charlie Wearne, a small son of the villa where Miss
Gleig lodged.
"Why don't you and boy Charlie come and take hold of my hand?"
"Because the maids is so pushing. If maid Bessie do lev go for a
moment one of the other maids gets a hold of 'ee so quick as nine-
pence."
"Well, you and Charlie must be quicker than ninepence."
"Then the maids do get in some frizz. I'd be brim glad if there
wasn't no maids to our school."

After this I was always careful to see the boys were allowed to demonstrate their affection on equal terms with the maids. I felt that,
apart from stories in the Gospels children could understand, no attempts should be made to explain theology, and I avoided any story
from the Old Testament. I could not believe that Abraham's or
Jacob's behaviour was a good example for children.

I gave each child a money-box into which every Sunday I put various coloured counters unseen by my scholars. A white counter for some
act of kindness, a red counter for the reverse, a black counter for some
particularly reprehensible behaviour, a yellow counter for a display of
jealousy, a green counter for thoughtfulness about birds or wild-
flowers, and one or two others whose colours and significance I have
forgotten.

"And now, children, remember the Day of Judgment comes un-
expectedly," I used to warn them. So perhaps no more than a fortnight later I might decide to open the money-boxes, when the various
counters each child discovered in his or her box were recorded in a

[1] Faith Compton Mackenzie, *As Much As I Dare* (Collins).

notebook. I used to let them know what good deed or behaviour had been rewarded; if a child was able to remember why he had been awarded a red or yellow or black counter it was not entered against him or her.

Some of the chapel folk who had been having it all their own way for many years were worried by the increasing number of children who persuaded their parents to let them attend my Sunday school instead of the Methodist school. Feeling strongly as I did that John Wesley himself would have been greatly distressed to find how far away from his teaching the Wesleyan Methodists of this part of Cornwall had moved into a gloomy Calvinism, I could not feel at all apologetic. I cannot remember who the minister was, but he must have felt that revivalist action was called for, and a local preacher from Helston, notorious for his eloquent exposition of Hell, was brought in to admonish the tolerance that seemed to be in danger of corrupting the people of Gunwalloe. They must be thoroughly frightened about their prospects in eternity, and in an attempt to illustrate the heat of hell-fire he proclaimed that a white-hot poker in Hell would be no hotter than an ice-cream in Hell.

Some time in that February the agent of the Penrose estate let me know that he would give me a lease of the cottage we wanted in Gunwalloe. This was to date from Lady Day, by which time he felt he could promise that the thatched roof would be repaired. Toy Cottage had four rooms, two above and two below; even after the walls inside had all been distempered in ivory it was still full of fleas. I am lucky enough to be antipathetic to fleas, but poor Faith found them a trial. She had persuaded her father to stump up in order to equip herself for making chocolate creams, which she proposed to sell to her friends in the hope of relieving our chronic state of impoverishment. Fortunately Christopher managed to let Lady Ham. So our interest on the mortgage could be met. This would mean a home would have to be found for my books, not to mention the furniture, almost all of which was mine.

I could not go to Burford because Bernard Walke had booked me to preach once a week for him at Polruan during Lent. So Faith went and arranged for the furniture and books to be stored. As I remember, Percy Wyatt who ran the Lamb Inn kindly found us a space in one of his out-buildings until we knew where we were going to live. Toy Cottage, as I wrote at the time, was about the size of a walnut.

Although I preached in it on five Wednesdays during that Lent I can remember nothing of the mission church except a crowded con-

gregation and the pulpit. Three of my sermons were on the three
theological virtues—Faith, Hope and Charity. The reason why I chose
these virtues on which to hold forth was my anxiety to express the
importance I attached to Hope. I felt then and I feel just as strongly
to-day that Hope is not sufficiently contrasted with Faith. I argued
that if one has Faith one must have Hope, but that if, in spite of finding
it impossible to preserve absolute and unquestioning Faith, one pre-
served Hope, such a state of mind to some extent took the place of
Faith. "I cannot help believing that something is true, though I hope
it is not." "I hope something is true, though I cannot help believing it
is not." I argued that the Hope expressed in that second asseveration
was at least as valuable as the Faith declared in the first.

One of my favourite poems was, and still is, Browning's *The Statue
and the Bust*, the tale of that equestrian statue in Florence which gazes
for ever up at the Della Robbia bust of that "passionate pale lady's
face".

> *Make me a face on the window there*
> *Waiting as ever, mute the while,*
> *My love to pass below in the square!*

She and the Duke loved one another but could never make up their
minds to an elopement, she being married to a man she hated. In the
end both of them died, and Browning asks:

> *So! While these wait the trump of doom,*
> *How do their spirits pass, I wonder,*
> *Nights and days in the narrow room?*

> *Still, I suppose, they sit and ponder*
> *What a gift life was, ages ago,*
> *Six steps out of the chapel yonder.*

> .   .   .   .   .   .

> *I hear your reproach,—"But delay was best,*
> *For their end was a crime!"—Oh, a crime will do*
> *As well, I reply, to serve for a test,*

> *As a virtue golden through and through,*
> *Sufficient to vindicate itself.*

> .   .   .   .   .   .

> *And the sin I impute to each frustrate ghost*

C

Was, the unlit lamp and the ungirt loin,
Though the end in sight was a crime, I say,
You of the virtue, (we issue join)
How strive you? De te, fabula!

I must have been saying those lines of a great poet over to myself
that summer in Gunwalloe before I was preaching to a congregation
of summer visitors on the parable of the talents, and that buried talent
which was so sternly rebuked.

In a *John o' London's* article of January 1953 Joyce Weiner wrote:

"He knows clearly what he wants and applies his gifts to achieve
this. An incident of forty-five years ago told me recently throws some
light on this. It was Sunday night in the small church of Gunwalloe, in
Cornwall, and the narrator, a small girl, had been amazed at the sight
of a beautiful young layman in the pulpit who, taking as his text the
theme of Browning's *Statue and the Bust*, had earnestly exhorted his
congregation of fishermen and labourers to sin if they felt they must,
but, above all, to do something."

I do not recall that particular occasion, but the story rings true.
Apparently the summer visitors were astonished by those sermons.

Faith recorded in her reminiscences hearing a young golfer say, "By
Jove, if that chap had any education he'd make his name as a
preacher."

Bernard Walke and I were completely in accord over what we believed to be the vital essence of Christianity which, as we saw it, was
in danger of being choked by the dead wood of mere conventional
acquiescence. Some time that Lent Dr Harry Roberts spent a night in
Polruan and I thought him as much the ideal figure of a doctor as
Bernard Walke was the ideal figure of a priest. Harry Roberts was the
father of Denys Kilham Roberts, the Secretary of the Society of
Authors.

Another doctor I met at this time was Dr Boger of Fowey, a small
rather plump man of indefatigable energy with a tall, charming, kind
and very hospitable wife. Boger had a passion for amateur acting; hearing that I had played Gratiano for the O.U.D.S. five years ago, he
asked me to play the same part in four performances of *The Merchant of
Venice* that the Fowey A.D.C. were giving in the town hall at the end
of April, when Boger himself would be playing Shylock. I did not feel I
should be interested by a part I had already played but Boger was
insistent on my being in the show, which A. T. Quiller-Couch was
going to direct. So I offered to play Antonio if Quiller-Couch would

accept my conception of the way I thought the part of Antonio should be played.

I well remember my first meeting with Quiller-Couch in that book-lined study of his at The Haven, the windows of which looked out across that enchanting harbour on which I have not set eyes for over fifty years. I still see Q's library at dusk with the windows blue as sapphires and the fire burning brightly and the half-covered sheet of paper on his desk where he had left off writing. I felt rather shy of that literary figure whom I so much admired and was careful to avoid saying anything about my *Poems* in case he should feel compelled by kindness to suggest my sending him the volume. Q was wearing a brown tweed suit with a *café au lait* shirt and a tie the colour of a *clarissimo* cigar. The D.N.B. says that Q was celebrated for "his kindness of heart and the care he took in choosing and wearing his picturesque clothing".

I told Q I thought it was a mistake for the Merchant of Venice himself always to be played with a greying beard and be apparently twenty years older at least than his gay young friends. I said I thought Antonio should be dressed like Bassanio, Gratiano and the rest of them until the trial scene, when he should appear in a black doublet, open at the neck as if he were already prepared for Shylock to cut that pound of flesh. Q agreed with me that if Antonio looked fairly young the audience might transfer some of their compassion to him instead of giving it all to Shylock as played for the sympathy of a modern audience.

Q was Commodore of the Royal Fowey Yacht Club, the cosy headquarters of which were by the harbour's edge. I was made a temporary member and spent much of my time there in the intervals of rehearsing. Most of the cast were members and the endless "shop" in which both professional and amateur actors indulge must have been rather a trial for the yachtsmen who were not acting.

Most of Great Britain was snowed under in that last week of April, but what upset Q more than the blizzard was the news that Winston Churchill had been defeated in the bye-election in North-West Manchester, after his being made President of the Board of Trade.

"Who is this comic Tory solicitor?" he demanded.

Even more ludicrous than the election of Joynson Hicks were the adventures of some floral experts from Kew. Scepticism had been expressed over the sub-tropical plants that the Cornish gardeners were exhibiting at R.H.S. shows, and Kew was invited to send some experts to see for themselves that they really were being grown without glass protection in the benign climate of the Cornish Riviera. The Truro flower show when the rhododendrons would be in their glory was suggested as a suitable occasion for the visit.

So the experts set out, and when near Camborne their train was buried by a snowdrift for several hours the floral experts were more sceptical than ever about the claims of the Cornish gardeners to grow New Zealand tree-ferns and flowering shrubs from Chile and Queensland without protection.

That blizzard over south-west England at April's end in 1908 remains in my memory as the most successful demonstration of eccentricity by our eccentric climate during my lifetime.

On May 1st when the performances were over I went to say goodbye to Q; the date is fixed by his inscription in a copy of *The Westcotes*.

"I think we'll have to do *Hamlet* next year with you playing Hamlet," he said to me. "I'd like to produce *Hamlet*."

Back at Cury I found that Faith had not yet returned but that some furniture had arrived from Lady Ham for Toy Cottage; a letter from her said she was bringing Althea Gyles to stay with us in Gunwalloe for the summer.

We had met Althea Gyles in the previous autumn and had visited her in the room where she lived in Chelsea. I cannot remember visiting anybody else living in an atmosphere of such squalid poverty. She was an Irish painter who had illustrated Oscar Wilde's poem *The Harlot's House* and at one time, rumour said, had been the mistress of Leonard Smithers. In the last known letter of Oscar Wilde, written to Frank Harris on November 20, 1900, he referred to Althea Gyles as "an artist of great ability". She designed the cover for Yeats's *The Secret Road* and for the new edition of his *Poems* in 1899. Yeats wrote an essay on her work called "A Symbolic Artist and the coming of Symbolist Art" which was published in the *Dome* in December 1898 but never reprinted.

Faith went to see her in Chelsea that April and found the squalid poverty of Althea Gyles had become destitution. She spent most of her time lying upon a broken-down truckle-bed. Faith felt that something really must be done for poor Althea Gyles and suggested she should come and live with us in Toy Cottage. Althea offered to paint portraits of us both if we could provide her with the necessary materials. This was the bait Faith offered her father to extort out of him Althea's fare and the money for paint and brushes and easel. It was also the bait I offered my mother to get the £17 I wanted to buy a pony and jingle I had seen at Helston Fair; a jingle was what was called elsewhere than Cornwall a governess-car, a square box of a vehicle to seat four, one of whom drove. Edward the pony was an aged gelding who did not seem likely to be able to do more than ten miles in a day when I bought him. With plenty of food and good grooming by Ernie Bolitho, who was engaged at five shillings a week to look after him, Edward became a really dashing animal for his age, with a determination to overtake and pass any vehicle he saw in front of him.

Edward rendered me one great service for which I shall always be grateful to him. I had been to the Furry Dance in Helston but had not taken part in it because I did not have my top hat and tails down in Cornwall. The municipal worthies of Helston dancing in and out of the houses all used to wear the clothes they would wear for a wedding. No doubt their ancestors had put on ceremonial woad for this dancing relic of two thousand years ago. Driving back to Cury, I had taken a short-cut by a lane which descended a steep hill to a wooded hollow with a stream flowing through it and a ruined farm-house called Tiddlywits, reputed to be haunted by a ghost without a head. It was an entrancing place, a steep lane with high-banked hedges on either side leading up out of it toward Cury. The children and I used to visit Tiddlywits, where we always found the first adders' eyes, as they called the little white flowers that starred the banks. Here too were the first primroses and the first bluebells. Best of all, in one of the fields of that derelict farm there were cowslips galore; I never saw them anywhere else in the Meneage.

I may have been thinking about the progress of *Curtain Wells*, of which by the beginning of that May I had written over 50,000 words out of what I expected would be 120,000. I may have been deciding that, much as I enjoyed preaching and much as I enjoyed my Sunday school, I did not have a vocation for the priesthood and that to her relief I should tell Faith as much when she came back from "up along". I may have been constructing a play round the name of a place called Cannebrake of the Starlings which I had come across in some chronicle. What that play was to be about I have completely forgotten: the only evidence I have that it ever existed is a page in a notebook with a deplorable attempt to draw my idea of the set for—

Act I. The Hall at Cannebrake of the Starlings

Anyway, I was lost in a dream about something or other when I suddenly came to with the jingle almost vertical and Edward above it trying to reach some coveted vegetation at the top of the high bank that bounded the lane; I was just in time to check his further advance before the jingle must overturn. I realized that if I was subject to fits of absent-mindedness like this I might easily be a menace to traffic. At that moment I decided never to learn to drive a motor-car, a decision to which I have adhered, thereby greatly adding to my pleasure in motoring and much to the advantage of the public.

By the time Faith arrived with Althea Gyles I had got Toy Cottage furnished with the stuff from Lady Ham, and Janie Bray had promised to look after it for us. She was the wife of Sam Bray who kept the cemetery of Gunwalloe church fairly tidy; he was the only son of old Bray who had been promising to mend John Williams' gate for nine years. Sam Bray was an unpleasant fellow with a reputation as a Peeping Tom. I could never imagine how Janie Bray came to marry him. They had one daughter called Violet, who was in my Sunday school.

Mrs Williams was inclined to be jealous of Mrs Bray's reign at Toy Cottage, and I told her we would rather have had her services if she could possibly have found time to give them. Mrs Williams was sensible enough to recognize this and if any jealousy remained she managed to hide it successfully.

When I stood on Helston platform and saw Althea Gyles alight with Faith my immediate thought was that we had made a mistake in bringing her to Cornwall. She looked rather like a part of the decorations of a harvest festival which had been caught up unwittingly by one of the congregation and dragged outside. Her large-brimmed black straw hat was wreathed with poppies; her green silk dress hung upon her, not in graceful folds as it should, but in the depressions one may see in a field of hay-grass beaten down by heavy rains. Her cheeks, no doubt once rosy and bloomed with youth, were now pale; her hair, no doubt once autumn-gold, was now as dead as a faded rug; her pale blue eyes lacked lustre. At this date she was just forty. In a tiny cottage she was an intolerable nuisance because not only did she never offer a hand in help either with the cooking or with keeping it tidy, but she was constantly bringing in armfuls of flowers and grasses which she stuck into any receptacle she could find; in the course of arranging those armfuls she used to throw on the floor whatever vegetation she did not need for her vases.

"I'll sweep Miss Gyles herself up one of these days," Mrs Bray declared, "and put her into the dustbin."

Knowing it would annoy Miss Gleig, Althea used to beguile Wason with memories of the 'nineties when she was in her early twenties and by implication the golden girl of all the poets and painters of that decade. By June Faith and I felt we could stand no more of her. Although she had been equipped with all the materials for painting, she did not once bother to put her easel together and it was obvious that there would never be a portrait or a landscape or a seascape from her idle brush. Fortunately by the middle of June we had an excuse for getting her back to London, because my mother was coming to Cornwall in order to decide about a house I had found at Phillack on the other side of the Hayle estuary.

"Ah, that's near St Ives. I know quite a few of the painters there," she said.

"Yes," I put in hurriedly. "But we shan't be settled in there until the autumn, and I must keep a spare-room for my mother here when she comes down to Cornwall from time to time."

So Althea Gyles was mercifully eliminated from Gunwalloe, and Miss Gleig's apprehension that she would lure Wason into marriage was allayed; not that there was ever the most remote chance of Wason's eccentricity being quite as eccentric as that.

The other day I wrote to dear Rupert Hart-Davis to let me know anything he had discovered about Althea Gyles for his great edition of Oscar Wilde's letters, and he sent me with other information this extract from a letter of W. B. Yeats to Florence Farr in this very year 1908:

I have a fine tale of Althea Gyles. She brought a prosperous love-affair to an end by reading Browning to the poor man in the middle of the night. She collects the necessities of life from her friends and spends her own money on flowers.

I was glad to read this because it has relieved my conscience of the last faint prick for having banished Althea Gyles from Gunwalloe. She used to tell us that one day she would inherit money from a family estate in Ireland. Perhaps this was one of those rare occasions when she spoke the truth. Anyway, she lived on until she was over eighty in 1949; she certainly could not have survived that squalid room and truckle-bed in Chelsea for forty years.

After my mother sold the bungalow at Beech she began to think it would be a good idea to take a house in Cornwall, where Fay could spend a year of country life before she went to be "finished" in Paris, where my second sister Katie was going presently to spend a year to study acting under the tutorship of an actress of the Comédie Française. Now that Lady Ham was let Christopher wanted a place where he could retire to write, and the plan was for him and me to contribute our share of the rent and rates of Rivière House.

On May 16th I wrote to my mother:

Now about this house which I went to see. It is a Georgian house of three floors. Hall: large dining-room and large drawing-room: large study fitted with splendid book-shelves. Magnificent kitchen: small kitchen: pantry, scullery, etc.

Underneath in the basement are splendid cellars like the crypt of a Gothic church.

1st floor. Main staircase. 3 large bedrooms. 1 large bedroom and dressing room, and a large powder-closet.

On the servants' staircase. Two rooms and a bathroom.

On the top floor 5 bedrooms and two large powder closets.

Nearly all the rooms have old hob grates and magnificent shelves, drawers and cupboards.

There is a good stable and outhouses. Tennis court and paddock. Also an acre of potatoes and other rough plants. Also a walled garden of one acre, full of fruit and flowers with a large green-house and vines—one of the most charming wall gardens I ever saw, also a rockery and shrubberies.

The Hayle estuary is in front of the house and the sea two miles away at the back.

The West Cornwall golf-links are over the ferry by Lelant. They are the finest in Cornwall.

St Ives is 4 miles away, Penzance 7. It is on the north coast with glorious sands and only 6 miles from the south coast. Altogether a fascinating house and only £50 (!) a year. The main-line station is about a mile away.

I want you to come down and see it. I think you couldn't resist it. It would let for 15 guineas a week in the summer (furnished). I don't think I ever saw a house for the money which would suit us so well.

It is only 14 miles from Gunwalloe, so that I can keep up my work there quite easily every week end. Let me know by return what you think.

Mr Edmund Hockin, the squire of Phillack, was a bachelor of almost sixty who lived in a small house at the top of the village he owned. Here, with an elderly housekeeper to look after him, he devoted himself to two passions—growing vegetables better than anybody else in Cornwall, and the preservation of old Cornish apples like Sops in Wine, Cornish Gillyflowers, Irish Peaches, Tom Putts, Sweet Larks, and many another the names of which I have forgotten. He seemed doubtful at first about letting Rivière House because it would mean parting with that acre of potatoes on the left as one entered the gates of the drive up to the house. Also there was a Canadian woman to whom he had half promised to let the house the previous year when she was visiting some relations in Hayle. However, in the end he decided to let it to us on a seven-years' lease with the option of renewal.

Rivière had been built by the chief owner of a long abandoned copper-mine at the end of the eighteenth or beginning of the nineteenth century, and it had a large copper roof. Another relic of that mine was an adit, at the back of the house, which pierced the slope above for at least a hundred yards; it was a dark, gloomy and tiring business to walk up to the end of that adit with bent head and shoulders; I need hardly add that it was an expedition I inflicted on any male guest we had.

Behind the house rose the great sweep of towans, many times larger than those between Church Cove and Cury Churchtown, and stretching for most of the length of St Ives Bay, being bounded on the west by St Ives itself and on the east by Godrevy lighthouse below the cliffs of Dead Man's Cove. To my pleasure I saw that the towans at the back of Rivière were covered with cowslips.

Mostly these towans presented to the beach a low line of serrated cliffs some thirty feet high; from time to time they would break away to gullies full of fine, drifted sand, whose small cavities hoarded snail-shells wind-dried to an ethereal lightness and rabbit-bones bleached and honey-combed by weather. The beach itself was at low water a very wide and flat and completely desolate expanse, shining near the sea's edge with whatever gold or silver was in the air, shot with crimson bars at sunset, crinkled by the wind to a vast replica of one of its own shells, ribbed and ploughed by tempests.

Beyond that acre of potatoes with which Squire Hockin had been at first unwilling to part was the walled garden sloping down to what from a gardener's point of view was a pestilent row of elms beyond which at high tide the water of the Hayle estuary glittered, at low tide presented an expanse of mud. On the other side was the town of Hayle, which had grown up round the famous Hayle Foundry where that engineering genius Richard Trevithick had done at least as much as if not more than Watt and Stephenson to develop the steam engine. He married a Harvey and in 1908 there were still Harveys in control of the Hayle Foundry and Engineering Works, where once upon a time were built, besides the engines used in the lead mines, what were considered the best railway locomotives in Great Britain. By 1908 the great foundry was almost still and Hayle itself had become a small industrial town living in its past.

The north side of the walled garden was sheltered from the wind by a large shrubbery of laurels and a grove of those elms; these sheltered the west side of the house, against which grew right up to the gutter round the roof two large trees of *Magnolia grandiflora*. When they were in full August bloom the air of the lawn was scented by their great flowers. The lawn itself sloped down into the elms through the laurels, under which a path led to the road along the estuary, ending by the Lelant ferry a mile or so along. The ferryman was a captivating figure who stood in the bows and ferried his passengers across the hundred yards of river with the power and grace of a gondolier. I see now his slanting eyebrows as he told me that autumn of a tragedy. Throughout the summer a baby seal which had lost its mother had made a habit of following his boat backward and forward each time he crossed.

"It was like a child," he told me, "and belonged to cuddle up against me when I would stroke his head. Then one day in August month when I was ferrying over some of these furrin visitors I asked them what they thought of my baby seal and one of they bloody visitors up and shot my baby seal. Man, I don't know how I didn't throw him into the river; I suppose the Lord stopped me because if I had thrown him in he'd have drowned dead sure enough because the tide would have swept the bugger out to sea. I believe I'll give up the ferry come October month because I'm for ever looking behind for my baby seal and you never know what I might do to the boat one day."

W. H. Hudson has told the story of that baby seal in his book *Land's End*. I met him some time that summer, and being a devoted admirer I was suitably thrilled. However, Hudson was disagreeable and I decided his prose was much better than his manners. To my taste Hudson and Cunninghame Graham were writing the best English prose during the 'nineties; both had the advantage of being bilingual in English and Spanish. Shaw was writing polemical prose better than anybody since Swift; but he could not write evocative prose like Hudson or Cunninghame Graham.

I have run ahead with that story of the ferryman and the 'furrin' English visitors and must get back to the month of May when my mother returned from making arrangements for my sister Katie's year in Paris and came down to look at Rivière House. She agreed we should take a lease, provided my father did not object to the place.

Before she went back to London she insisted on standing the Sunday school a treat. This was to be an expedition to Praa Sands, which were near the south-east corner of the Meneage beyond the Lizard. The hire of the omnibus was to cost twenty-five shillings. Mrs Williams, Mrs Bray, Miss Gleig and Faith came to help with the picnic lunch and the picnic tea; Wason came too. It was a glorious day at the end of May and we had tremendous games on those wide sands. Yet what comes back to my memory most vividly is walking down a small narrow cove not far from Cadgwith and finding at the bottom of it, sheltered from the sea by a thrust of the cliff, a six-roomed cottage the walls of which were covered by a pink ivy-leaved geranium, and not merely the walls but the tiled roof as well. I forgot all about Rivière for the moment in my desire to live in this cottage. However, enquiries offered no hope of my doing so; it belonged to some people who would be arriving next week to spend the summer there. Even to-day I am still haunted by the pink flowers and ivy-leaves of that luxuriant geranium.

On the day after we unloaded that omnibus full of sleeping children round about nine o'clock of a warm May night I wrote to my mother:

Glad that Father has said Yes, but I don't at all care to have the house if it means giving up your carriage. So if those are the conditions I simply can't accept them. Unless that is to say you will live premanently at Rivière.

We had a glorious day yesterday and a most successful treat.

I am glad to say that my mother did not have to give up her brougham.

My mother was not greatly interested in the campaign for women's suffrage. No doubt when she agreed to accompany a demonstration of actresses in favour of the vote she may have felt she owed something in return for the support some of them had given to the Actors Church Union, the Theatrical Ladies Guild, and the rest of the pious concerns in which she was interested.

A letter survives from that June from one of the organizers:

I am so delighted to think you will come with the actresses on Saturday. . . . It has been very difficult to get anything of a number together and I do fear the group will be lamentably small. Therefore I venture to ask if your daughters could start walking with the group. The carriages will not actually form part of the procession—at least not with the banners—the police will not permit it—and will follow indiscriminately. . . .

I think a good many of us will not get as far as the Albert Hall from the Embankment—it is a long walk, but I would like to have a good start off. . . .

I enclose a notice of Instructions and have marked the spot where the banner will probably be on the Embankment—behind the Artists and in front of the Musicians. The banner has two masks—tragedy and comedy—and the name of Sarah Siddons on it.

We expected to move into Rivière early in September, and during the summer I worked hard at my novel, of which I had written more than three-quarters by the time the house was redecorated and furnished, partly with Lady Ham furniture, partly with furniture that

could be spared from Nevern Square. My week-ends were given to the
children of Gunwalloe.

I look back to that paradise of childhood, finding in their mirth and
innocence the emotion which of all who have ever lived on this earth
and written verse or prose or music or painted pictures only William
Blake has been able to express:

> *'Such, such were the joys*
> *When we all, girls and boys,*
> *In our youth time were seen*
> *On the Echoing Green.'*

Under my direction the children used to play denominational games
of Indians, Pirates, Smugglers, Cavaliers, Early Christians and Ancient
Greeks. I recall by the shores of the Looe Pool Alec Bolitho as King
Arthur receiving Excalibur in the shape of a yard of lead piping from
Violet Bray whose pinafore of white samite was sadly spotted by hiding
among the bulrushes, those same bulrushes among which on another
day Lily Francis, the daughter of Pharaoh, discovered the infant
Moses, one of her own dolls, lying in a basket. Nobody found a silver
dollar or a golden doubloon or a drowned mariner; but Alec Bolitho
found a coconut husk on the very day he was Robinson Crusoe, and
once they came upon the carcase of a dead porpoise which, though it
smelt very heavy, as Leslie Williams said, was not on that account less
to be gloated over. There was the day when Alec Bolitho saw the blue
bird of Spring; this was a wheatear, and I asked him why he called it
blue when it was really grey.

"We belong to call it the blue bird of Spring," the children cried in
chorus. Argument was out of the question when a Cornish man or
child belonged to say or do anything.

One day when we were walking along the cliffs between Mullion
and Poldhu we saw an adder basking in the sun. "Kill 'un, kill 'un,"
they screamed.

I intervened; the snake flowed like a stream of jewels across the
sunny path, and in a trice his jetty lozenges and glistening scales of
silvery green vanished in the herbage beside the path.

"But adders belong to kill you," one of the children protested. I was
told stories of being chased by adders. These were followed by the tale
of a man who was once chased by seven badgers. If I had been James
Robertson-Justice I should have been able to cap their stories with
one of my own of having been chased by a pack of weasels.

The weather became so hot in July that I suggested the children should celebrate it by learning to swim. The provision of bathing-dresses was a problem for Gunwalloe. Mr Wearne, Miss Gleig's land-lord, could afford to buy proper bathing-suits for his two boys, striped affairs such as little visitors wore and as grand in their way as the sailor suits they sported on Sundays. Leslie, too, would probably have been given a new equipment, if a girl visitor of two years ago had not left behind a red bathing-dress which Mrs Williams declared it would be a sin and a shame not to use. Leslie might have objected to the frills on the shoulders if all the rest of the children had appeared in any-thing remotely like bathing-dresses; but compared with theirs this was so clearly what it was intended to be that he did not grumble at its having been originally designed for a girl. Mrs Francis cut up an old willow-pattern curtain for Lily and Nellie, but made the dresses so much too baggy that the two little girls looked like a couple of ginger-jars when they stood hugging themselves at the water's edge. The equipment of the Bolitho children taxed even their mother's optimistic extravagance. No doubt if she could have found a Helston tradesman to give her credit she would have indulged herself in a burst of sheerly luxurious shopping. In the end she bought a lot of fondants, which gratified her sense of colour but left her children clamorous and un-clothed. At last Mrs Bolitho applied herself seriously to the problem, and for a start took her husband's solitary pair of pyjama trousers, which had been washed ashore from a wreck eighteen months previ-ously, and cut them down for Beatrice. For Bessie and her younger sister Lily a pair of poor Bolitho's underpants and a vest were cut about and stitched to provide two costumes, while for Alec, having robbed the males of the family for the females, she took Beatrice's only chemise and sent him into the water looking like a small clown. Of the other children I recall only Violet Bray's appearance in a confection of oil-skin.

The first bathing expedition was one warm and misty Saturday morning in a sea of oxidized silver, but these children who had spent all their lives on the brink of the Atlantic were horribly frightened of entering it when the moment came. Each one urged the other to go in first; but nobody would advance beyond his or her knees. As far up as that their bodies were familiar with the sea when they went washing feet, which was what they called paddling; the moment the scarcely heaving water rose an inch higher all the children leapt back as if they were going to be bitten by a savage fish.

No reproaches of mine for their timidity were of any avail until Alec Bolitho decided to set an example at Charlie Wearne's expense by suddenly giving him a push in the back which sent him face-downwards with a splash into the water. Fired by her brother's action Bessie did the same thing to her sister Beattie, and a moment later Charlie Wearne and Beatrice Bolitho were running back across the sands to the caves where they had undressed.

"Look out for red counters in your money-boxes when the day of judgment comes," I warned Alec and Bessie; so Alec and Bessie decided they must try to win whatever coloured counter was awarded for a brave action and agreed to pull each other down into the water. Leslie Williams let them pull him down too. When I teased them about not being true daughters of a sailor Lily and Nellie Francis sat down, and they were followed by the rest. On the way back to dress in the caves there was much bragging about their bravery, at the expense of Beatrice Bolitho and Charlie Wearne, who had refused to join the others in the water.

Suddenly Bessie exclaimed,

"My gosh, where's boy Leonard to?"

Leonard Bolitho, three years old, was sighted a quarter of a mile further along the beach. Wrapped in a faded flag, a relic of the Diamond Jubilee celebrations, he had, in accord with the interior life he led, wandered away from the noisy bathers to pursue his own thoughts. When his sisters overtook him and were about to shake him for his truancy, he produced from the folds of his flag two small crabs with which he frowningly threatened them. Then with grave unhurried steps he followed them back to be dressed. I told the others that Leonard would learn to swim before any of them; by the end of that summer most of them could swim.

I have just come across over a dozen notes, some of which must have been written in the spring of 1909 when Faith and I were still driving over from Phillack to Gunwalloe every week and then staying in Toy Cottage. When we moved in to Rivière in the autumn we took Ernie Bolitho with us to act as a diminutive groom for Edward. I cannot resist reprinting some of those notes of nearly sixty years ago.

Here is Alec Bolitho who had been in bed with a bad cold:

Mr Compton Mackenzie.
I hope to be to church on Sunday if I am well. if it is ruf and I amnot allowed to come to church I will try the best I can to comme your truley
                              Alec Bolitho.

Here is Lily Bolitho:

Dear Sir. Leanord said that he is very sorry for not coming Singy school.

With eleven crosses for kisses, as postscript.
Here is Bessie Bolitho:

Dear Sir. I am very sorry for all my noughtyness in the Sunday school. I will try to better in the futcher. I hope you are very well. Your truly Bessie.

With eighteen crosses for kisses.
Here is Beatrice Bolitho also apologizing for naughtiness. I wish I could remember this outbreak, but it has vanished from my mind.

Dear Sir,
I very sorry for our naughty ness in the Sunday school And I will try to be better for the futcher. I hope you are very well has it leaves me at present
                    Your truly
                              Beatrice Bolitho

With nineteen crosses for kisses.
Leslie Williams with the advanced age of eleven in his favour made only one mistake in spelling and moreover dated his note.

                    Gunwalloe
                    Oct. 29, 1908
Dear Mr Mackenzie.
I am so sory because I was such a naughty boy in School last Sunday. I will try not to be a naughty boy again. Hoping to see both Mr and Mrs Mackenzie upon Saturday.
                    Yours truly,
                              Leslie Williams

Two more apologies:

                    Coast guard station
                    Gunwalloe
Dear Sir,
I am so very sory I was such a bad girl in sunday-school. Please will you forgive me. I will be a better girl next time. Mother is able to walk about with a stick now. I hope it will be beter soon. The baby is getting on nicely. I am writing with red ink because we have no black. Love from Lily to Mr and Mrs Mackenzie. From your affectionate scholar
                              Lily Francis

                    Coast Guard Station
                    Gunwalloe
Dear Mr Mackenzie,
I am very sorry I was a naughty girl in Sunday-school last Sunday. I shall always be a good gril [*sic*] *at Sunday-school. Mother is getting much better on*

her leg and Baby is getting on nice. father is much better. I hope as we shall all see you on Saturday. With my kind love to Mrs Mackenzie and the same to you

From your
Affectionate Schoolar

Nellie Francis

Nellie Francis was hardly seven when she wrote that letter.

Just about now George Francis received notice that the Coastguard Station at Gunwalloe was to be closed down in November and that he was to remain as caretaker until notified where his next station would be. His wife, who had recently produced a baby boy, had fallen down and hurt her leg. Francis himself had been laid up with bronchitis. The prospect of moving in midwinter was not attractive. I forget what strings I pulled to keep him in Gunwalloe until the spring; anyway, I was successful.

The next three letters must have been written some time early in that spring of 1909.

Coast guard station
Gunwalloe
Helston

Dear Sir

I am very sorry that I was not in church Sunday morning. I will try to come next Sunday. Jack's arm [her baby brother] *is getting better now. How is Edward now. I have not seen him for a long time. His Hayle very pretty place? Bessie and Beatrice goes to school now. the sea is very rough now. I have no more news now. Give my kind love to Mrs Mackenzie and the same to you from your*

very sincerely

Lily Francis

If the weather is fine mother says that she will have the baby Chrisening next Sunday. Mother said that she would like you to be God Father and would you and Mrs Mackenzie come to tea.

Lily Francis was enquiring after Edward the pony because we were now driving each week to Toy Cottage in a dog-cart behind a chestnut mare with Ernie Bolitho in a tiger's livery much admired and envied by the boys and girls of Gunwalloe. Nellie Francis in the following letter was enquiring after Bob, our much loved sheepdog who used always to accompany us with rests in the dog-cart from time to time during the fourteen miles:

Bessie and Beatrice gos to cshool [sic] *now. I hope you and Mrs Mackenzie*

are quite well. Mother and the Baby and Father is quite well. Jack arm is quite
well to. I hope Bob is quite well to. I will be a good girl in sunday school and in
church. I have no more news now. Give my kind love to Mrs Mackenzie and the
same to you from your

very sincerely

Nellie Francis

One more of those letters that remind me so poignantly of the
Echoing Green:

Dear Sir
I am very sorry that I was not in church Sunday morning I will try to come
next Sunday. hope you and Mrs Mackenzie are sciet [quite] well. hope Ernie is
well tell him we had his postcard and we hope to see him on Sunday. Lenord says
he coming church on Sunday morning. Lill bath her dolls every morning no more
nues to tell for now

Good by for the time
Your sincerely

Beatrice Bolitho

I look back to that August of 1908 and see John Freeman walking
very slowly backwards and forwards along the road above the Helzephron cliffs, in his hand a large spray cut from a furze bush. He would
be on duty like this every day from sunrise until noon; he was the
"huer" of the Gunwalloe Fishing Company. That means he was gifted
with eyes that could detect the change in the appearance of the sea
which marked the presence of a shoal of pilchards. The huer would
then wave his branch of furze in the direction of the shoal, shouting as
he did so "Heva! Heva! Heva!" That meant fish in Cornish, a language
which unlike Welsh or Breton had been a dead language for a century
and a half. The cry of "heva" was echoed all around by those working
in the fields who would at once throw down spade or pick or whatever
implement was in their hands and rush helter-skelter down to launch
the boats and cast the net before the shoal moved out of Gunwalloe's
territorial waters. An oar stuck up on the beach of Church Cove half-
way between Church Cove and the Poldhu cliffs marked the boundary.
Beyond that the territorial waters of the Gunwalloe Daws became
those of the Mullion Gulls, and many a fight had there been in the
past over the position of a shoal and the right to net it.

All through that summer there had been no sign of a shoal, but
John Freeman had continued his watch until the end of October. We
were lucky enough to be in Toy Cottage when on the very last day of

D

his watch the huer was able to shout "Heva!" and I with the rest of them ran to help in the launching of the boats. John Freeman himself was in the "cock boat" whose job it was to direct the casting of the net; I was given a seat in it.

An echo of that excitement can be heard in an attempt by Leslie Williams to write a poem about it:

> *Heva*
> *Pilchards again, Tom,*
> *His yow a wacking great school,*
> *Plenty of colour too.*
> *Look out here comes the men*
> *Jim is going some rate*
> *There goes Bill down grunter.*

I am at a loss to-day to understand that last word.

> *Hurah!!! Hurah!!! Hurah!!!*
> *Get a jar of Beer put in the bow,*
> *A launch a boat a launch,*
> *Keep her going go-a-head-go-a-head*
>
> *Out with the oars*
> *Pull away pull away boys*
> *No anchors on board!*
> *Then the men started shouting*
> *I wont say what it was too awful.*

What the hitch was that caused so much bad language I have forgotten. The shoal was safely taken before it reached the territorial waters of Mullion; the amount of money netted by the Gunwalloe Fishing Company after they had taken that shoal and sold it in Penzance was over £2000.

The farmers of to-day may have all sorts of mechanical improvements and government subsidies, but none of them will share in the profits of the Gunwalloe Fishing Company with its capital of £100. No shoals of pilchards visit Mount's Bay any more; the huer with his furze bush will never be seen again; the cry of "heva!" is for ever silent.

The excitement of that great shoal of pilchards had been too much for the music of Leslie's verse, but about the same time he was inspired to write another poem about our Sunday school which may commemorate the bad behaviour apologized for in those letters already quoted.

A School

There was a little school
And a lot of little children
Some had all brains
Some had none,
This is the way the school
the school did run

Some had light hair
And some had black
What a row there was
When they went out to play
Some skipping and some slipping
I cannot say any more to-day.

I do not know how many words of the Cornish language still survive in colloquial speech; I recall from that very week-end of the great "heva" cutting my finger and being told by Mrs Bray that what I needed was a bisgon. A bisgon was a finger-stall. I was told at the time that "vis" was Welsh for finger. I wonder whether "bisgon" is ever heard to-day?

A letter from J. H. Scholefield, the Vicar of Mullion, tells me that I stayed with him for the following week-end in order to preach in his church. This is dated September 29th:

Come over on Saturday the 7th Nov: and stay with me and preach next day Nov: 8th, our Feast day, a great day with us—the Feast of the dedication of the church. Take the same subject morning and evening—23 minutes in M. and 30 minutes in E. and so give yourself a chance. What say you? You will be more or less settled down by then and it will not be too great a rush: and it will be nice for us all to anticipate. 5 weeks to think of it.

In the middle of November C. F. Rogers, the Vicar of Penzance, was writing to ask if I would preach a course of sermons to children next Lent.

We would have the service at 5.15 on either Tuesdays or Wednesdays. If you can arrange to do this I shall be very much obliged and I am sure that the children will benefit.

It may have been all this preaching which decided me that I should be bored if I committed myself to a life of preaching by taking holy orders. Moreover, I was beginning to have faint doubts about the ability of the Church of England to play a truly influential part in what I felt might be the great struggle ahead for Christianity in this twentieth century. At this date I had no thought of quitting the Anglo-Catholic fold for Rome. Nevertheless, I could not recapture the fervour by which I had been animated before my engagement to Ruth Daniel was broken off. I began to ask myself whether in recovering from the fever of atheism which succeeded that broken engagement during most of 1905 I had managed to recover more than a religious temperature that was sub-normal. I asked myself whether my Sunday school was inspired by a genuine desire to teach those children the Catholic faith or whether the pleasure of disconcerting the Methodists was not the sharper stimulation. As I write that it sounds as if I was deep in intro-version at this date. In fact I never did and never have consciously set out to think about myself or my beliefs. My attitude has always been and still remains that of the hippopotami in *Johnny Crow's Garden* who when the stork gave a philosophic talk exclaimed impatiently "Ask no farther what am I."

I suppose what was happening was that, although I would cling to Toy Cottage and those children for some months yet, my imagination was beginning to decide that one passion must gradually die and be replaced by another passion. So it has been all my life; fortunately for me, these successive passions, although they may be dead in the present, have remained vital in my memory and therefore are all of them really still alive.

When Lady Ham was let Christopher left Search in charge of it "until such time Monty has decided in what county he is going to rent, buy, or build a house" he had written in May. When I was certain we were going to rent Rivière I offered Search the job of gardener, and in September he arrived with his wife, sister-in-law and two children to live in the cottage which Squire Hockin let me have for a small weekly rent; it was only about a couple of hundred yards beyond Rivière beside the estuary.

Christopher, who had been spending much of his time with the Chinnerys, came down to help in the process of moving in and, feeling that my mother was taking too much charge of the domestic arrangements to Faith's disadvantage, proceeded to give her a little lecture. Considering that my mother was forking out for almost everything this was tactless.

"I'm afraid I cannot be lectured by Christopher," she said. "He's not a schoolmaster himself."

Faith, who had suffered from the lectures of those elder brothers who were schoolmasters, though never one from that dear old father of hers, difficult though it was for her to hear a word of criticism of that much-loved younger brother, agreed to ask him not to lecture my mother again.

Almost immediately after this Christopher went back to the Chinnerys who had moved by now from their very large house at Chobham and were living in Surrey in a house not quite so large at Witley. Presently he wrote from Abingdon to Faith, telling her that he might be married by the time she saw him again.

Faith in a spasm of tactlessness that surpassed Christopher's display with my mother sent him a postcard:

Not to Mrs Chinnery!

I hastily wrote to poor Christopher my congratulations and assumed that he *was* going to marry Mrs Chinnery.

A long letter arrived from Christopher in Abingdon. Most of it was about the future of Lady Ham, but significantly he told me that he had been to Hall's, my favourite tailor in Oxford, to say he was buying a certain amount of clothes.

The man there is priceless. "I think I may say, sir, that I have met many thousands of gentlemen of all sorts, but Mr Mackenzie is the nicest gentleman that has ever stepped inside this shop, sir."

This testimonial from Harris was gratifying and I hope I repaid it by the portrait I drew of him sixteen years later in my book *The Old Men of the Sea*, a new edition of which was issued this year 1964 under the title *Paradise for Sale*.

Then, after keeping off the subject for the greater part of the letter, Christopher reached it:

I hope to God I shall get married, but I don't believe it till it's done. Now I'm all nerves and Mrs C. is ill too with a cough and worry. I'll write again. The news is all over the place. Logan is pleased and Ned and Laura and in fact everyone so far.

By the end of the year Christopher and Alice Chinnery were married; she was a little more than twenty years older than himself. Few marriages have been so completely successful.

Soon after we had moved into Rivière I met Charles Marriott, who was living at 2 Porthminster Terrace in St Ives. Marriott's success with *The Column* in 1900 had not been maintained as a novelist. He was at this date working at a three-novel contract with Eveleigh Nash by whom he was being given an advance of £150 on each one, which he just about earned and no more. By great industry he was able to write and get published at least one other novel every year. He was now on the edge of forty, married to a woman whose directness of speech I much admired. His eldest daughter Vivien, aged fourteen, was a beautiful girl with that fair hair the French call *cendré*. She and her sister Dulcie were away at school that autumn and I recall with amusement their indignation at having to do so much housework in their holidays. Mrs Marriott did it all herself in term time. There was a small son called Basil, and I have a souvenir of him at this date in the shape of Wolf Cub military orders. These were discovered by his father who typed them out from Basil's scrawl and gave them to me for a laugh:

Raven patrol
   My dear feel-marchel plese will you clect as many troops as you can we are going to catch a boy corled denis Yours truley basil Marriott.

Oter patrol
   My dear captin-cole we are expecting the raven patrol to atac us please will you revvu your troops incase of an atac suddnly. But we must cath denis cellithi [stealthily?] clecting all the armour that I can. I am going scouting soon. 5 miles south and a ¼ of a mile west. Yours truley Coprol.

In that September Hugh Walpole, who earlier that year had been sitting at Marriott's feet, his pink face aglow with hero worship, came for a brief visit to St Ives. He called on me at Rivière with the typescript of his first novel and asked me if I would like to read it. I was no keener then than I am now on reading other people's novels in typescript, but I did not have the excuse of failing eyesight in 1908. When Hugh came to collect it I told him I did not think he was really a novelist. To my amazement he said that Charles Marriott and E. M. Forster had both written long letters to tell him how good *The Wooden Horse* was. Hugh Walpole was a schoolmaster at Epsom in this year, and that would give him the material in *Mr Perrin and Mr Traill* for a much better novel than *The Wooden Horse*, even although in describing somebody climbing up a Cornish cliff he did make him grasp with one hand a tuft of sea-pinks and with the other a tuft of sea-anemones. I suppose I must have told Hugh that I was writing a novel myself: otherwise he would have had no reason to suggest my reading his. Some time in the new year I had a postcard from him, telling me that Smith, Elder had accepted *The Wooden Horse* for publication.

In December 1908 he wrote a "fan" letter to Henry James, which was Hugh's way of getting to know writers he thought would help his career. Soon the Marriotts were forgotten. It did not worry Charles Marriott, but I remember Mrs Marriott's bitterness about the way Hugh ignored them when they left St Ives about a year later and went to live in London. I told her not to worry.

"Hugh Walpole rises on stepping stones of his dead friends to higher things."

In his masterly biography of Hugh Walpole Rupert Hart-Davis quotes Charles Marriott on this subject:

"Not long after we were settled in London in 1909 Hugh had engaged to dine with us but threw us over for an invitation from old Lady Lovelace, saying quite frankly that she would be of more use to him in that stage of his career as a writer. Personally I was not scandalized; given Hugh's temperament, his determination to get on, and his uncertain position at the time, his desertion seemed to me at least logical, and what interested me most was Hugh's candour and his apparent inability to see why it should have given offence; but it upset the feminine part of my family a good deal."

Charles Marriott put me up for the Arts Club in St Ives, and during that autumn I would sometimes bicycle over and take a long walk with him, Marriott dressed in corduroy breeches and jacket. He had been a photographer and dispenser before he wrote *The Column* and by now he was disheartened by his inability to repeat the success of his first book. Nevertheless, he continued to write novels until in 1924 he became art critic of *The Times*.

It has never occurred to me to ask a writer senior or even junior to myself to read a book of mine in typescript or in print. When my first novel was rejected by publisher after publisher I found it difficult to understand how publishers could be so stupid. If Hugh Walpole could get that unpromising first novel of his accepted by Smith, Elder, a firm which had published the Brontës and Thackeray, why should my first novel be steadily refused? I am running ahead. That first novel of mine is not yet finished.

I only used my library at Rivière for work by day. Here I wrote a play for my father which failed to attract him. I have forgotten what the play was called; indeed, the only thing I remember about it was that the name of one of the characters was Henry Penry. The MS. has vanished.

At night I wrote in Faith's bower, as we called it, with memories of Lady Ham, a small room looking west and south. Here I wrote on, often until one or two in the morning while Faith would play sometimes for three hours at a stretch on the cottage piano. I had acquired, and presented to her, all Beethoven's Sonatas, all Schubert's and

Schumann's piano music, and of course Chopin's. I also gave her the piano scores of Beethoven's symphonies. That habit of writing to music, at first to Faith's piano and later to the gramophone, would last for over forty-five years.

Faith had been a pupil of Fanny Davies, herself a pupil of Clara Schumann, and if only she could have brought herself to work really hard at the piano she might have reached the top. However, she would not practise and was quickly bored by any composition she could not read right off at sight without a mistake. Instead of the piano she insisted on going on the stage, where she could never hope to rise above obscurity, being much too self-conscious for a good actress. Fortunately she did not, like all too many young women, suppose that she was a great actress whose only lack was opportunity, and therefore it was never necessary for me to disillusion her about her histrionic ability. Besides being a good pianist, she had much skill at drawing, and might, if she had bothered to work at that, have become a comic-strip writer. Then she took up sculpture. Finally, after she had pottered about for a long time with fragments of short stories or single chapters of possible novels I set her down to writing a series of studies of operatic composers for my paper, the *Gramophone*; these were so good that I egged her on into writing a life of Christina of Sweden. Finally she wrote three volumes of autobiography which had a great and well-deserved success.

However, these were many years away in this autumn and winter of 1908-9 when I was toiling away to finish that first novel of mine to the accompaniment of Faith's music and the company of a delightful tabby cat called Tootoose.

My habit of writing to the piano was not because I wanted the emotional effect of incidental music. The benefit I derived from music being played while I wrote was its power to occupy the waste places of the mind. Instead of wandering from the task in hand to worry about unpaid bills, and at this date there were all too many of them, or to start thinking what I was going to preach about at Gunwalloe or Mullion or Penzance or Polruan, or indeed about whatever else was going on outside that eighteenth-century spa of Curtain Wells, I would be half listening to the music and half considering what my characters were going to do next or how I was to describe a piece of natural scenery; the vacancy would be filled by music. Thus it was that the unrevised *Curtain Wells* was finished on the eve of my twenty-sixth birthday. Little did I think when I wrote *Explicit* that two years would pass before *The Passionate Elopement* was published on my twenty-eighth birthday.

TWENTY-SIX YEARS OLD: 1909

I SENT the manuscript of my novel to Miss Champion; since her husband was killed in the South African war she had been trying to augment by typewriting the thin pension of a captain who had died in the service of his country. I had been animated only by gratitude to that help she gave me to escape from the tyranny of my old nurse, twenty years earlier; I had not realized quite what a task it would be to decypher that wretched handwriting of mine in pencil. There were so many words that neither she nor any other typist unfamiliar with my handwriting could have read that I had to spend many hours making corrections and filling in blanks, after which I had to send it to be retyped.

Faith was expecting a baby at the end of June; she did not tell me about this while I was working away to finish *Curtain Wells*, because she thought I should have refused to let her go on playing the piano for so long at a stretch, as indeed I certainly should. Not until the book was finished did she tell me on the morning of my birthday.

I have a letter from Henry James to my father from the Reform Club a week later in that January 1909 which lets me know that by now my father had acquired his first motor-car:

My dear Compton,
    This is but a word to say how sorry I am to have missed your call on me the other day at Rye. I am spending this month in town—but should have been glad to be at my little old house—for which I am in fact very homesick. I hope you are master of a motor and enjoy it as much as I do—though I only know the thing by charitable lifts from friends. I am working again—hard—for the theatre, you may be interested to know—and with prospects of good productions which in due and I think not distant time you and your wife must come and see. I send my kind remembrances to Mrs Compton and am yours ever,
            Henry James

Things were prospering with my father and he had just bought a large Mercédès car. It was typical of him not to buy a car until he could afford to spend £2000 on that Mercédès; that was a lot of money for a car in 1909. My mother may have heard in the autumn of the prospect of the Mercédès and thought it gave her an excuse to buy that dog-cart and chestnut mare in which Faith and I used to drive to Toy

Cottage almost every week-end. Faith handled the reins perfectly. When we met a motor-car, and we rarely met more than one in the course of that fourteen-mile drive, Ernie Bolitho, our tiger, used to jump down and hold the mare's head until the fearful vehicle had passed.

My father must have written to Henry James to ask about those plays of his mentioned in his January letter, for on July 5th James was writing from the Reform Club:

My dear Compton,

It has given me pleasure to hear from you even though I can't tell you that I am doing anything that could be of any calculable use to you. I have returned to the attempt to work again for the Theatre—with the idea of trying to get some good of that before I give up all things: which seems an odd undertaking at my age— but I have all along, and in spite of immense deterrents, felt it was inevitable. I am trying it, however, on lines that now at last are the only lines for me—and am at any rate trying it hard, and am up to my eyes in it—I have engaged to supply 3 plays—and have 3 or 4 more in my head. You and Mrs Compton to whom I send my kindest regards, must at least see them all—even if you have to come up from far Cornwall for the purpose. I hope you are enjoying that peninsula —and the very thought of that sea-breeze drives me home to-morrow. Do knock at my door again—I mean make occasion favour it—and believe me yours ever,

Henry James

Before I went down from Oxford Jack Murray,[1] who was a year junior to me, had told me to remember 50 Albemarle Street if I ever wrote a book. This I promised to do. That spring when the fair copy typescript of *Curtain Wells* came back I sent it to John Murray junior, who wrote to say that a special interest should be taken in it. I felt sure I should later receive an enthusiastic letter to say that *Curtain Wells* would be in the autumn list of that famous publishing house.

The letter came soon enough; but it was not enthusiastic: Murray wrote that two of their best readers and he himself had all read it and that none of them could quite make out what I was trying to do. It was a great personal disappointment to him to have to let me know that *Curtain Wells* was being returned to me with regrets. This was an extreme surprise to me because I had thought that Jack Murray was such a sensible chap; it did not occur to me for a moment that there was anything the matter with my novel. I now sent off *Curtain Wells* to Methuen. In due course I received a pleasant letter to say that much as they admired the book they could not see any possibility of its

[1] Sir John Murray, K.C.V.O.

attracting enough readers to secure them against loss. However, if I was willing to publish the book at my own risk they would be happy to put their name to it. I wrote to say I was not prepared to be financially responsible, and back came the typescript. My mother now wrote to Frankfort Moore, who advised me to send it to Hutchinsons, his own publishers. He would ask them to pay special attention.

After *Curtain Wells* came back in a few days from Hutchinsons I sent it to two more publishers; not being perfectly sure which they were, I shall leave their names out of it. Eveleigh Nash was the next, to whom Charles Marriott wrote to ask for attention to the book. Back it came within a few days. The next on the list was Heinemann, and my father told me he had written to ask Henry James to recommend it to the attention of Heinemann himself. James wrote:

> Lamb House
> Rye
> Sussex
> *August* 18*th* 1909

My dear Compton,

I ought already to have let you know that I wrote with pleasure to Heinemann to call his attention to what your son has sent him. He won't publish it, the book, alas, for any reason but that he likes it and thinks it may do—any word from me will be vain about that. But I may have the effect of the packet's having a little earlier attention and judgment, and I give Monty all my cordial hopes for its acceptance and success. I don't know whether most to rejoice with him or to weep over him on his entering that so alluring but so arduous and so crowded field!

> *Yours most truly,*
> *Henry James*

P.S. I hope you have been girded up by your holiday.

The only apparent effect of the trouble Henry James had taken was to get my book returned to me more quickly than by any publisher—in three days. I decided that from now on I would send *Curtain Wells* to publishers without any recommendation from kindly seniors; I decided at the same time that I would waste no more money on registering the typescript. After two or three more publishers it reached Constables by the end of the year. I was by then completely indifferent what happened to *Curtain Wells*, and was beginning to wonder if publishing as a profession deprived its practitioners of common sense. While I felt that *Curtain Wells* was unquestionably a *tour de force*, I felt that the same could be said of some of my poems. Was that enough? Was I capable of expressing either in verse or prose the emotions of the contemporary world in which I lived? If my destiny was to be a novelist my first novel would be accepted in due course; I must leave it for destiny to decide. I was not prepared to attempt another novel until I was able to turn the pages of that first novel, printed and bound. What had happened was that I had been bewitched by the fascination of gardening in Cornwall; that I was indeed so utterly absorbed by a new passion that the fate of my first novel was seeming less and less important. My mother was rather worried by this; she was apprehensive that this preoccupation with gardening might be another temporary interest pursued for a while to the detriment of my finding out what I really wanted to do. She had been disappointed when I told her that my lay readership was not going to be a preliminary to my ordination. She had been worried by coming to the end of her marriage settlement. Fortunately my father's affairs were flourishing, and in that spring of 1909 *The Arcadians*, in which he had a third interest with Robert Courtneidge and his own partner, Milton Bode, began its career at the Shaftesbury Theatre, where it would run for two years; with the mind's eye I see that wonderful woman Ciceley Courtneidge in her teens playing an ingénue.

As a sign of that paternal prosperity an H.M.V. gramophone arrived at Rivière with about two dozen polychromatic celebrity records, some black-label orchestral records and all of Harry Lauder's output. I much enjoyed the sextet from *Lucia di Lammermoor*, Destinn singing *Un bel dì*, Caruso, and Harry Lauder, but orchestral music and even solo violin recordings at that date did not seem worth the trouble of putting on. Fourteen years would pass before the gramophone would join the list of my passions. It may have been in the hope of diverting my obsession with Flora that my mother had sent a copy of my *Poems* to Henry James that autumn. He had written:

Lamb House
Rye
Sussex
Nov. 14th 1908

Dear Mrs Compton,

   I am horror-stricken at the way I have suffered delays to accumulate and pile themselves up in the matter of my acknowledging your gift of your son's very interesting and charming volume of verse. I have at most times two or three volumes, of sorts, on my hands, and on my mind, to acknowledge (and appreciate!) and that complication appears to have blocked the way a good deal, in combination with other blockings. I wish all the appeals to appreciation, or half of them, were really as worth attention as this little book of your accomplished young Monty's has all the while struck me as being. His verses have, to my sense the positive note of distinction and grace and style—and you're not for a moment to think, nor is he, that my slowness to give you this assurance has had to do with anything in them more unpropitious than their having disposed me to take them in piece by piece. I find in him a real interest in poetics—that is in verse forms and varieties, and a great deal of skill and art in using them; a great deal of fancy and tenderness and taste—and above all a great deal of youth! But he must tackle prose with some of that latent energy, and I hope he is to have—or has had—good news of his novel from Heinemann. Having let me see his verses, you must some day let me see him—for I remember his infancy and one of his birthdays somewhere. How far that time seems now—though Compton appears so unaware of the lapse of the interval. Give, please, my friendly blessing to the artful young Monty—"that hansom rattles like a castanet!"—I wd. give much to have written that!—and tell him that I congratulate him much on his sense of the quality of words and of images, and that I am most truly his and yours.

Henry James

I read that remark about tackling prose and his hope that I had good news from Heinemann about my novel with a kind of wry amusement. At this point let that mood continue without talking any more about it, and let me get back to that spring of 1909. I was hard at work gardening; Faith was hard at work on a layette for the baby that was to arrive at the end of June. At the beginning of May my father wrote from Chester, where in partnership with Milton Bode he owned the theatre, as with Bode he was part-owner of theatres in Reading, Leicester, Northampton, Huddersfield, Wolverhampton and Dalston, to say that he had arranged for me to produce a Pageant there in July. Pageants were all the rage about now; even Oxford had succumbed to having a pageant. I was not at all attracted to the notion of producing a pageant at Chester, and I obviously suggested as much when I wrote to my father to say I had heard nothing yet from Chester. On May 12th he was writing to me:

The offer is probably delayed a day or two because of the forming of a preliminary Committee etc., but it should come all right. If found necessary the Pageant could be the week of July 19th in place of the 5th or 12th.

The Garden must be left to the gardener and the Novel proofs you can correct at Chester. I said nothing about Railway Fares and out of pocket expenses, but no doubt they will find these, though I wouldn't haggle over them in the face of such good payment. I should merely accept offer, and say you presumed they would pay your 3rd Return Railway Fare, Hayle to Chester and back, and pay all out

*of pocket expenses in connection with the Pageant and leave it at that. Yes, I think
you will have to write something for it. One thing I foresee will be an address
for me to speak as a Prologue to the Pastoral on the Opening Day in the second
dress of Garrick. I hope he played Chester once! If a great success you could
speak it on the 5 following days. Nobody else has written anything. All the
acting will be in the Pastoral Play, though I think in addition to the Procession
through Chester . . .*

What my father thought I do not remember, and the rest of that
letter has vanished. In May I must still have been feeling optimistic
about the prospect of my novel's being accepted when I used that,
together with the garden, in a vain effort to discourage the idea of
going to Chester.

I was there for about a fortnight and soon realized that there was no
likelihood of a pageant's being produced at Chester. Other cathedral
cities all over England might be doing pageants; the Mayor and Cor-
poration of Chester did not want to have a pageant.

I was summoned urgently from Chester to Abingdon, where Faith
had gone to await her confinement.

The births in *The Times* of Tuesday, June 1, 1909, recorded:

"Compton Mackenzie—On the 27th May, prematurely, at Abing-
don-on-Thames, the wife of M. Compton Mackenzie, of a son (stillborn)."

I doubt if any man can appreciate the full bitterness of a woman's
disappointment when so much travail leaves her with nothing. Perhaps if the father were longing for an heir to a title and estate his own
disappointment might compare with that of his wife. In my case the
prospect of fatherhood had been clouded over by the insecurity of my
financial position and the uncertainty evoked by the first refusal of my
novel. I had hoped for a daughter, for whom I had chosen Corinna as
a name; it was almost a relief when I was told that the stillborn child
was a boy. I ask myself now whether I should like to have a son fifty-
five years old with grandchildren and perhaps great-grandchildren. I
can say with complete certainty that I should not. I have never felt
the faintest desire for a son, and although I should have liked a daughter
or two I reflect that they would probably have presented me with
sons-in-law whom I should have deplored. This is not entirely an ad-
mission of intolerable egotism. I should always have felt that a son of
mine would have been handicapped after his early childhood by a
father with what might be called an excess of personality. True, I had
never felt the least handicap from having a father who was at home

equally with both old and young and had been for years a well-loved actor all over Great Britain and Ireland. At the same time, from my early 'teens onward it never occurred to me that he knew as much about life or understood people as well as I did. I respected him and recognized his integrity, but I used to feel faintly sorry for him when he talked of his own father with such obvious belief that "father" was always right.

My brother, who had been in Crete with his regiment, that Crete which seemed then to offer a more insoluble problem than Cyprus now, was in Malta. He had had to call on his father to pay for polo ponies; now the regiment was ordered to Tientsin, which meant a good deal of expense for a new uniform that involved fur. His father must have written a severe letter, and in a moment of exasperation Frank sent in his papers. What was an ex-Fusilier to do? In Frank's case the answer was the stage. I think if his father had had imagination he would have let Frank start by playing at least "third walking gentlemen", that is Careless, Fag and the rest. Instead he insisted on Frank's starting at the very bottom as junior prompter at a pound a week and sharing rooms with himself and his sister Viola. Frank and his father were not on speaking terms almost at once and in the end he went off to Canada, where Faith's brother Guy gave him hospitality for a while until, after earning a living for some time by driving round in a fur-coat with a pony and cart, selling milk, he got an engagement with a touring company going to Australia.

My father was disappointed about the failure of the Chester pageant to materialize, but the success of *The Arcadians*, the Mercédès car, and good health, made his vacation in that July enjoyable. He had taken up golf and believed with what I have always felt was the pathetic credulity of middle-age in its being the healthy kind of exercise a man of fifty-five required. All three of my sisters were at Rivière that summer and were given the whole of the top floor to themselves.

When Faith came back from Abingdon we resumed our weekly visits to Toy Cottage; we were much touched by the warmth of sympathy over that stillbirth.

My Sunday school outing was not quite as successful as it had been last year. We decided to visit Praa Sands again; when we were half way there it began to rain, and it continued to rain relentlessly for the rest of the day. I found a little shelter under some trees along a wall against which the children and I sat, most of us in oilskins, while I tried to keep them amused with stories. Presently came along a starry-eyed young visitor from up along, who asked eagerly if we had been wrecked and in which direction she should go to see the vessel in which we had been driven ashore. When I told her that we were a school treat, her starry eyes were clouded as heavily with disappointment as the sky was with rain.

Soon after this I met Owen Seaman, the new editor of *Punch*, who was staying at the Poldhu Hotel for golf. I had always admired his verses in *Punch* but could not detect in himself any of the grace and wit which inspired them. He was solemn, and on the edge of being slightly pompous. I told him the story of the girl who had hoped for a wreck and was given a Sunday school treat; I rather expected it might be illustrated in *Punch* presently. He did not seem to think it as funny as I did.

On another occasion that summer Sich drove me over to lunch with P. D. Williams at Lamarth on the eastern side of the Meneage. Percy Williams was one of the great pioneers of the daffodil and raised some of the most famous varieties. With us at lunch that day was E. A. Bowles, famous for his feats with crocus species in that garden of his beside the river Lea. The dining-room window looked on a green slope covered with yuccas. I hear now Bowles's squeaky voice expressing his astonishment that one of these yuccas had seeded without being pollinated by hand.

"I don't understand it. I don't understand how one of your yuccas can have seeded without the help of Pronuba yuccatacella."

Seeing Sich and myself looking rather puzzled, Bowles in his squeaky voice explained:

"*Pronuba yuccatacella* is a moth which collects pollen and in collecting it fertilizes the yucca and at the same time provides board and lodging for her own family."

After lunch we walked round the garden; Percy Williams told us that he was beginning to become just a little less interested in raising new daffodils and was becoming extremely interested in raising new rhododendrons. We went into a small greenhouse, and he showed us pot after pot of two- and three-year-old seedlings from which he hoped great things some ten years hence. Those who have followed rhododendrons will know how abundantly his hopes were rewarded.

That was the day I first met *Sollya heterophylla*, and I have never seen it so well placed since, a mass of bluebell-like flowers falling over a red brick arch. There, too, I first saw *Calceolaria Burbidgei*, a superb bush about five feet square growing against a wall in what seemed a solid sheet of lemon-yellow blossom. I was to grow this hybrid between *C. pavonii* and *C. fuchsiafolia* from the Dublin Botanical Gardens with

Sunday school outing. Gunwalloe 1908

Toy Cottage

Faith

Monty 1913

fair success at Rivière, but I was never to see it growing as well as I saw it growing in the garden of Lamarth. Near it was a fine bush either of *Cassia floribunda* or *C. corymbosa*, the orange of which, or better the honey-gold of which, made a beautiful contrast with the calceolaria. That day, too, I saw for the first time *Clematis Davidiana*, whose pale-blue hyacinthine bells made a great impression on me. I well remember my delight when Sich and I got into the dog-cart to drive home and Percy Williams said he had told his gardener to dig up half a dozen plants of the clematis I had admired and put them in a basket for me to take back to Rivière. Later on I acquired from Lemoine of Nancy all the varieties they had raised of those herbaceous clematises, but none of their many shades of blue ever gave me quite the pleasure of those first clumps of *C. Davidiana* presented to me on that summer's day in 1909.

I find in a ledger surviving from this period a catalogue of the shrubs, herbaceous plants and bulbs I had planted at Rivière between 1908 and 1910 and am slightly awed to find that the number of different varieties exceeded three thousand.

This collection was obtained from Britain, Holland, France, Germany, California, British Columbia, New Zealand and Australia; mostly in seeds, of course, from overseas.

A bill has survived from 1909 of John Lewis Childs, Floral Park, New York. Childs was one of the great pioneers of the gladiolus we have to-day. One item is twelve bulbs of New, Odd and Beautiful Gladiolus at $1.50. I read also of one tuber Sweet Potato, Early Triumph. No doubt I was hopeful of growing sweet potatoes for my mother, who often sighed for those sweet potatoes of her American youth.

And from Ukiah, California, in October 1909 I read:

Dear Sir, Your order for Primula Suffruticosa filled by this post. They were collected in the Sierra Nevada Mountains at nearly 8000 feet in early October. They grow on a south slope near the crest of the ridge in a very light soil. I would plant in a cool situation and keep well covered with leaves in the winter.
Yours truly
Carl Purdy

That was a well-known name in horticulture fifty years ago.

I find, with what some gardening readers may consider the almost intolerable self-confidence of a fool jumping in where angels fear to tread, that as early as the end of the year I was in communication with

E

the publishers Kegan Paul about the possibility of my writing a book on gardening in West Cornwall for the autumn of 1910.

I have played with the notion of writing a book about my gardening life ever since, but something has always intervened and, although I still play with the notion, I doubt if that book will ever be written. However, I shall indulge in an abstract of those gardening years in Cornwall; it will be easier to anticipate 1910 and 1911 now because there will be much else to record then.

When I first saw Rivière I had been attracted by the shelter those elms seemed to provide against the sea-wind; what I overlooked was the soil, which was the worst I could have chosen for the particular plants and shurbs that had caught my imagination. If I had searched all Cornwall I could not have discovered a less suitable habitat for Himalayan rhododendrons and all those peat-loving plants I had been admiring in the magnesian soil of the Meneage. Leaf mould there was in plenty, but the leaf mould of elms I found valueless for any plant and positively harmful to many, with its shiny blue and white streaks of fungus. Farewell to tree-ferns!

Compensation was not far away; I discovered as soon as I began to learn something that the light soil, swift drainage, southern slope and modicum of lime in the walled garden at Rivière with its 10-feet walls of slag as nearly ideal as any ground could be in England for all kinds of difficult bulbs and for quite enough sub-tropical shrubs and herbaceous plants to make up for the lack of the suitable natural conditions for the particular glories of the usual Cornish gardens.

Within two years of starting I find the following note in *Gardening Illustrated* of June 4th 1910:

The Cultivation of Bulbous Irises

I fancy that I answered Mr Fitzherbert's questions (page 219) more or less in my last note. I should add, however, that most of the irises mentioned have bloomed with me two successive seasons, and that imported bulbs of *Iris alata* did not throw one flower this year, while those already in my garden had larger and more richly coloured blooms than any I have seen since. The soil is a very light sandy loam, which has been worked for a hundred years or more. I dress heavily with bone meal, and surround each bulb at planting with sand from the towans at the back of my house; the latter contains a large proportion of lime from broken sea-shells. Most of the Junes are found in limestone. The Persica class has an annoying habit of growing well and throwing a bud which turns brown and suddenly topples over; it reminds me of *Lilium auratum* in this habit. I wondered whether some muscular worm had shifted their roots; they behaved quite decently the following year. The black fungus seems an insuperable barrier to certain success with the *I. reticulata* class. I believe the best thing to do is to plant them within reach of hungry roots, as one does with white daffodils. Some bulbs of *I. histrio*—the trickiest of all—were better at the foot of an old peach-tree against a south wall. Mr Herbert Chapman told me the other day that early bees fertilised for him, but his garden is later than mine, and personally I never met a bee that would look twice at any iris. All my tall Junos like *bucharica* have set seed through the agency of those weary-looking flies that loaf round a garden in early spring. Sir Michael Foster said that Cushion irises were naturally short-lived and wanted hand fertilisation as bees were frightened by their strange appearance. It is the beard more than anything else. They suspect the presence of spiders.

I think that shallow planting is the first step in the cultivation of all Asiatic bulbs. This applies particularly to the Turkestan tulips. It is absurd to say that because they are found a foot deep in clay we should plant them under similar conditions. In the west of England, where the sun is never powerful, this shallow planting seems more than ever necessary. The second step to successful cultivation of Eastern irises is the presence of lime. I believe this to be as important for Junos as for Cushion irises. Then, they must be ripened with a light in summer, and they ought to have the glass put over them the moment their flowers begin to fade. The other steps are sharp drainage through the medium of beds raised six inches above the surrounding soil, care against slugs, August planting (if one can induce nurserymen to send them out in time), and finally a perpetual optimism. By the way, I do not think that peat is at all a desirable addition to the soil, nor do I think that leaf mould in the proportion of a quarter is necessary.

With regard to irises in bloom to-day (April 22nd) *I. hauranensis* is blooming in solitary and sombre glory. The colour is that sad purple which you find in ten-week stocks—the variety that Parkinson calls the Melancholy Gentleman. It is netted with darker lines, and has glossy black and large signal blotches. The beard is straw-coloured. The rest of the Cushion irises will not be fully out for a week or so. *I. tol-long* (*tolmeana* X *longipetala*) looks well with a group of *Camassia Leichtlinii* seedlings. It rather reminds me of some forms of *I. stylosa*, but the net-work is clearer, and of course the standards are much smaller. I wish all your readers could have seen the Rev. A. T. Boscawen's bunch of *I. tingitana* at Truro Daffodil Show. It was magnificent.

M. C. MACKENZIE

This is a cutting that survives from the various notes I used to send to the gardening papers at this period of my life, and I am amused by the dogmatic self-assurance of a young gardener with hardly more than two years' practical experience. Yet in justice to myself at that

age I can boast that I did flower all the Cushion irises then in cultivation every year for at least three years, a feat which I never succeeded
in equalling later, either in Capri where the soil and climatic conditions were far more favourable than at Hayle, or in Jethou where the
climatic conditions were the same and the soil required for Cushion
irises should have been easily managed. During the 'nineties of the last
century the Rev. H. Ewbank, whose name is kept alive by a tulip, used
to have similar triumphs in the Isle of Wight. In 1911 I had no less
than twelve *I. paradoxa* in flower at once and in the same Spring
I. Lortetii and *I. Gatesii*, the two most beautiful irises of all; I wonder
how many amateur gardeners to-day can show the sublime flowers of
Lortetii and *Gatesii*.

I was exceptionally fortunate in having within reach so many of the
great Cornish gardeners, all of whom were always willing to give their
advice, and what was more, some of their rarities, to a young enthusiast.
Every visit to the Rev. A. T. Boscawen's garden on top of that hill at
Ludgvan was a fresh inspiration. I remember his telling me that he
was thinking of giving up everything except New Zealand plants, but
as in a corner of his garden he had hundreds of seedlings from one of
Forrest's or Kingdon Ward's Chinese expeditions I doubt if the resolution was kept. Celmisias were his particular passion at the moment, a
passion with which he fired me; he grew them wonderfully at Ludgvan
Rectory; I never succeeded, with all his advice, in making much of
any celmisias except *coriacea*. On the other hand I was able to grow
that other New Zealand daisy *Olearia insignis* to perfection; I even
dreamed of crossing it with one of the shrubby Olearias in order to
produce an eight-feet bush covered with those fat *Insignis* daisies which
remain as fresh as a daisy for nearly two months. I grew it at the foot
of a wall where it could keep as dry as it liked.

In a field near Ludgvan Rectory I saw what I believe I can call the
most perfect combination of land- and sea-scape I ever saw. It was a
ten-acre field of that vivid green Cornish grass, surrounded on three
sides by a belt of dark pines—*insignis* probably—underneath which
was growing a line of that black-stemmed hydrangea with panicles of
intensely blue flowers. Southward the view was open to Mount's Bay;
between the dark pines and blue hydrangeas St Michael's Mount
seemed to float on an azure sea beneath an azure sky. The sky, the sea,
the narrow bosket of blue hydrangeas, the emerald grass, and the dark
green of the pines created an unforgettable vision of severe yet immensely rich colour to which was added the supreme simplicity of
design one finds in a Chinese picture. I wished that one of the St Ives

painters would preserve the picture of that field but nobody who is not a painter ever succeeds in recommending a landscape or seascape to a painter; Julius Ohlsen, Arnesby Brown, Lamorna Birch and others less renowned listened patiently to my plea for that field, but none of them was inspired to take a look for himself and preserve on canvas those pines and hydrangeas and grass with the sea and the sky and that castellated islet beyond. Perhaps I should have pleaded with the Newlyn painters at Mousehole: Ludgvan was more convenient for them.

Lionel St Aubyn, a grandson of the first Lord St Levan, had been at Stone House, my father-in-law's prep. school, and his grandfather invited Faith and myself to lunch some time in that summer of 1909. I recall arriving at Marazion station and being met by a brougham with wooden seats instead of leather cushions because the sea-damp was too much for leather. It was low tide and so the brougham was able to drive across the causeway to St Michael's Mount. It was quite a climb up winding stone staircases to the top of the castle, and all the way up there were large stuffed tropical fish, souvenirs of Lord St Levan's prowess as a fisherman. The tide was high when it was time to leave after lunch and we went back to Marazion in the barge. I must have sent Lionel St Aubyn a copy of my poems from Rivière; that copy appeared in a second-hand book catalogue over fifty years later priced at eight guineas.

Back to my gardening. I recall four trees, the first sight of which is in my mind's eye to-day. I have already mentioned the magnificent specimen of *Benthamia fragifera*, that great dark-green glossy mass of leaves hung with hundreds of glowing crimson strawberries, in the garden of Cury Vicarage. The next revelation was *Embothrium coccineum* growing in the garden of Bochym in the heart of the Meneage. Those who have seen that Chilean tree blazing will need no words from me; those who have not should take the first opportunity available of curing their ignorance. The third revelation was a large *Eucryphia pinnatifolia* in full bloom in the great Bolitho garden near Penzance, the August air heavy with its hawthorn scent, the ground beneath covered inches deep with fallen snowy petals. Finally in that same garden was the largest *Lomatia ferruginea* I should ever see, a truly noble piece of vegetation exceeding in beauty any tree-fern. I planted a *Lomatia ferruginea* at Rivière where in spite of the substitution of peat and leaf-mould for the light limy soil it did not thrive. Many years later I planted a small specimen of this Chilean tree at Jethou where it stood up to the east wind with great courage, for the fern-like foliage, rusty brown underneath, is extremely tough. Wherever *Lomatia ferruginea* can be planted without extremes of frost in a soil free from lime it should be planted, and that as soon as possible, for it is a slow grower.

The development of the "German" iris which has been such a conspicuous feature of post-war gardening spared my anxious purse when I was gardening in Cornwall. At that time the garden variety erroneously called *I. pallida dalmatica* was about the largest iris we had. My passion remained concentrated on the *oncocyclus, reticulata,* and *juno* sections. I must elaborate a little on that note from *Gardening Illustrated* quoted above. Search and I later made a raised bed about two feet above the level of the garden and added to the already well-limed soil a generous amount of chalk and bonemeal. The rhizomes were planted deep enough to allow boards to be put over the top of the bed on which Search and I used to jump as hard as we could to press the soil tight. The rhizomes were planted as early as I could get hold of them in the summer. Lights were then placed above the bed at a sufficient height to allow air in all round but extending far enough on either side to prevent so much as a drop of rain reaching it. These lights were removed at the end of October and the bed was then covered with about a couple of feet of dried bracken. This bracken was not put there to protect the rhizomes against frost but to supply the nearest substitute I could think of for the heavy covering of snow under which so many Cushion irises spend the winter. At the beginning of March the bracken was taken off but the lights were not put over the bed again until there were signs of flowering; during the years when I was able to superintend the operations myself the results were satisfactory.

After the First World War when I tried the same method again in the islands of Herm and Jethou I did not have much success; I attributed this partly to the fact that the soil of the Channel Isles had no natural lime in it and partly to the decrease in the vitality of all stocks of *Oncocyclus* iris during the depressing years of the war. Moreover, the species available for distribution were not nearly so various as once upon a time; during the war the stock of many varieties had been exhausted owing to the impossibility of sending collectors to their natural habitats. Finally the comparative ease with which Tubergen's beautiful *regelio-cyclus* hybrids could be grown was making most gardeners content with them.

Far be it from me to criticize the beautiful varieties now obtainable in the *Pogoniris* section, the old "German" irises, but I must maintain that they cannot compare with the aristocrats of the *Oncocyclus* section. They are to them as the triumphs of cement in modern architecture to the triumph of the Parthenon; for one perfect bloom of *I. Lortetii* I would give the lot. And *I. paradoxa!* There is an effect of violet as supreme in its own shade as the blue of *Gentiana acaulis*; no Tyrian dye ever achieved such intensity.

The usual method of cultivating Cushion irises was to lift the rhizomes every year when the foliage had ripened off and replant them in October, but no rhizomatous irises like being disturbed. In my father-in-law's garden near Broadstairs, which had formerly belonged to Archbishop Tait, *I. susiana* grew as freely as *I. germanica*; my *I. susiana* at Rivière in that raised bed was no more robust than any of its relations. The strange thing about *I. susiana* is that nobody knows where its native habitat was. It reached Western Europe at the end of the seventeenth century and is mentioned in Parkinson's herbal as the Great Spotted or Turkey Flower de Luce.

As well as with *Oncocyclus* irises I was successful with *Junos*, and mention of them reminds me of a mystery I never solved. I was sent a tuberous root of *I. Wilmottiana* which flowered with me three years running without increasing. The flowers of what was sent to me as *I. Wilmottiana* were a vivid Cambridge blue with an equally vivid Oxford blue patch, and to no description I could find of *I. Wilmottiana* did that colouring apply; nor did it apply to any *Juno* iris I have seen or read about. The original *I. Wilmottiana* came from Tashkent and was described as blue-purple with a conspicuous white patch. I hope that some fellow-member of the Iris Society who reads this may be able to correct me when I say that *I. Wilmottiana* is no longer in cultivation, having apparently with other *Junos* died out from inability to provide them with the heavy soil they like and the sun to ripen them.

Juno bulbs loathe being disturbed on account of the damage done to their fleshy tuberous roots. *I. bucharica* is the one best able to stand up to our soil and climate. I had one in Cornwall in 1909 which was sent out to me in Capri in 1913, and from Capri sent to Herm in 1922, whence it was moved to Jethou, where it was still growing and seeding when I left Jethou in 1930. Its lovely companions, my Oxford and Cambridge *Wilmottiana*, my gold and violet *Warleyensis*, and my yellow and white *orchioides* were by then faded and gone. Dykes mentions a hybrid between *sindjarensis* and *persica* of a wonderful turquoise blue; my *Wilmottiana* was another *sindjarensis* hybrid; but *sindjarensis* and *persica* have a spun-silk texture and my *Wilmottiana* had the porcelain quality which is characteristic of *bucharica*.

I wonder if any Cornish gardeners to-day have specimens of that beautiful prehistoric iris *Moraea Robinsoniana*? The plant was originally found on the remote Lord Howe's Island until it was exterminated, fortunately not before it had passed into general cultivation in Australia, where the flowers, resembling white Spanish iris, are used in wedding bouquets. It was a superb affair with great sword-shaped leaves five feet high and as many as three hundred flowers on a stem six feet long; I had one plant which was doing well when I gave up my Cornish garden.

Prehistoric plants always had a fascination for me. Is *Primula gigantea* still in cultivation? It is found high up on some mountain in Java, and it grew well with me in Cornwall. The flower is insignificant—a feebly coloured kind of overgrown cowslip—but the leaves are prodigious, quite two feet long, in the shape of our own native primrose leaves. I am glad to think that the prehistoric forget-me-not from the Chatham Islands, *Myosotidium nobile*, is to be found nowadays in many gardens. This is just as well; I believe that cattle on the Chatham Islands have eaten up the stock.

I had little success with lilies, no doubt because I had no time to grow lilies, as they should be grown, from seed. I shall never forget the impression made by my first visit to the R.H.S. gardens at Wisley in this year 1909 when I first saw groups of lilies sown by Wilson in that patch of Surrey woodland. There was a group of *L. giganteum* which has haunted my memory ever since; there must have been twenty stems twelve feet high scenting the wood in majesty.

I never saw any outstanding lily-gardens in Cornwall. I tried importing *L. auratum*, *L. speciosum* and others direct from Japan; the result was always failure, and the expense of buying home-grown bulbs was prohibitive.

My greatest success was with lemon-yellow *L. monadelphum* from the Caucasus; perhaps if I had stayed long enough at Rivière I might have seen one of my *monadelphums* flower above the boughs of an apple-tree. Nearly forty years ago I found myself one stormy night in the snuggery of a small inn in Wester Ross. Into the snuggery from a coach, as he still called the 'bus, came a minister with whom I had one of the most absorbing horticultural talks I ever enjoyed. I cannot remember his name, but he once had a daffodil called after him, a daffodil rather like *W. P. Milner*, a favourite in its day. In the course of our talk he related how once upon a time he had planted a bulb of *L. monadelphum* under an apple-tree where it grew rapidly in a dressing of manure which had been dug in round the tree to restore its fruiting vigour. Indeed, the lily throve so well that its stem finally grew up through the branches of the apple-tree until it was able to spread a parasol of yellow blooms above the tree not less than ten feet high. I have seen specimens of *L. monadelphum* up to eight feet, but never a giant of ten feet, and as I ponder in fancy over that mighty lily the name of the little minister comes back to me; it was Williamson.

By an agreeable coincidence, after writing about *oncocyclus* irises, I read in the *Royal Horticultural Society's Journal* for March 1964 a vivid account of Lebanon and of the author's disappointment at not finding any of the irises he longed to see in full flower, until in a sheltered southern spot he found *I. sofarina*, of which there was a coloured photograph. As I looked at it I was back in Cornwall in this year of 1909 and looking at my own *I. sofarina* in the garden of Rivière.

My imagination had been fired by reading about Max Leichtlin's garden in Baden-Baden and I had visions of establishing a comparable garden at Rivière. With all their climatic advantage most of the Cornish gardens lacked the ideal soil for growing bulbs or the kind of plants that were classed with bulbs in the nursery catalogues. It was Max Leichtlin's triumphs with such plants which made the tale of them my Eldorado. With a sandy soil well limed but not chalky, with a southern slope, and with the ten-feet high slag wall that ensured the amount of extra heat in summer which the unaided Cornish sun could not provide, I might reasonably hope to achieve wonders. Moreover, youth was still mine and that exhilarating inexperience which tempts a man to try for miracles. The extent of my optimism may be gauged when I confess that my first ambition was to cross the freesia with the ixia and sparaxis. I saw in the mind's eye and smelt with the mind's nose brilliant flowers of every hue from fiery scarlet to sea-green, all of them with the orange-blossom scent of the freesia. Before I had an opportunity even to arrange for the simultaneous blooming of the subjects for my proposed experiment in cross-pollination, I saw the first result of Herbert Chapman's success in giving diversity of colour to the freesia without any help from the ixia or the sparaxis. Deciding that he had struck on a much more promising method of development than myself, I abandoned the project to raise 'frixias' and turned my attention to kniphofias.

It was appropriately *K. Leichtlinii* which incited me to tackle the kniphofias. This plant, introduced from Abyssinia in 1886, is described in Nicholson's *Dictionary of Gardening* as having dull pale vermilion-red and yellow flowers; Chittenden in the Royal Horticultural Society's *Dictionary of Gardening* follows Nicholson. Neither by any word to the contrary suggests that the flowers are not deflexed like the rest of the genus. The plant growing in my garden as *K. Leichtlinii* had light canary-yellow flowers with a protruding tuft of brilliant crimson stamens like a panache, and the flowers were not deflexed but almost erect. I have not noted *K. Leichtlinii* in any catalogue for fifty years, nor have I seen the variety I acquired as *K. Leichtlinii* in any other garden. It certainly was a grand kniphofia, as vivid in my memory to-day as if it were still growing before my eyes. I wrote about it once in the *New Flora and Silva* but heard no news of it. Does *K. Leichtlinii* exist anywhere to-day? Is it not time that some expert collector explored again the flora of Abyssinia?

K. comosa had a tuft of protruding yellow stamens with erect flowers; I grew that also and am not confusing it with my *K. Leichtlinii*; it was a much smaller plant.

Apart from the loss of practically all the species kniphofias from cultivation, all the best hybrids of the past except *Ophir* seem to have vanished and their places have not been taken by others. *Chloris, Heroine, Lachesis, Obelisk, Pfitzeri, Solfaterra*, and noblest of all *Star of Baden-Baden* were all grown by me to make the part of the garden they occupied look like a Turner sunset. Above the kniphofias at the head of the slope I planted a *Romneya Coulteri*, which grew into a superb specimen. A corps de ballet might have looked tame beside that Californian tree-poppy covered with hundreds of golden-hearted ballerinas whose perfume scented the air for yards around them as they danced for the orange and amber and scarlet and yellow kniphofias eyeing them like military connoisseurs of feminine charms.

K. Tuckii was the earliest in the year to flower, and moreover the most rapid to do so from seed. To my fancy it was the ugliest and dullest of the kniphofias, with a particularly crude red tip to the washy yellow, closely deflexed flowers. The ease with which it could be grown made me ambitious to cross it with some of the brilliant later varieties. I used to sow *K. Tuckii* in pans in August, bring them under glass in October, transplant them into pots in January, and take the risk of planting them out in the open in mid-March. I remember a day, bleak and raw and near to frost, when I was planting out *K. Tuckii* and refused to come in to tea, racing the melancholy dusk to get my task finished. I was justified in taking that risk; that batch of *K. Tuckii* grew at such a pace that some of them flowered at the end of August, a year after they were sown. Normally they would not have flowered until the following June. As it was I was able to cross them with the aristocratic beauties in full floral display. The cross was not successful, but I now knew I could get *K. Tuckii* to flower in August instead of June; if I had persevered and gone on with my cross-pollination experiments I might ultimately have achieved something worth while.

One of the joys of the Rivière garden was the ability to grow with complete success in the open *K. Nelsonii*, that brilliant little scarlet kniphofia from the old Orange Free State; the lateness of its blooming period in October prevented its seeding. I tried to marry *Nelsonii* to a dull little lady from Natal called *modesta* and perhaps with the help of her rather dingy white flowers raise a family of pink and carmine children. *K. modesta* herself is only worth growing as a curiosity, though in her native land she may have a purer white than here. Another white-flowered kniphofia from South Africa also blooms in October, but *K. multiflora* is much more distinguished than *modesta*. The flowers are more of an ivory than pure white, and the spikes are somewhat loose. At Rivière both of my clumps reached eight feet; during a gale the very long leaves used to lash the ground beneath as smooth as a billiards-table. Growing against the wall beyond *K. multiflora* was *Buddleia auriculata* also from South Africa and flowering at the same time. The creamy flowers deepening almost to buff smell exactly like a honeycomb. Those two plants will always be associated together in my mind, but I have not seen *K. multiflora* since Rivière. I succeeded in crossing *multiflora* with *longicollis*, another South African species flowering late, with blooms of a lovely shade of lemon-yellow. Unfortunately I abandoned my Rivière garden before my seedlings flowered; I was hoping for primrose-yellow blooms on one of them.

In those days *K. Northiae* was always providing controversial notes in the gardening papers. People used to write and brag about the foliage, which was as handsome as a blue-green yucca and grew in a tough rosette. The flower spikes were ugly, a dirty yellow turning to a dirty red. No sooner did somebody mention *K. Northiae* than somebody else would write to say that it could not be *K. Northiae* from South Africa but must be *K. quartiniana* from Abyssinia. Thereupon somebody else would write to declare that both the preceding correspondents were wrong and that it must be *K. foliosa*. In fact the last two were identical and my *Northiae* differed from my *quartiniana* by its leaves being glaucous and indented whereas *quartiniana's* were a more yellowish green and smooth, but whether I had the right plants I do not know. *K. caulescens*, with brick-coloured flowers fading to a sort of decayed russet, was another kniphofia sometimes introduced into the argument.

K. Rooperi was handsome and usually flowered well into December, with orange-red flowers and fine foliage. Then there was a distinguished fellow called *Burchelli*, almost as bright a red and yellow as the old Spanish flag but tipped with green like some of the lachemalias. *Carnosa* was an impressive apricot-coloured kniphofia from Abyssinia with pro-truding yellow anthers. I also grew *Macowani, pumila, pauciflora, praecox, citrina, breviflora, corallina,* and of course every variety of *aloides,* as it used to be called in those days. The only desirable kniphofia I never succeeded in obtaining was *pallidiflora,* a white variety from the moun-tains of central Madagascar.

I have written at such length about kniphofias in a missionary spirit, in the hope that some of them will be brought back into cultivation. At present it looks as if the only kniphofias available are the old Red Hot Poker, *K. uvaria,* and the garden hybrid *Ophir.* I fear I shall never see my *K. Leichtlinii* again; he looked like an operatic hussar before the First World War and is probably as extinct.

The gladiolus offered another great opportunity to the hybridist at this date, when we called it gládiolus or sometimes gladíolus but *never* gladiōlus. The Oxford Dictionary recognized gladíolus as a permissible pronunciation but preferred gládiolus. To-day the Oxford Dictionary gives the barbaric gladiōlus as the pronunciation and does not even allow gládiolus, the correct pronunciation, to be mentioned.

Some five years earlier *G. primulinus* from the Victoria Falls had been first shown, and there were already plenty of pastel pink and cream and salmon-coloured *primulinus* hybrids. However, so far nobody had worked the *primulinus* yellow into the larger-flowered varieties, of which *gandavensis,* whatever might have been its complicated origin in Hol-land, seemed by now firmly enough fixed as a type to take kindly to the introduction of even yet another strain. Gladiolus growers had been working for years to achieve an unmistakable yellow but without better success than the sweet-pea growers. I had ambitions to emulate in yellow the triumphs achieved with scarlet first at Brenchley as long ago as 1848, and then even more remarkably in the United States where Van Fleet raised the superb *princeps* by fertilizing *G. cruentus* with *G. Childsii. Childsii* itself had been originally raised by my hero Max Leichtlin by crossing *gandavensis* with *G. Saundersii.* This had been bought in America and renamed after its purchaser J. L. Childs, from whom I was buying bulbs and seeds in 1909.

I heard of a reputedly fine yellow which had been raised in Ramsgate and travelled all the way from Cornwall to see it; good flower though it was, it was not my idea of yellow. I worked hard with *primulinus* pollen, not merely on the garden hybrids like *gandavensis, Childsii* and *Lemoinei,* but also on various species. Among other crosses I made were some with *G. tristis* in the hope of getting the perfume from the night-flowering *G. tristis* into a new race of gladiolus; although I did succeed in raising two or three *tristis X primulinus* hybrids, the only result was to lose both scent and colour. Yet if circumstances had ruled that I should persevere with serious gardening, I might in the end have produced something worth while from this cross. After all, the exquisite, popular and profitable *Bride* was a sport from *G. Colvillei*—itself a hybrid between the tender *tristis* and the tender *cardinalis*, a lovely flower but without perfume. I tried to obtain corms of *G. dracocephalus* and of the sweet-scented *G. recurvus* without success. Are they in cultivation now? Has their pollen been used in crosses? There are so many magnificent gládioli nowadays that further experimental crossing may seem a work of supererogation. Yet the blue gladiolus is still as far away as a blue rose and likely to remain so. *Baron Hulot*, which was still something of a sensation in 1909, was heralded as the first of a wonderful race of violets that might in time achieve a genuine blue; that wonderful race of blues has never appeared. Has the pollen of *G. byzantinus* or *G. communis* been used with any success? I did not have either in Cornwall, but later on I was to see them growing in such profusion in Southern Europe and Asia Minor that I used to wonder whether the vigour of them might not introduce a valuable power of resistance to disease.

With the prospect of ever getting my first novel published growing dimmer month by month through the rest of that year 1909 I resolved to become a professional gardener. That visit to the gládiolus raiser in Kent had convinced me that a bulb-grower's life was a hard one and that years must elapse before I could hope to extract from it anything more than a bare living. Nevertheless, I had enough faith in my own creative imagination to believe it would carry me further than the average bulb-grower, and that in the years when my new daffodils had succeeded my new gládioli I should be doing much better than earning a bare living. I was still under the glamour of that great daffodil *King Alfred*, raised from *maximus X Emperor*, or *Golden Spur*, by which Mr Kendall, the raiser, was rumoured to have made a fortune. As long as I was in Cornwall it was inevitable that any business I might build up as a bulb-grower would be built up first and foremost on the daffodil. "Daffodils and the green world they live in," wrote Keats, and nearly every Cornish gardener lived with them in that green world of theirs. My special dream was a white trumpet as tall, as shapely, as floriferous and as hardy as *King Alfred*; *Mary, Queen of Scots* was the name I intended to give that flower when I showed it first some ten years hence and received an F.C.C. It was no good dreaming of *Mary, Queen of Scots* with nothing more advanced in the way of white trumpets than dear *Madame de Graaf*. *Madame de Graaf* had been first shown in 1887; *Peter*

Barr, first shown in 1902, was the white hope of the moment, but one bulb of *Peter Barr* cost £30, which was a very large sum of money for me to find in 1909.

I told in an earlier Octave about my cousin Frank Greppo's deserting from the Chasseurs d'Afrique and of his mother's anxious wait for him at Victoria station when he had insisted on going back to France for a diary or something he had left behind in the house, and his arrest was expected at any moment. Afterwards he joined Theodore Roosevelt's Rough Riders in Cuba and later took to stage-management with E. A. Sothern. Then he married Irene Rooke, but they separated and he enlisted in the U.S. Army without saying he was married. This led to his discharge, and coming over to England he decided to enlist in a British dragoon regiment. His great object was to avoid responsibility; if he was given as much as a single stripe he took care to commit some breach of discipline which involved losing that stripe and relieved him of even as much responsibility as that borne by a lance-corporal. He was at this date serving with his regiment in India; his mother, who had come over to England from California, was anxious to buy him out. As it happened, when he received the suggestion an officer he liked had just died and he agreed to be bought out. He was expected back from India in about a month's time.

My aunt Ellen came down to Rivière and suggested that Frank Greppo should work with me for a while until he decided what he intended to do next. I owed that aunt of mine a great deal when, as I related in my third Octave, she dissuaded my mother from pursuing the foolish notion of my being articled to a firm of solicitors. So when my aunt Ellen suggested Frank's living with us at Rivière I naturally agreed. She to show her appreciation offered to buy a bulb of *Peter Barr* for my daffodil scheme.

When *Peter Barr* flowered next spring it seemed to me and other daffodil experts I consulted to be much more like *Earl Grey*. *Earl Grey* had been shown by Miss Wilmot in 1901 and was a creamy *Johnstonii* (*triandrus X Emperor*). I sent the bulb back to Messrs Peter Barr and Sons, and among the scanty relics of this period I find the following letter from them. It is typical of that firm's generous and, if I may use such an old-fashioned word, gentlemanly treatment of their customers:

July 29th 1910

We beg to acknowledge receipt of Daffodil bulb and as promised shall have much pleasure in sending you another "Peter Barr" to replace. The whole matter is truly a mystery to us. Certainly the bulb you send us is not "Peter Barr" which is absolutely distinct and as we have already informed you, we have never had the variety "Earl Grey" until this year so it would not be possible for us to have sent it to you in mistake for "Peter Barr", and "Peter Barr" being our own raised Daffodils naturally came from our own stock. However we shall be sending you on the "Peter Barr" very shortly which will put the matter right whatever may be the explanation of the matter.

During that summer of 1910 I had to be away from my garden for most of it, but I was still set on raising the supreme white trumpet and had made a start that spring by pollinating from *Peter Barr* my *Madame de Graafs* and using on *Peter Barr* the pollen of some *N. triandrus calathinus* I had. What I should have done was to lift that bulb of *Peter Barr* as soon as it had ripened off and looked carefully for the Mark of the Beast, *Merodon equestris*, the sinister and ruthless daffodil-fly; in the rush of London work I forgot to give the order to Search and it was not until July of that blazing summer that I wrote and told him to keep a sharp look out for the infernal pest, which was rampant in Cornwall. The previous year we had taken a good many daffodil-flies with a butterfly-net in May and June, but the harpies might still be working in July. Alas, the worst happened. Instead of devoting her attention to the hundreds of *Emperors, Sir Watkins, W. P. Milners* and *Mrs Langtrys*, that harpy went straight for *Peter Barr*; throughout the autumn and winter her loathsome grub was enjoying a £30 meal. The combination of this disaster in daffodil-growing with the success of my second novel *Carnival* put a stop to my dreams of one day reading in some daffodil book:

Mary, Queen of Scots (Mackenzie)—April 12, 1919. F.C.C. White Ajax. Huge flower. Pure waxy white trumpet. Substance and constitution as strong as *King Alfred*. Undoubtedly the best white Ajax yet raised.

Nothing brings back more sharply the remoteness of the last full year of King Edward VII's reign than the engraved trade-mark of Barr and Sons above that letter of theirs; it was a moss-rose with three buds, a bunch of diminutive thistles, and a spray of massive shamrocks, all tied up with a love-knot.

And here I must record my gratitude to Mr Mudge for much good advice and much help when I was supposing that it might be my lot to earn my living from flowers instead of novels. For many years he was in charge of the Barr stall at the various flower-shows of the period, and a friend of all who loved daffodils. I have never cared for bi-colour trumpet daffodils, but I felt bound to add one to my collection because it was called *Mrs Mudge*, and *Mrs Mudge* remains in daffodil catalogues to-day.

I must have had doubts about my ability to earn a good living from bulbs without financial help from my father on a larger scale than he seemed likely to offer. What I was beginning to regard as that confounded novel was coming back time after time from publishers.

My father arrived at Rivière that summer with his Mercédès and a jolly chauffeur called John Gray who sent me greetings on my eightieth birthday, an age he had just reached himself. He wrote of "some very happy times with the 'Dear old Governor'," and sent me a snapshot of the Mercédès being dug out of the snow when they were caught in the "Snake Pass" on their way to Sheffield. He wrote, too, of my taking him down to the beach to look at the seals.

The seals of St Ives Bay were not the grey Atlantic seal and were therefore unprotected. At the east end of the bay where the towans ended in the cliffs towering above Godrevy lighthouse students from the Camborne College of Mines used to come and take shots at the seals playing below in the water of Dead Man's Cove. In July, when I used to walk about the high ground to revel in the columbines, or Blue Men's Caps as they were called in dialect, which grew thick above Dead Man's Cove, I would sometimes come across a couple of those students shooting away and often wounding seals without killing them. I recall once asking a pair of them if they had ever thought of bathing in Dead Man's Cove.

"You couldn't get down there to bathe."

"No, I suppose not. It's a pity because I should so much have enjoyed taking pot shots at you both. However, all I can do is to wish that when next you go down a lead-mine something will happen to the lift and you'll go down so fast that you'll never come up again."

Being reminded of those seals in that letter from John Gray sent my mind back to those damned students, when I was going to say that my father was obviously beginning to wonder whether that novel of mine was another bubble I was blowing and whether my gardening passion was a matter of time. I do not recall a positive refusal by my father to finance the garden project, but I must have felt pessimistic because I began to consider the possibility of getting some land in Cyprus where I should be able to earn a living and at the same time indulge my passion for the irises and tulips of the Levant and Middle East.

Ned Stone was married now to Laura Bovill and the infant Reynolds had arrived in this world. Laura had a brother, W. K. Bovill, who was the Principal Forest Officer of Cyprus. He had a farm he wanted to

Edward Compton at the wheel. 1911

6 North Street

C.M. playing *Hamlet*. Fowey 1909

sell which Faith told me about after she came back to Cornwall that
June, having stayed with her brother at Eton when she left Abingdon.
I wrote to ask Harry Pirie-Gordon if he could find out something about
land in Cyprus and received a letter from the Anglo-Egyptian Land
Allotment Company in Famagusta. They gave details of various pro-
perties for sale, and wound up:

*Before we close this letter we wish also to give you some information concerning
the farm of Mr W. K. Bovill which we understand is for sale.*

*The property in question consists of nearly 500 acres of land and a considerable
number of young almond trees which we believe have now begun to bear fruit.
There are also a certain number of olive and carrib trees as well as vineyards
which give a return.*

*The farm is about 9 miles distant from the town of Larnaca and its position
is simply charming, being situated practically in a valley surrounded by small
hills.*

*Mr Bovill has spent a considerable amount of money in developing this place
and we have no doubt it is a valuable property on account of its extensive planta-
tions of fruit trees (mostly almonds) which should give a good revenue as they
grow year by year.*

*As to terms of sale we have no doubt that Mr Bovill will be glad to communi-
cate with you on the subject.*

The correspondence between myself and Bovill has vanished except
for a last letter of his written to me from Troodos on October 1, 1909,
in answer to one from me, telling him I could not accept his invitation
to come out to Cyprus and join him in some kind of a partnership.

*To give you some idea of what the business is that I propose in the way of
poultry farming, I have just executed the agreement to find someone to supply the
P. and O. SS. Company at Port Said with eggs and poultry which is a larger
business than any one man can undertake, to say nothing about the local Egyptian
market.*

How fantastically improbable it would have seemed in 1909 that
some fifty years later a street in Nicosia would be named after me!
As I write these pages Cyprus is again sadly in the news and as usual
the British Press and the B.B.C. are slanting the news in favour of the
Turks. I may observe that in 1909 the British, French and Russians
were handling Crete as ineptly as the British and Americans have been
handling Cyprus to-day.
My cousin Frank Greppo came back from India that autumn, but

F

he was in a gloomy mood and viewed the prospect of gardening in Cornwall with as little enthusiasm as I had viewed the prospect of poultry-farming in Cyprus. He drank a great deal of beer and compared life as a civilian in England unfavourably with the life of a dragoon in India. He left us after about a month; I fancy that he and his wife, Irene Rooke, were temporarily reconciled.

Most of December I spent in Fowey, where *Hamlet* was to be produced under the enthusiastic direction of Quiller-Couch. Faith was in London, but I was writing early in December to give my mother and her the best date for them to see the play. In spite of *Hamlet* the garden was as much the thing as the play. *Tremendous planting of bulbs all day and a pile of letters written. There is a beautiful Iris alata in bloom.*

I stayed with Dr and Mrs Boger at Cliff Lawn, Esplanade. Boger was playing Claudius, and Morse, the other doctor, a huge man, was playing the Ghost. The programme has not survived among my papers and except for the two doctors the only other name I remember is that of my Ophelia, Miss Norah Dove. We rehearsed, with breaks for meals, from eleven in the morning until eleven at night. The two doctors regarded patients as such intolerable interruptions of rehearsals that the Hippocratic Oath sometimes seemed in danger of violation.

Laurence Binyon was staying in Fowey. I had a great admiration for his poetry, but when I tried to express this his gentle and shy personality was embarrassed, and I talked most about *Hamlet*. He was forty years old then and had just become Assistant Keeper of Prints and Drawings at the British Museum. We talked, too, about our old school; although he had left it before I went to Colet Court we had shared quite a few of the masters.

I had some theories about the interpretation of certain scenes in *Hamlet*, in the carrying out of which I was indulged by Q. One theory was that Hamlet had seduced Ophelia, and that one of the reasons why he hesitated to kill the King was self-reproach for his own behaviour.

HAMLET: I did love you once.
OPHELIA: Indeed, my lord, you made me believe so.
HAMLET: You should not have believed me, for virtue cannot so inoculate *our* old stock but we shall relish of it—I loved you not.
OPHELIA: I was the more deceived.

I argued further that Hamlet's remarks in the play-scene which in those days were always cut suggested a relationship between them far from virginal:

HAMLET: Lady, shall I lie in your lap?
OPHELIA: No, my lord.
HAMLET: I mean my head upon your lap? Do you think I meant
country matters?
OPHELIA: I think nothing, my lord.
HAMLET: That's a fair thought to lie between maids' legs.

In the Nunnery scene it was usual for the Hamlet not to see Polonius
until he asks "where's your father?" I anticipated the sight of him.
At the end of the soliloquy Hamlet says:

> Soft you now,
> The fair Ophelia—Nymph, in thy orisons
> Be all my sins remembered.

OPHELIA: Good my lord,
How does your honour for this many a day?
HAMLET: I humbly thank you, well, well, well.

Most commentators want to make "all my sins" ironical. Dr John-
son, who had much more common sense than most Shakespearian
commentators, rightly maintained that they were uttered in "grave
and solemn mood". Dowden managed to think that Shakespeare's use
of the word "nymph" implied estrangement and that the repetition of
"well, well, well" implied impatience. Professor Dover Wilson thought
it implied indifference.

I think that the first "well" should be spoken with "grave and
solemn" kindliness, and that when Hamlet suddenly sees Polonius the
second "well" should be sharply suspicious and that when he sees the
King also he should say "well" with cold harshness.

OPHELIA: My lord, I have remembrances of yours,
That I have longèd long to re-deliver,
I pray you now receive them.

It is then that Hamlet should let his anger get the better of him.

HAMLET: No, not I.
I never gave you aught.

It was in Ophelia's mad scene that I suggested the sharpest departure from the conventional presentation. I believed, and still believe,
that Ophelia imagines Laertes to be Hamlet and that, instead of
wandering about the stage offering flowers to all and sundry, every
single flower should be given to Laertes.

OPHELIA (*to* LAERTES): There's rosemary, that's for remembrance—pray you, love, remember—and there is pansies, that's for thoughts.

In his commentary on *Hamlet* in the Cambridge University edition of Shakespeare's plays, which was started by Quiller-Couch, Professor Dover Wilson seems to think that Ophelia recognizes her brother. "Each flower has its meaning and is presented to an appropriate person." He cannot find one for "pansies". So he suggests "thought, especially love-thoughts, she keeps, (pansies) I think for herself". If she imagines Laertes to be Hamlet, she certainly gives them to *him* immediately after "rosemary".

OPHELIA (*to* THE KING): There's fennel for you and columbines.

There is no authority for giving them to the King apart from stage tradition, a tradition broken by the Roundheads and messed up at the Restoration so far as Shakespeare was concerned.
Fennel meant flattery. Columbines meant false vows. I cannot find anywhere that columbines ever meant cuckoldry as Professor Dover Wilson thinks. These, too, should be given to Laertes-Hamlet.

OPHELIA (*to* THE QUEEN): There's rue for you, and here's some for me, we may call it herb of grace o' Sundays. —O, you must wear your rue with a difference. There's a daisy. I would give you some violets, but they withered all when my father died.

Professor Dover Wilson comments "Rue = sorrow (for herself) and repentance (for the Queen). Daisy = dissembling. Violets = faithfulness; these she cannot give to anyone, as there are no more left in the world."
All of these flowers would be given much more appropriately to Laertes-Hamlet. On the daisy Professor Dover Wilson quotes Greene, *Quip for an upstart courtier.* "Next them grewe the dessembling daisie, to warne such light of love wenches not to trust every faire promise that such amorous batchelers make them" and adds that Ophelia would place (it) next the "pansies" in her own bosom as a warning.
Professor Dover Wilson might have connected with the "daisy" Ophelia's song before she went out to gather those flowers and herbs:

> *To-morrow is Saint Valentine's day,*
> *All in the morning betime,*
> *And I a maid at your window*
> *To be your Valentine.*

Then up he rose, and donned his clo'es,
And dupped the chamber door,
Let in the maid, that out a maid
Never departed more.

By Gis and by Saint Charity,
Alack and fie for shame!
Young men will do't, if they come to't,
By Cock, they are to blame.
Quoth she, Before you tumbled me,
You promised me to wed.

Professor Dover Wilson observes of this song that "its immodesty is attributed by most commentators to the influence of madness".

My theory that Hamlet seduced Ophelia makes this in the words of Laertes "a document in madness, thoughts and remembrance fitted".

In the final scene I emphasized a small pronoun I have not heard any other Hamlet emphasize.

God, Horatio, what a wounded name,
Things standing thus unknown, shall live.
If thou didst ever hold me in thy heart
Absent thee from felicity awhile,
And in this harsh world draw *thy* breath in pain
To tell my story . . .

Draw *thy* breath in pain as I am drawing mine at this moment.

When the entry of Fortinbras is cut the play is usually ended either with Hamlet's last words "the rest is silence", or with Horatio's "Good night, sweet prince, and flights of angels sing thee to thy rest!"

Beerbohm Tree used to have a celestial chorus of angels, a piece of sentimental redundancy which irritated Henry Irving.

We could not manage Fortinbras in our Fowey production but ended the play with a solemn drum-beat off and Horatio's saying "why does the drum come hither?"

At the first performance in the small Fowey hall the audience laughed when Hamlet drew his rapier and killed Polonius behind the arras. In order to avoid a repetition of this I discarded the rapier and used a dagger. When Hamlet says "I will speak daggers to her, but use none" I made him touch the dagger's cross at the top and then cross himself. On the way to the Queen's Chamber Hamlet carried a lighted candle and when he saw the King kneeling at prayer he blew out the candle and made the speech that begins "Now might I do it pat", with the stage in complete darkness. Q and I thought that a blue lime on the King and Hamlet to represent moonlight would make Hamlet's speech sound ridiculous on so small a stage. That small stage was a handicap; when Dr Morse entered as the Ghost he seemed to fill half of it. I am glad to remember that when Hamlet cried "A rat? Dead, for a ducat, dead," and stabbed Polonius behind the arras with a trick dagger the audience gasped instead of giggling.

I have seen seven Hamlets in my lifetime. I never saw Henry Irving, but I did see his son H. B. Irving, and he remains in my memory with John Barrymore as the best; easily the worst was Martin Harvey.

I have lost the kind notice of my performance that Q wrote for the local paper; indeed, the only relic of it that remains is a letter from Norah Dove, my Ophelia, to thank me for sending her the volume of my *Poems*.

It is a delightful reminder of a very happy time and the first Hamlet I have seen who lived. You were by no means "a fretful manager"—on the contrary a most patient one. I shall always be very grateful to you for your ungrudging help.

It was all very well sending Miss Dove my *Poems*; her opinion of them one way or the other would not affect me. It was quite another to send them to Q; an adverse judgment from him would confirm the doubts that were gathering about my literary future; that wretched novel was still without any prospect of being published. I felt it was hardly fair to ask Q to read the *Poems*; he had so much to read for his own work. I felt I might get a letter from Q saying "you were a good actor but you are not a good poet". However, when I got back to Rivière I decided to risk a pail of cold water over my head and sent him the volume. My relief when he wrote me the following letter can be imagined:

The Haven
Fowey
Cornwall
Dec. 26th 1909

Dear Mackenzie,
 The book is full of beautiful stuff, it is indeed. I spent a part of yesterday idling through it, and again this afternoon I have had an hour with it when by rights I should have been compiling notes for electioneering speeches. What's worse, it has put me out of the mood for doing that necessary work, and I am scribbling this instead. Of the longer pieces (and barring "A Song of Parting", at which I was lucky enough to open—and it's right good and jolly) I like best

the Harvest Moon and the Hill of Death, but I wish you could have contrived it without a shift of metre. You pulled me up in full flight just as the thing had complete hold of me, and fine as the ending is, I felt that Ophelia's back hair had got itself hitched. Of the Harvest Moon I like each page better as it goes on. The imagery—a trifle stiff at first—gets lovely in the moonlight passage. "So close they sat, the thinnest moon-wrought blade" kind—that made me sit up. I was brutal enough to say "He won't keep this up, not he" when I came to the subtle surprise of the last two pp. It is, really and truly a beautiful thing. So is "A Tragedy of Provence" or would be entirely for me if the climax were a bit more clearly indicated [I am a trifle dull at seeing in shadows, and like to be told precisely what happened. It's childish, but I like to read e.g. of Judith that she cut off the gentleman's head, and tumbled the body down on the floor and dragged down the canopy from the pillars to cover it.] I like the Bracelet poem, too, and all the sonnets—"Dream Love" and "In Red and White" particularly. Avoid one little trick. The word "some" in a simile always puts me off, e.g. "like some strange rune". I could invent a reason, but have only room here to set down the fact. Oh, by the way there's a line that particularly likes me—"There's no sweet living where there are no flowers."

Did you tell me you had never seen Polperro? If that's so, I've a mind to book you for a Saturday meeting there—fishermen have a Saturday night—and we'll go over early and see the place—and the Sunday we'll devote more or less to the Muses. . . . On Wednesday I go to Liskeard to help in planning out the campaign and I am going to take you at your word. Our best wishes to you both.

Yours sincerely,

A. T. Quiller-Couch

After getting that letter I was naturally anxious to do all I could to help Q's passionate Liberalism. The fight in South-East Cornwall might be tough and from now on until the General Election was over by my twenty-seventh birthday I was spouting in three Cornish constituencies like a whale. I felt less strongly about the Lords' behaviour or Lloyd George's 1909 Budget than I felt about Home Rule for Ireland. At the same time, I wished the Liberals would gain a clear majority without the help of the Nationalist members.

On January 4, 1910, Q was writing:

You are a good man. The meeting is at 7 p.m. on Thursday (Jany 6) and I want you to talk to 'em for 25 or 30 minutes. I shall say only a few words, being booked for Polperro Saturday, Paignton Monday, Helston Tuesday or Wednesday. Life is REAL, Life is EARNEST!

Next business—you are to let me know if Mrs Mackenzie is coming with you. It seems the obvious plan—we shall be delighted—and you can get off to Penwith together next day. It is understood that we put you up: and though we have to bed you out [horticultural expression] next door, I dare say you'll forgive.

The meeting being at 7 o'clock, a meal at 9 is plainly indicated, but we will have a light one beforehand. I shall be at Truro all day—Education Committee —returning by the 4.25 from that city. But do you turn up at your own time.

My blessings on you! And a happy new year to you both.

On January 9th the Agent for the Liberal candidate in the Mining Division was writing from Redruth:

Our mutual friend Mr A. T. Quiller-Couch was here a few days ago.

He said you were doing grand service to the Liberal cause and urged us to endeavour to enlist your help in this Division.

I want you for our last meeting at Redruth, but I owe you an apology for asking at such short notice. Can you possibly come and give us a speech at our meeting in the Druids Hall on Wednesday evening next?

My old Magdalen friend Norman Chamberlain was the Unionist candidate for the Mining Division and I wrote to invite him to stay at Rivière. He wrote back to say he could hardly stay with me when I was tub-thumping all over the place for the Liberals.

I have never been able to take party politics as seriously as politicians are able to take them. I felt strongly about Home Rule in 1910; I felt strongly about the Unionist cabal against Winston Churchill in 1915; I felt strongly about the Coalition Government's handling of the Irish situation during the Troubles; I felt strongly about the betrayal of Greece and the ignominious surrender to the Turks after Bonar Law, Baldwin and Co. had managed to eliminate Lloyd George; I felt strongly about the slow slide downhill to disaster of the National Governments of the 'thirties; I feel strongly to-day about what I believe to be the Conservatives' pathetic belief in the Nuclear Deterrent as a status symbol for Great Britain and their failure to recognize it as a bad example to the rest of Western Europe. At the same time, I have never been able to make personal friendship depend on political opinion.

I am glad to find that a note of mine on bulbous irises which I sent to some gardening paper has survived what I thought and said about that General Election of January 1910.

"Perhaps the most beautiful bulbous iris now in bloom with me is *Iris Tauri*. It opened on January 9th and is still perfect a week later. The colour is deepest claret violet suffusing the tube like wine in old-fashioned glasses. The ridge is orange and the leaves scarcely show at flowering time. In catalogues I find it classed as a variety of *Iris persica* and priced at its lowest at 7/6 a dozen.

"*Iris Vartani* from Palestine with flowers sometimes of an exquisite Sèvres blue, sometimes of a dark slate-colour, was out of bloom by October's end. *Iris Histrio* has also finished for this winter, but *Histrioides* is in its glorious prime, rich blue dappled with gold and silver.

"*Iris Danfordiae* is beautiful at present but does not display its form like the others. If Herr Leichtlin is right in distinguishing between this and *Bornülleri*, I possess the latter form, since the green stripes along the ridge are very conspicuous, against the yellow.

"*Iris reticulata Krelagei* is going to be beaten this year by plain *Iris reticulata*, which will be in bloom before February. A vile mouse gnawed *Iris Bakeriana*, that violet-scented and violet-coloured beauty from Mesopotamia; I fear only one bulb will recover. *Sindjarensis* looks like an emerald fan at the moment, and a new batch of *alata* is showing flower; last year's bulbs bloomed before Christmas. *Iris stylosa* is flowering profusely, notwithstanding a dull summer and an unexpected transplantation in November."

I may add to this note of January 1910 that all these bulbous irises continued to flourish and increase with me until I abandoned Rivière in 1913.

TWENTY-SEVEN YEARS OLD: 1910

O N January 24, 1910, Q wrote from Fowey when the General
Election was over:

My dear Mackenzie,
*I tell you it was the beast of a fight. This side of the division won it: for along
the Tamar we were snowed under by (1) Navy vote (2) out voters and (3) the
General's[1] personal popularity.*
*He took the result beautifully. Their figures were quite abnormal owing to
these 3 causes: and the Launceston figures give a far better index. So dont be down
about the Truro-Helston result. All over the county we held our own well on
Saturday: and the rot may very likely be stayed.*
*In any event I am grateful for your help. This end of the division was the only
hope and we amassed enough votes in Looe, Polperro, Polruan, Fowey, and
Lostwithiel to down 'em.*
*That false message was a blackguard's trick. Redruth Brewery blew its hooter
for an hour and a quarter. At Lostwithiel, ladies drove about the streets, waving
flags. At Bodmin the Unionists marched in procession. And all the while 20 or 30
very pale-faced men were keeping a tight lip around the table at Liskeard.*
Well, this all means that I am grateful, very grateful for your help. I mean it.
*The Boy has opened his artless course at Trin. Coll. and by latest advices is
enjoying himself hugely. Best regards.*

Yours

A. T. Quiller-Couch[2]

A week after this letter from Q I heard from Norman Chamberlain:

West Woodbury House
Newbury
Berks

Jan. 31, 10

Dear Monty,
I would have written earlier, but haven't had time. Of course I didn't mind

---

[1] Lt.-General Sir Reginald Pole-Carew, K.C.B. He became M.P. for the
Bodmin Division of Cornwall at the second General Election in 1910.

[2] Q was given a knighthood in the first birthday honours of the new reign.
No man ever deserved one better.

your spouting against me and am only sorry your fears for your majority were so
unnecessary!
I shall be down again soon I hope and will then come and see you, I hope.
                                       Yours
                                       Norman Chamberlain

From what a member of our audience told me of your speech, it was *tub-
thumping and no mistake. A pity there were no reporters: oh, Monty, how are the
mighty of the '97 ...!!*

That last allusion is to debates in the Magdalen College Debating
Club, the '97. Norman Chamberlain would all too soon be killed in
the First World War. He was a great loss to his country. Neville
Chamberlain wrote a moving memorial of his cousin for private
circulation.

That General Election of January 1910 unfortunately gave the
Unionists enough gains for them to exploit in their own political interest the Irish situation and to tempt Germany to suppose Britain would
not stand by France.

The agent of the successful Liberal candidate wrote on February 3rd:

*I hasten to return my grateful thanks for the zealous efforts you made on behalf
of the cause. . . . Your kind action in lending a conveyance on election day was
indeed helpful. We were, as you know, terribly handicapped for vehicles and
therefore your help in this direction was doubly welcome. The majority of 2,446
shows that the Mining Division is Liberal to the core.*

Early in that February I received a letter from my old friend Philip
Sergeant, who had returned from the editorship of the Hong Kong
paper and was now one of the directors, with Oscar Parker and A.
Wilson Barrett, a son of the actor, of the Authors' and Playwrights'
Agency at 110 Strand. At the time Constables had the typescript of
Curtains Wells, indeed they had had it for about three months; I had
written once or twice to enquire about their verdict and had always
received evasive answers. So I decided to put *Curtain Wells* in Sergeant's
hands. On February 14th I received a valentine from Constables to
say they had not yet been able to come to a final decision about *Curtain
Wells* and were about to send it to another reader. "We regret that we
have been obliged to keep it so long, but we have been very busy, and
we are anxious to give this book our most careful consideration." This
letter was signed "O. Kyllman per W.M." W.M. was Will Meredith,
son of the novelist, who two or three years later would become a friend

and tell me that the real reason why Constables had kept my book so long was because it had been mislaid.

In the end Constables refused *Curtain Wells* and the agency sent the book to Melrose, who at the beginning of May seemed on the verge of accepting it, but in May I was writing to Faith in London:

The King's death has polished off Curtain Wells for this year. Melrose won't risk it. A mysterious man called Secker came into Sergeant's office and said he heard they had a novel by me. He's going to set up as a publisher next Spring and is taking the Curtain Wells typescript away with him. He wouldn't tell Sergeant how he had heard of Curtain Wells. But Sergeant seems to think it may lead to something . . . such amazingly beautiful irises are out in bloom. You'd better come back quickly before they fade.

Everybody in London, rich and poor, felt King Edward's death as a personal loss. The death of Queen Victoria had awed London, but there was no feeling of grief like that roused by the death of that son she had always resented.

Martin Secker made up his mind at once and Sergeant, with the prospect of the novel's being published, wrote to ask if I had any unpublished stories or articles. I told him that the only potentially negotiable work I had was the dramatization I had made of H. G. Wells's *Kipps*. The Agency wrote off to Wells who said he had no recollection of any dramatic version of *Kipps* having been made by anybody, still less of having "approved" such a version. Fortunately after a terrific search the correspondence between H. G. Wells and myself in 1906 was found, and copies of it were sent to him. Wells wrote to say he should like me to call on him; Wilson Barrett wanted to come with me, but I insisted on going by myself. On a chilly May evening after dinner I went to 17 Church Row, Hampstead, feeling slightly shy of meeting a man for whom I had such admiration.

H.G., in that high voice of his that seemed to float about in his nasal breathing, was friendly.

"About this Kipps play of yours. As a matter of fact I had completely forgotten about it, but these letters of mine from Sandgate seem to show that I must have read it. But this Mr—what's his name—Wilson Barrett. . . . Is he anything to do with the actor? His son, eh? Wasn't there a play called *The Sign of the Cross?* Terrible nonsense. Well, this Mr Wilson Barrett talked about James Welch being interested in it. That's out of the question because I have just arranged with a promising young dramatist whose work I admire to dramatize *Kipps*."

I asked who it was.

"I can't tell you that, but he has had a very good idea. He's going to make Coote the chief character and is building his play round Coote. And of course I'm more or less collaborating."

"Are you going to call the play *Coote*?"

"Oh no, it will be called *Kipps*."

"Then you'll have a failure. No audience will go to see a play about Kipps and find it's all about Coote without feeling disappointed."

"You're a very self-confident young man."

"I do know a great deal about the theatre."

"I'd like to have another look at your version," said H.G.

"No, Mr Wells. There is only one way to construct a play about Kipps. You and your promising young dramatist may have hit on that way. But suppose I let you read my version again and found when your play was produced that it was constructed like mine I should always wonder if you had got the idea from me. On the other hand, if when your play is produced I find it is constructed like mine, I shall know that it was your idea or the idea of the young dramatist whose work you admire."

H.G. sat in silence for a minute or two. I recall that, although it was May, there was a fire in the grate and hearing a clock tick above H.G.'s nasal breathing.

"You say James Welch is interested in your play?"

"According to Wilson Barrett," I replied. "But Wilson Barrett is an optimist. I never pay any attention to what actor-managers say about possible productions in the future. They seem as little able to make up their minds as publishers."

"You don't think James Welch really is interested?"

"He may be."

"Look: if James Welch makes a firm offer I may feel inclined to authorize you to go ahead. At the moment the idea of a *Kipps* play has not gone beyond talk. Nothing has been absolutely fixed. But if James Welch turns down your *Kipps* it will be better for me to carry on with the young dramatist. He has already had a great success with a play. You are quite unknown."

I did not feel that the great H. G. Wells would be at all impressed by my telling him that an equally unknown publisher had just accepted my first novel.

James Welch finally decided not to produce *Kipps* as dramatized by me and Wells stuck to the young dramatist; he was Rudolf Besier, who had had a great success at the Haymarket with *Don* in the previous year. *Kipps* was produced at the Vaudeville Theatre in 1912 not long after the success of my book *Carnival*; it ran for hardly a week.

Faith found herself sitting next to H.G. at some dinner party soon afterwards.

"I think I may have made a mistake about your husband," H.G. said to her.

When I came to write that second novel of mine I realized what an invaluable experience my dramatization of *Kipps* had been. Without it I doubt if I should have handled Cockney dialogue as well as I did, thanks to H. G. Wells. I never lost an opportunity of declaring in print what I owed to him; and H.G. and I were friends to the end of his life.

A few days after this interview with H. G. Wells my father presented me with something like an ultimatum. Would I come to Reading where he and his partner Milton Bode wanted to see me about something? He must have been playing in the County Theatre that week, and staying with his partner at Caversham. Here, he told me that they wanted me to play a part in a Hall Caine drama which they were putting on at the Garrick in September.

"Mr Hall Caine wants somebody to play the part of a young priest who is cast ashore on the Isle of Man and gives absolution before he dies to the Bishop's son who had been banished for some offence. He told us he wanted somebody who looked like a young Savanarola, ascetic and spiritual. Mr Bode at once suggested you, and you will have to go up to the Isle of Man and see if Mr Hall Caine approves of you for the part."

I doubted if Milton Bode knew the difference between a Savanarola and a Saveloy.

"But I do not want to go on the stage," I protested.

"I can't afford to go on making you an allowance indefinitely. You believe you are a novelist. Well, you must admit that the time it has taken for a publisher to accept that novel of yours doesn't sound as if it would be a great success."

My father's eldest brother had written three or four novels, none of which had been successful enough to prevent his having to borrow money from his younger brother; he took a poor view of the financial prospects of a novelist.

"You will be paid a salary of £10 a week," my father went on, "which you must admit is a handsome salary for somebody taking his first stage engagement. I started on 18s. a week."

"You wanted to go on the stage. I don't. However, if you insist, obviously I must fall in with this plan of yours. But if Hall Caine thinks I look too fleshly for this young priest I hope you won't expect me to try to get a stage engagement elsewhere. After all, my novel *has* been accepted at last; having waited so long for it to be published, surely I may ask you to wait a little while longer to see if it is a success. If it falls flat I will recognize I was not meant to be a novelist and will go on the stage."

That visit to Hall Caine was a memorable experience. I sailed from Fleetwood in a paddle-steamer, probably the same paddle-steamer in which I had first crossed to Douglas nearly twenty years earlier. Somebody had told me the best way to avoid being sea-sick was to drink Guinness; in spite of drinking three bottles one after another, I was pretty sea-sick.

Hall Caine himself met me at the quay with his car; although I could not help finding him a little ridiculous, I could not help liking him more and more as we drove to Greeba Castle. The Castle, which I had supposed would have some signs of Gothic grandeur, turned out to be a medium-sized red brick villa. In the small dining-room, which opened on a small conservatory full of brown and yellow calceolarias, was an engraving of *The Blessed Damozel* in the frame of which was stuck a card, "From D. G. Rossetti to Hall Caine 1881", a souvenir of the days when Hall Caine had attended the poet during his last days at Birchington-on-Sea.

The garden at the back ran up in a fairly steep slope to level ground on which Hall Caine had built himself a granite study, furnished inside with massive and severe furniture which included a bare table as large as a four-post bed.

"It's all so simple," Hall Caine commented, in a dreamy, slightly sepulchral voice. "So simple, so utterly in keeping with the simple life of this little island, and if I may say so with the books I write here in complete seclusion."

Remembering the music-halls and dancing palaces of Douglas, I did not fancy that life was quite so simple in the Isle of Man as Hall Caine suggested, but I felt I ought to play up to his mood.

"Yes, indeed," I said. "One can imagine Aeschylus writing his plays in surroundings like this."

"Thank you," Hall Caine almost intoned, "thank you, Mr Compton, that is one of the nicest things ever said to me." (I had dropped "Mackenzie" for the family stage-name.) "I shall cherish that observation of yours. Yes, that is one of the nicest things ever said to me. And so true!"

When Hall Caine came down to breakfast next morning he enquired how I had slept.

"Splendidly. I hope you had as good a night as I had, Mr Caine."

"I hardly ever sleep," he replied in his most sepulchral voice. "Go on with your breakfast, Mr Compton. Pay no attention to me. I hardly ever eat breakfast."

His hands were small and seemed all the smaller on account of the way he wore his cuffs, which came up to the base of his thumbs, tightly buttoned. I remembered Max Beerbohm's cuffs at that undergraduate breakfast in Oxford. Hall Caine had been a feature of Max's caricatures; I wondered if he knew they both wore the same kind of cuffs.

Later that morning Hall Caine took me in his car to see the Tynwald.

"In one sense we shall be profaning that sacred spot by arriving in a motor-car," he assured me solemnly, "and I must confess there are moments when I reprove myself for having surrendered to such a blatant method of transport. But . . ." he opened his arms and shrugged his shoulders in a gesture intended to convey the corroding advance of progress against which not even he could hold out.

When we arrived at the Tynwald, which was a green glen between grey hills, Hall Caine took off his hat and, as the gentle breeze of early summer played through the hair above that domed forehead, he delivered a kind of elegy upon the "rude forefathers" of Mona, who in that glen had made the first laws of the island.

"And yet," said Hall Caine when his elegy was finished, "there are some people incapable of responding to the poetic and spiritual influence of this sacred spot. When his late Majesty King Edward visited the Island I was privileged to show him the original site of the Tynwald Court. He seemed completely unimpressed. Indeed, his only concern after I had tried to tell him about the Tynwald was to know what time lunch was."

Hall Caine put on his hat with a sigh for King Edward's lack of imaginative response.

"And yet," he went on, "he was not incapable of responding to romance. His wife—Her Majesty Queen Alexandra—told me that what must have been the last book he read before his fatal illness was my novel *The Eternal City* . . . and graciously assured me that King Edward had much enjoyed it."

I crossed next day to Liverpool on a glorious first of June in a steamer with turbine engines instead of paddles and was so much pleased with myself for not being sea-sick that I wrote to Faith on board:

Hall Caine was quite priceless but very kind and nice. He told me he wanted somebody who looked spiritual! Apparently he was satisfied with my appearance, so that more or less settles us in town for the autumn. I have only one scene so perhaps it won't be necessary for me to go up when rehearsals begin in August. I'm a Roman priest who has been wrecked on the coast of Man and die at the end of the scene.

The contract with Martin Secker was signed on June 9th, by which I granted to him the sole and exclusive right to print and publish a "certain work provisionally entitled *A Tragedy in Porcelain*".

Two days later Secker was writing from Churchgate, Iver, Bucks:

Dear Mr Mackenzie,
*   I am returning you the typescript of your book, for you to run through it and make any alterations which may occur to you, before I send it to the printer. I shall have to set up early so that I can send a set of proofs to America, and do my best to get off an edition over there for simultaneous publication.*
*   I like the flavour of* The Passionate Elopement—*both that and* A Tragedy in Porcelain *are good titles—and it is difficult to know which to decide upon. It would not be hard to persuade me that the first were the better, but there is something very attractive about the second. Has it occurred to you to use "A Tragedy in Porcelain" as a descriptive* sub title?
*   Yours very truly*
*   Martin Secker*

I am glad that letter has survived. There in Secker's attractive and completely legible handwriting is the foundation stone of a career. I had learnt by now how he had come to hear of *Curtain Wells*. He had inherited a legacy, some of which he had spent on learning publishing for a year with Eveleigh Nash, and with the rest of which—£1000— he proposed to start as a publisher on his own. When he was with Eveleigh Nash he read the typescript of *Curtain Wells* and strongly recommended it for publication. Another reader whose judgment Nash trusted more than that of the novice who was learning publishing turned down *Curtain Wells*. Somehow Secker heard the book was still going round, probably from one of the readers at Melrose who had believed in it.

On June 16th Secker was writing again:

Let us decide upon The Passionate Elopement. *As regards the old spelling, please retain it, at any rate for the present. I like it personally, and if there is not overmuch of it I don't think the public will find it tedious. I will instruct the*

G

printers to put in the "turn overs", for all these things, I think, give the book character, and help to create atmosphere.

I had asked for "ic" to be "ick" at the end of a word and for lashed "ct" and "st" as well as for the "turn-overs"; I abstained from asking for the long "s"; that I knew the public *would* find tedious.

I was much annoyed that August by Wilson Barrett's arranging with my father without consulting me for a copyright performance of *Kipps* at the Dalston Theatre, the first news of which I had being a bill of two guineas, the Lord Chamberlain's fee for the censorship.

In answer to a letter from me asking what the hell they thought they were doing Philip Sergeant wrote:

The copyright performance of "Kipps" was decided on by your father and Mr Parker as soon as the period allowed by Wells expired. It was thought best to safeguard your interests in the play by this means in case there was anything going on of which we were not aware. I was under the impression myself that you were informed of it. Sorry—but in this affair I was not a principal. Naturally it may be rather startling to hear of it in the way you have heard, but it was not our intention to keep you in the dark.

On August 18th I wrote to the Agency:

I am still unable to see any justification for not consulting my wishes. I am placed by your precipitate action in a most ridiculous position with regard to Mr H. G. Wells, who as an author will scarcely appreciate my inability to control my own work.

In February of the following year when Herbert Trench announced he was going to produce *Kipps* by Mr Wells and Mr Besier at the Haymarket Parker wrote to ask if the Agency should notify Herbert Trench that my rights to the dramatization of *Kipps* had been secured by a copyright performance.

This ludicrous suggestion determined me to cancel my connection with the Authors' and Playwrights' Agency as soon as possible.

My mother persuaded Milton Bode and my father that Frank Greppo would be the right stage-manager for the production of *The Bishop's Son*. He had been Sothern's stage-manager with great success in America, but the life of a dragoon in India had blunted his stage-sense, and he was not a success. It should be realized that in those days "producers" as they were called in the theatre, "directors" as they would soon be called in the films, were only just beginning to appear.

In those days the actor-manager, with the help of the stage-manager, took charge of rehearsals. Frank Greppo was not too bad with the scenery and the furniture and the movement of the supers, but he was unable to direct the individual performance of an actor or actress. However, Hall Caine himself enjoyed trying to do that, sitting in the middle of the dress-circle.

Bransby Williams, the banished son of the Bishop, was a favourite in music-halls with his impersonations of characters from the novels of Charles Dickens, but he was not really at home in a theatre. He believed that the whole play rested entirely upon him and that what the other actors did lacked importance unless they were helping him to be the centre of the stage. It was Hall Caine who had chosen him for the part and how my father and Bode had been foolish enough to suppose that Bransby Williams would be a successful lead at a West End theatre was incomprehensible to me. The rest of the cast were good— particularly J. D. Beveridge as the Bishop, beautiful Elaine Inescourt as the heroine, and best of all Shiel Barry as Davy Fayle, the young fisherman devoted to Dan, the bishop's son. Hall Caine had not had much of a success in the provinces with *The Manxman* fifteen years earlier; why should he or anybody else have supposed that a re-hash of *The Manxman* would attract a London audience in 1910?

I recall two moments from those rehearsals. When I was giving absolution to Bransby Williams with open hand raised shoulder-high, Hall Caine protested from his seat in the circle.

"No, no, Mr Compton. That is not the way to give absolution," raising, as he spoke, his arm above his head with fingers pointing, appropriately, up to the gallery.

I pointed out that this was more like an episcopal absolution.

"Are you trying to teach me how a priest gives absolution?" Hall Caine asked. "Please remember I spent six months in Rome when I was writing *The Eternal City*."

The half-drowned priest had to make a long speech to Dan about his spiritual position now that he had been absolved. It included some exaggerated rhetoric about the joy his repentance had given to millions and millions of angels in Heaven.

"Mr Caine," I asked, "would you mind if I said 'thousands and thousands' instead of 'millions and millions'? It is difficult to express emotion with those narrow labials. The broad vowels of 'thousands and thousands' would make it easier."

I can see the expression of stupefied amazement on Hall Caine's face and hear the quaver in his voice as he leans over from his seat in the circle to ask, "Mr Compton, are you now trying to teach *me* how to write?"

Just before the rehearsals for *The Bishop's Son* ended Faith and I had moved into the Muirhead Bones' flat at 28 Church Row, Hampstead. Horace Taylor, a brilliant young caricaturist, who was a friend of the Marriotts, in whose house in Brook Green Faith and I had met him, had written to Faith:

I saw Muirhead Bone to-day and looked at his flat. It is on the first floor of a house in Church Row. The "lobby" door shuts it all off from the rest of the house. It is a charming place but may not be large enough for you and Monty. He rather wants to shut off the studio and store his etchings etc. in it.

The sitting-room is nicely furnished with lots of old stuff and jolly pictures—a Corot, some Augustus Johns, Clausen, Dodd etc. The walls are all white-painted, wood-panelled and the room faces south, very sunny, and looks out over trees to the heath at the side.

The flat above belongs to one Aitken,[1] something to do with Whitechapel Art Gallery (curator I think) who has built himself a roof garden. He is a very decent sort and I think you would get on with him and that he would like Monty to "use his view" of the heights of London. I am thinking of taking the studio in Aitken's flat and have in fact almost decided.

The Bones' flat at £4 a month is ridiculously cheap but he seems not very anxious to let and would I think rather leave it shut up than hand it over to an agent. I told him you wanted a place for about six months.

Write at once and let Muirhead Bone know at once if you want it. He is off to Glasgow in a few days.

If you think the one bedroom looking out on Church Row with folding doors between it and the sitting room is not enough, I think you could often get a bedroom in Aitken's flat as he has three at present. One I propose to take with the studio.

Muirhead Bone goes to Italy at the end of September for a year or more.

I think that's all the information. There is a nice small kitchen, but no bathroom!

I forgot to mention the dog!

Faith and I were worried about leaving Bob by himself at Rivière. Muirhead Bone wrote:

About the dog. I am sorry to say the place is very inconvenient for a dog, as there is no backyard.

[1] Charles Aitken, C.B., *d.* 1936.

And Mrs Bone wrote:

About the dog. We once tried to keep a little terrier in these rooms and we had to send him into the country in a little while. The close quarters seemed to affect his health very much. That's why I shouldn't advise you to try a country bred dog in a flat.

Horace Taylor wrote:

It's rather sad about the dog and the Bone, but Bob is rather large.

So in the end we had to leave Bob at Rivière; those rooms at 28 Church Row were much too precious a bargain to lose.

I shared a dressing-room at the Garrick with Shiel Barry, a gifted and delightful young Irishman married to Dorothy Minto. She had just been playing with Gertrude Kingston in the Court Theatre production of *Lysistrata*. When I was writhing over the torture of that ghastly caricature of Aristophanes perpetrated recently on television by the B.B.C. I gave myself a sedative by recalling Dorothy Minto's enchanting Myrrhina at the Court Theatre over fifty years ago.

Shiel Barry had been engaged by H. G. Pélissier to play the lead in a revue he had contracted to write for an Alhambra production before Christmas, and told me he was going to suggest me for writing some of the lyrics. I did not take this seriously; I had seen too much of the theatre's ways to blow bubbles about possibilities.

The Bishop's Son ran for only a week; I was tormented at the time by neuritis, and I was much relieved when I took my £10 on the Friday to hear that to-morrow would see the end of my week-old career as a professional actor.

Frank Greppo vanished that night and did not appear in the theatre on the Saturday. This worried my mother and next day I went to enquire for him at some rooms he had by Swiss Cottage. The landlady told me she was to tell anybody who called that Mr Greppo had enlisted.

"Oh, he paid his bill all right yesterday morning before he left," I was assured.

He must have re-enlisted in his old regiment, for a few days later he was on his way to India. Two years afterwards my brother Frank met him in Melbourne. He said he had been finding it too hot in India and had left the army. He then joined the Australian artillery as a driver, and served right through the First World War, enjoying himself tremendously. On the day before the armistice he was shot through the heart, which was just the end he would have wished for himself.

Half way up Fitzjohn's Avenue on my way back to Church Row that Sunday I was seized by *la grippe*. It is a pity we do not call influenza the grip: we should hear less then about the influenza colds so dear to sneezers on television who are advertising remedies for something they would be completely incapable of curing if sufferers from a cold in the head really did have influenza.

Faith had a nasty experience that week. In her own words:[1]

"Monty was ill with influenza, and I left him in bed one morning to go shopping in Heath Street. As I came out of the greengrocer's shop opposite Church Row I was ferociously attacked by the greengrocer's horse which was standing unattended outside. He lifted me twice off the ground, his powerful teeth firmly planted in my left upper arm. I screamed and became momentarily unconscious. By the time I reached the ground a second time a crowd had collected and I was rescued before he got me down to savage me.

"I was helped up to the flat followed by a crowd of excited women who thought I was just going into the first available doorway and wanted to see what happened next. The room was cleared by the girl who helped me up. She turned out to be a nurse in mufti, engaged with an elderly gentleman the details of whose case gave us a good deal of ribald amusement later on, for she came every day to dress my arm. . . .

"I put my head in at the folding door.

" 'I've been bitten by a horse.'

" 'I thought it sounded like you screaming,' said Monty.

"He was feeling too ill to deal with the situation, so I shut the door again, and Nurse cut the sleeve off my arm and found the muscle wrenched, though the skin, strangely enough, was not broken. . . . The greengrocer had a heart attack, so we did not press damages upon him. The only result on his side was that the horse was thereafter seen wearing a muzzle—with a very sulky look.

"I blame the enormous hats that were in vogue then, and my own carelessness in crossing too near him. I was wearing a hobble skirt too, which he may have disliked."

Women's fashions in that autumn of 1910 were as absurd as any in my lifetime. The balloon sleeves of 1895 were pretty bad but at least they did not make a woman walk as if her feet were nibbling the pavement.

On top of the *grippe* my throat began to threaten tonsillitis; on the Saturday morning of that week after the closing down of the play I received a telegram from Shiel Barry to say that Pélissier wanted to

[1] *As Much As I Dare.*

see me about the revue. Would I come to the Apollo that night and meet him?

Although I felt wretchedly ill, I knew it was imperative for me somehow or other to get to the Apollo; the ten pounds of my salary were coming to an end. After the failure of *The Bishop's Son* with heavy financial loss for my father he would be in no mood to finance me until my novel came out. Moreover, we had not been on the most cordial terms since that tiresome copyright performance of *Kipps*. I could not afford to miss this opportunity; somehow I managed to pull myself together and get down to the Apollo.

After the show I accompanied Pélissier, Morris Harvey and Dan Everard to Verrey's in Regent Street for drinks. After some small talk Pélissier gazed at me with those great eyes of his like violet saucers and said abruptly:

"I suppose you understand that I shall want all these lyrics by Monday night?"

"Of course," I agreed as airily as my throat would allow.

"You seem to be the kind of young man I'm looking for," Pélissier grunted. Then quickly he added, "You'd better come back with us to Elm House now."

I divined that, if I were to make any excuse about the pain I was in or even to hesitate one instant, Pélissier would take no more interest in me and that my chance of writing lyrics for him would vanish for ever.

"Could we drive to Finchley by way of Church Row, Hampstead?" I asked. "I'll have to let my wife know where I am, and get some things for the night."

We reached Elm House, Church End, in one of his two Daimler Silent Knights which were at this date the latest thing in speed and comfort. In the dining-room an immense cold supper was waiting with places laid for at least a dozen people.

If I call that supper Gargantuan I am not using a trite epithet; since Gargantua himself there may never have been a man who was so much Gargantua as Pélissier was. Not that he ever saw himself in the pages of Rabelais. "Do *you* think Rabelais funny?" he once asked me, and I knew by the contemptuous pouting of his lips that he did not, in spite of the luxurious edition of his works he would have bought. Indeed, except over some of Dickens our literary tastes seldom coincided. I remember his annoyance because I would not admit that *The Dop Doctor* was a supremely great novel. Pélissier loved it and must have presented three or four dozen copies of it to different people.

After supper, at which the host himself carved with a tremendous gusto, and which I had to pretend to enjoy, though every mouthful was an agony to swallow, we adjourned to a room that seemed full of grand pianos.

"Now, this is the idea of the revue."

The author and inventor gave a muddled account of his conception.

"And this is the first song."

We wrestled with rhythms until five or six o'clock of Sunday morning, when I was allowed to go to bed.

At half-past eight Pélissier's face rose like a sun above the foot of my bed; he was wrapped in a brilliantly-coloured dressing-gown.

"Aren't you up *yet*?" he exclaimed. "Look here, come into my room, I've got a new tune."

I followed him, and found another piano at the foot of his bed. All that Sunday, interrupted by gigantic meals, games, and quantities of visitors we talked about the revue. In the evening after a colossal supper I insisted on being driven back to the seclusion of Church Row to work out the lyrics. Pélissier, when he took a fancy to anybody, wanted him or her round him all the time; having apparently taken a fancy to me, he was most unwilling to let me go.

"Never mind about this damned revue. Go on talking. I like to hear you talk. You interest me."

I insisted on going home. I was determined he should have those lyrics by the following evening, even if I offended him by going off to work when he wanted me to talk to him; on the following evening he did have those lyrics.

After that he demanded my company all the time. The first thing Pélissier always did when he made a new friend was to present him or her with a wrist watch, and next day, Tuesday, when of course I had to lunch with him, probably at Kettner's, I was taken along afterwards to the Goldsmiths' and Silversmiths' shop in Regent Street and presented with a wrist watch; it cost £20 and is on my wrist as I write these words fifty-four years later. One of Pélissier's traits was to be prodigally generous over presents and hospitality, but not so extravagant in his payment for work done. His first collaborator had been Arthur Davenport, the father of John Davenport and husband of Muriel George. Known as "Fish", he shared with Pélissier a quenchless thirst, and by 1910 was no longer writing what had been by far the best lyrics the Follies ever had. Davenport had been succeeded by Arthur Wimperis, but by now "Wimp", after the success of *The Arcadians*, still running at the Shaftesbury, was not prepared to work for Pélissier at what Pélissier was prepared to pay.

This attitude of his was not due to meanness but to his deeply felt conviction that everybody round him—the other Follies, the men who wrote his words, even Hermann Finck, the conductor at the Palace Theatre, who by putting his tunes into musical shape was indispensable—were really contributing nothing. No man was ever more aware of his own creativeness than Pélissier. "What does Hermann do? Nothing. It's the tune that counts." Yet even Pélissier had to admit that *In the Shadows* was a good tune, though he did his best to spoil it by making me write some idiotic words to it. "I've got a good idea for a song to that tune of Hermann's. Something like this. *You can take me if you want me or leave me if you don't.*" And on this fatuous verbal theme I had to build. In most cases (Arthur Davenport was an exception) Pélissier was justified in believing himself to be everything and his collaborators very nearly nothing. His fear of paying too much was justified when one compared what he was with what we did; but inasmuch as no man ever made such exhausting demands upon other people's devotion (so that to work for Pélissier meant one was at his beck and call for work and play for literally every hour in the twenty-four) that lack of generosity was not so justifiable. "You'll lend a hundred pounds to any actor that comes to your dressing-room and flatters you," I once told him, "but you'll argue for an hour whether you ought to pay me five pounds or six for a week's work." "Ah," replied Pélissier, "but I despise *them*." At the time I might have put up with some of the contempt for a little more of the cash.

Somehow or other *All Change Here*, as the revue was originally and (after innumerable other titles had been debated) ultimately called, was finished; it was a hard task in those days when the theatres and the music-halls were quarrelling over what was and what was not a stage play. The theatres resented the music-halls putting on what amounted to a play without having to submit it to the Lord Chamberlain for censorship. I cannot understand why theatres are not fighting television by demanding that the archaic censorship of the Lord Chamberlain should apply to plays on television as much as to plays in the theatre. The Alhambra management insisted that to avoid an action by the Theatrical Managers' Association there was to be no dialogue spoken without music; this meant every line of it had to be written in verse or free verse and set to music. On top of that Pélissier, whose comedy was of the most intimate kind, was overwhelmed by the size of the Alhambra and incapable of constructing an entertainment in which he was not going to take the chief part himself. His own shows were essentially improvisations, and all through the rehearsals of that

revue we felt Pélissier was treating them as he treated rehearsals of the
Follies, with the consciousness that he would be there on the first night
to fill in with his own immense personality any gaps. He declined to
have a producer. He would show the principals what he wanted and
"You," he said, turning to me, "can manage the rest."

Now the rest consisted of the Alhambra ballet, and my feelings when
I confronted over a hundred girls in practice dress for the purpose of
turning them into temporary Follies touched the poignancy of despair.
I had only the mistress of the ballet to help me, and whereas she
naturally wanted to use her best dancers I was searching for the best
potential actresses. The Alhambra traditions of fifty years were broken
when I picked the girls I wanted for each scene.

The theme of *All Change Here* was some bargain made by Shiel Barry
as 1910 with Father Time by which he was able to have the whole
year over again and change things for the better. London had had a
very wet summer in 1910. It was as if the great city were shedding
tears for that King it had loved so well. The weather had been beautiful in May when he died. Many years later when I went to see the
Kaiser at Doorn in May 1939 he said to me how beautiful the chest-
nuts must be looking in Bushey Park.

"I remember them so well when I was in London for King Edward's
funeral."

And in his vivid blue eyes was a moisture; except for a very brief
visit in 1911 at the unveiling of the memorial to Queen Victoria that
had been the last time he had seen London.

The second scene of *All Change Here* was Primrose Hill in the rain
with all the girls in mackintoshes. Then Shiel Barry waved his wand,
and the girls turned into primroses, to sing

> *It's primrose time in London*
> *And the primroses are here.*

Then there was another scene in which a rhyming recitative was
addressed to the driver of a hansom cab by Shiel Barry. He was warned
that his day was done and presently the stage was filled with taxi-
drivers singing a loud triumphant song in ragtime. There was a scene
with the unemployed complaining of the rain and Shiel Barry turning
it into snow so that they could earn more money by sweeping the
streets. The biggest scene of all was Covent Garden with a performance
of Strauss's *Electra* at which about sixty of the ballet rose in desperation
to protest in a song which began:

> *"Oh, Doctor Strauss, do give us a tune to sing."*

Finally there was a scene with the House of Lords above on their red benches and the House of Commons below on green ones; that must have cost the management a lot of money to mount. I seem to remember that in the new Cabinet of *All Change Here* Harry Lauder was to be First Lauder the Treasury, Thomas Lipton Home and Colonial Secretary, and Mrs Pankhurst Hearth and Home Secretary.

It can be imagined that the problem of rehearsing the Alhambra corps de ballet to act and sing was not an easy one to solve. Indeed, it would have been insoluble without the unbroken co-operation of all those marvellous girls.

I once wrote in an introduction to a volume of reminiscences by my sister Fay called *Rosemary* which was, published in 1926:

"I look back at *All Change Here* with an affectionate emotion that no other production ever has evoked or ever will evoke, and wherever you are now, you dancing London ghosts, I salute you with a very deep and a very humble gratitude."

I echo those words nearly forty years later. In a tiny notebook which has survived, are the now almost illegible pencilled choices I made for the parts the various girls might play. Among them are *Bella Davis Old Maid, Nellie Browne Old Maid, Nellie Digby Old Maid, Chrissie Maude Old Maid*, after I had scratched out *Japanese* against the last name. These were the girls I had picked for a quartet which began:

> *"Chintz and china,*
> *Milk for Dinah,*
> *Tea for you and me"*

in which four old maids suitably attired as such were transformed by the magic influence of "All Change Here" into four girls with short skirts dancing ragtime.

How far I was from realizing when I said "Miss Maude, will you learn these lines by eleven o'clock the day after to-morrow. We shall rehearse the steps with Madame Claire and I will rehearse the words," what Miss Maude would mean to me presently. Miss Maude not so long hence would be the inspiration of my second novel *Carnival*, which would sell over half a million copies in various editions, be the subject of two stage-plays, three films, the first full-length B.B.C. play, a B.B.C. opera, a B.B.C. reading, and translated into French, Spanish, Dutch, Danish, and American.

Miss Maude was twenty-four in that October; when these words are published she will be seventy-eight, the wife of my lifelong friend John

Mavrogordato, to whom I dedicated the second volume of *Sinister Street*.

One afternoon I came out from a long rehearsal during which I had leaned back in the dim, empty stalls, watching the corps de ballet flit like grey ghosts about the shadows of the stage. I came out just before the shutting in of a rainy autumn dusk, and noticed an inquisitive figure waiting by the stage door. He was not unlike that Cornish farmer I wrote about in 1907, as he stood there to eye the girls hurrying home to rest before the evening performance, and suddenly I fancied one of them, gay and lovable, transported by circumstance to a storm-beaten farmhouse. That was the seed of *Carnival*, but some time would pass before the first leaf appeared.

Some fairy arranged on the following evening that, after I had been at the Alhambra discussing with Alfred Moule, the managing director, various points in connection with the forthcoming revue, I should go behind to give Clarence Hunt, the stage-manager, the result of that discussion. As I came out of the stage-door into the courtyard outside the old Alhambra filled with the girls of the ballet talking and laughing together as they waited for boy-friend or girl-friend or husband, Chrissie Maude's slanting eyes caught mine. She was standing there with her great friend Lily Clarke; I asked them if they would like to come along to the Café de l'Europe in Leicester Square for a drink.

I was as much bewitched by Chrissie Maude's gift for story-telling as the Sultan was by Scheherazade in the Arabian Nights. Songs of Araby and tales of old Cathay would have seemed dull beside that phantasmagoria of London she could evoke, as she related some of the adventures she and her friend Lily Clarke had enjoyed. I recall that the girls drank Guinness and that I drank French and Italian vermouth, to be asked what the unnatural stuff was that I was drinking. At half-past twelve when the Café had to close they were going to Leicester Square tube-station, Lily bound for Camden Town, Chrissie for Finsbury Park. I offered to drive them back with me in a hansom; taxicabs were still scarce. I wonder how many who read this will see in their minds' eyes those particularly rare salmon-coloured taxis which took the fare two miles for a shilling and every additional quarter of a mile for twopence, like other taxis in more sombre hue.

After dropping Lily Clarke in Camden Town, Chrissie Maude and I drove on to the corner of the road of little two-storied houses in Harringay where she lived with her widowed father and crippled younger sister Violet. Thence onwards I used to meet the two girls every night at the Café de l'Europe, though I could not afford to drive them home by hansom. My father's allowance had stopped; Harry Pélissier was paying me £6 a week. Every night Chrissie Maude's tales used to make that hour in the Café pass in what seemed five minutes. Tales of the Alhambra ballet went back to tales of the time when she was in the ballet at Covent Garden, swinging high up as a Valkyrie or being the girl in the sack after Rigoletto had stabbed his daughter, and how, when the plump soprano took her place, Caruso, singing off-stage as the Duke, always kissed her when she came off. Tales of provincial pantomimes in a quartette of little dancing girls before she went to Covent Garden led farther back still to tales of herself in Islington when she first began to learn ballet-dancing.

I used to sit in the Café de l'Europe with the proofs of *The Passionate Elopement* which as signature by signature came in from Ballantyne's I passed for press. On a December evening shortly before the production of *All Change Here*, when I was sitting tired out by rehearsing all day and a long argument with Harry Pélissier at lunch, I was turning over the pages of the complete packet of signatures, when I read the opening of the first sentence: "For thirteen pallid February days." In a moment of aberration I crossed out "thirteen" and substituted "fifteen". "Thirteen" seemed an unlucky word with which to begin my first novel. Early next morning I was ringing Secker to get Ballantyne's to make that alteration before they started to print *The Passionate Elopement*. Secker managed to get it changed only a minute or two in time; my superstitious mind was at rest that night, only to realize next morning that in my moment of aberration I had overlooked the fact that Valentine Day is on the fourteenth of February not the sixteenth. There was nothing to be done about it, and now the very scarce first edition of *The Passionate Elopement* can be recognized by that ridiculous "fifteen".

All Change Here had a great reception on the first night. Alfred Moule had insisted that only Pélissier's name should appear on the programme as author, which from the Alhambra's point of view was quite right.

In her book *As Much As I Dare* Faith quoted from a letter she had written about that first night to my mother who was in Sicily with Fay, recouping after a bad go of pneumonia.

There were tremendous calls for author at the end. Pelissier took two calls. The management wouldn't allow Monty to go on. But a sweet thing happened. About thirty ladies of the ballet got hold of Monty, and not in fun, but like furies, tried to force him on to the stage. He had to cling to ladders and things to stop it. He was nearly torn to pieces. They simply adore him, and every one says that no one has ever been able to make the ballet do so much with no grumbling and everything going smoothly all the time.

When I look back on the first three years of this Octave I see the children of Gunwalloe, the flowers of Rivière, and the corps de ballet of the Alhambra as equal passions, all of which gave me a great deal more than I was ever able to give to them.

In spite of that enthusiastic first night, *All Change Here* must be called a failure. The Apollo Theatre was as tightly packed as ever for the Follies, but the Alhambra was far too big for a Folly show however elaborately it was mounted. The Follies had started like many another Pierrot show. After performing first on seaside piers they were enjoyed in due course by music-halls in London and the provinces where their programme would last for hardly half an hour. Their popularity was so great that Pélissier made the bold experiment of taking the Apollo Theatre and giving a whole evening's entertainment. Here the house was packed every night and at every matinée. Pélissier himself with his perfect foil, Lewis Sydney, would be on the stage all the time. Even if Pélissier and Sydney had both been on throughout *All Change Here* it would not have succeeded. Pélissier was a master of improvisation; even his comic genius could not have made the same lines live every night.

Apart from its size the Alhambra, with its paid claque at each corner of the gallery to applaud the *ballet divertissement* which opened the evening's entertainment and the grand ballet which ended it after an interval in between of jugglers and acrobats, could not furnish an audience for *All Change Here*. Those comfortable fauteuils in which elderly gentlemen sat with opera glasses to look at the female form, not dressed so scantily as it would be to-day, but nevertheless scantily enough to make a stall worth 10s. 6d., were only half-filled for a show in which all the girls were fully dressed. The claque clapped at the end of every song as they sat up there playing cards, but the claque could not rouse the house to applaud with them. The circle with the promenade behind it paced by expensive tarts had no attraction for a Follies audience. *All Change Here* was taken off after about a month and the regular Alhambra audience was lured back by a *prima ballerina assoluta* supported by ballerinas wearing less than ballerinas had ever worn before.

The failure of the revue hit Pélissier a great deal harder than anybody knew except myself. Outwardly he was setting to work as usual to prepare a new show for the Follies at the Apollo. The immense meals at Finchley, the flock of visitors on Sunday afternoons, the drives to Ramsgate or Brighton after the performance on Saturday night were as they had always been; but Pélissier himself was brooding over his first failure, and for ever asking me unanswerable questions about his future. He divined that he had reached his climacteric and that from now onward the struggle to maintain himself would become harder and harder. "Some great change is coming," he would assure me, his heavily lashed violet eyes seeming as large as the Pierrot moons by the light of which he had always performed, "and I shall either go completely to pieces or do something. But what, I haven't the slightest idea." Then he would lie back and roar with laughter. "What are you laughing at?" "Myself, of course." After this he would turn abruptly serious. "I like you, because you really do understand what I feel." Then he would look at me, his lips turned down at the corners, like a giant baby about to weep. "You do understand, don't you?" he would plead. And then he would sit in a melancholy, trying to solve the problems of life with the mind of a child. I guessed that the malaise which now constantly oppressed him was his own premonition of adolescence. How was it possible to say this to a man of thirty-seven? Yet that was in effect what was troubling him. He had outgrown the simplicity of childhood and he was frightened by the complications of grown-up existence.

It may have been a good lesson for me how not to let success go to my head that besides Pélissier I should have seen what a shock failure could be to Hall Caine, a much older man than Pélissier. I had divined what a blow to Hall Caine the failure of *The Bishop's Son* must have been and I wrote him a letter to express my sympathy. He had hurried away from 2 Whitehall Court, his London address, to Greeba Castle. From there he wrote to me:

I have been feeling extremely unwell since I left London or I should have written before to give you my most hearty thanks for your kind letter and to express to you my deep regret for the great disappointment you must have suffered owing to the disastrous termination of the run of "The Bishop's Son." After twenty-two years of rather unusual success, it is a new experience to me to encounter so absolute a failure.

I wrote just now that the effect of failure on two successful men may have been a lesson to myself; on reflection I doubt that. I do not believe that I should ever have been in the least danger of having my head turned by success because I cannot recall any time when I was wondering with the least anxiety whether I should one day be successful. Somerset Maugham was noting in this very year of his first immense success as a playwright that he did not think his head was being turned by it because he had always expected to achieve success. When that first novel of mine was being refused by publisher after publisher I had taken to growing flowers, determined not to write another novel until that rejected work was accepted and published. If it had never been published I should have been perfectly happy in concentrating the whole of my creative energy on flowers. I might have continued to write plays; if I had done so it would have been solely in order to make the money necessary for me to finance my floral aims. I had already abandoned the idea of expressing myself by play-writing because, as already told, I had realized I was too good an actor to be a good playwright from my own point of view. I already knew that for me the only satisfactory performance of a play would be when I read it to the proposed cast, after which for me the performers would deprive the characters of life, however successfully they might convey them to an audience.

Hall Caine, deluded by his own success, was no longer capable of self-criticism. If I say he had no background of the arts that does not mean a writer needs such a background to be a good writer. What it does mean is that a good writer without it is almost always ready to blame everybody and everything except himself for the failure of a book or a play to win the favour of the public.

At this date Hall Caine's novels were still selling as well as ever; he did not realize that the failure of his play was a portent of what would happen to his novels within a few years.

It must have been about a week before my birthday on January 17, 1911, that side by side on Secker's table in his office at 5 John Street, Adelphi, I saw his first two novels—*The Imperfect Branch* by Richard Llewellyn, bound in light green, and *The Passionate Elopement* by Compton Mackenzie, bound in light peacock-blue. The jackets of both were plain with nothing except a decorative colophon; both of them looked more attractive externally than any other novels yet published.

As if it were yesterday I see those two volumes side by side on Secker's desk, and as I look at them, equally attractive to look at, I have something like a feeling of guilt in recalling the fate of those two books.

There were no repeats from either the libraries or the book-shops for *The Imperfect Branch*; the rest of the 1000 copies printed remained undisturbed for ever. *The Passionate Elopement* had to be reprinted almost at once and is still in print to-day. Two women were at the well. One was taken and the other left.

TWENTY-EIGHT YEARS OLD: 1911

O N the morning of my twenty-eighth birthday a telegram came from Martin Secker:

Many happy returns of the day   total subscription two sixty one.

In the *Westminster Gazette* that evening appeared this advertisement:

Love and Fine Thinking
"I shall fall
Like a bright exhalation in the evening
And no man see me more."

The New Machiavelli
The New Machiavelli
By H. G. Wells

"The New Machiavelli" contains a striking picture of the unequal contest between love and duty, and a stern moral of the inevitable consequence. It is a remarkable exposition of the political condition of the present day, and a masterly indictment of the fundamental hypocrisy of the modern point of view.

At *ALL* Libraries
By H. G. Wells   The New Machiavelli   6s.
The Finest Novel of the Century
Ready To-day
John Lane. The Bodley Head. Vigo Street. W.

Immediately under *The New Machiavelli* was:

A Brilliant First Novel
THE
PASSIONATE
ELOPEMENT
By Compton Mackenzie
Ready to-day at all the best Bookshops
Price Six Shillings
Martin Secker. Number Five John Street, Adelphi.

H

The New Machiavelli had been turned down by Macmillans because that conflict between love and duty had been the "subject of all the town talk" the previous year. The father of the heroine was well known and had expressed his intention of shooting H.G. at the first opportunity. They were both members of the Savile Club, and the outraged father used to sit at one of the small tables in the big bow-window at 107 Piccadilly with a pistol beside him, waiting for H.G. to approach the Club from either direction. The Committee were naturally disturbed by the prospect, and H. G. Wells was asked to resign. After the outraged father died some years later H.G. was warmly welcomed back to the Savile, which had by now moved to 69 Brook Street.

The New Machiavelli had been offered to Secker; the advance asked was £1200. I recall urging him to raise the money somehow, but he felt such an advance would be too much of a strain on his small capital and prudently withstood the temptation.

The first review I received with some sentimental pleasure was in the *Scotsman* on January 19th. It was friendly and encouraging, but in those days the *Scotsman* column devoted once a week to fiction gave three dozen friendly lines to every novel reviewed; the Scottish reviews that counted were those in the *Glasgow Herald* and the *Aberdeen Free Press*. The *Scotsman* regarded novel-writing as a harmless amusement to be patted on the head with a tolerant smile. Scotsmen who themselves wrote novels wrote them with rare exceptions under a pseudonym.

There were several good reviews during January, but the libraries did not repeat. That was just as well because Secker managed to sell 450 sheets to the John Lane Company in New York and 250 to Fisher Unwin for the Colonies.

I remember well the interview with Fisher Unwin. He sat at the desk in his small room in the Adelphi like a great bearded Buddha; as Secker and I were trying to look suitably grateful for his decision to take those 250 sheets at a cut price, a young man with the faintest fluff on his chin came timidly in to ask his formidable uncle some question and slid timidly out again when it had been answered. That timid young man would one day be Sir Stanley Unwin, as formidable to-day in his own urbane way as that formidable uncle of his.

The sheets for America and the Colonies would leave no copies available for any repeat order by circulating library or bookshop, but Secker was able to have a second edition of 1000 ready by February 3rd. This was just as well, because a long review in the *Spectator* next day brought 150 repeats from the libraries and when on February 10th the *Times Literary Supplement* made it the first of the three novels picked out each week to take up a third of the fiction column we felt that *The Passionate Elopement* had arrived. We were right; all through February and March one review after another came along without even so much as a slightly tepid notice. One that pleased me particularly came from *Country Life*, which had been so severe on my *Poems*:

"A real triumph . . . in the kindliness, the humour and the gentleness of the treatment it comes as near to Thackeray, and to Thackeray dealing with the same subjects, as any man has come since Thackeray."

I naturally felt I should like as many people as possible to read remarks like that, and I offered Martin Secker a deal. I would give up any royalties if he would give up his profit and spend the money on advertising. Secker agreed and as a start we had a quarter page of quotes in the *Spectator* and half a page in the *Saturday Review* on February 11th.

Then I had a bright idea. On my way down in the deep Hampstead tube lift it occurred to me that no publisher had taken space in that lift to advertise his wares. Yet I could see passengers all the long way up and all the long way down in that lift reading about baby foods and tobacco and toilet accessories with apparently profound attention.

"What does it cost to have one of those panels you see in tube lifts?" I asked Secker.

He enquired and found that it cost ten shillings a month.

"That's pretty reasonable," I said. "Why don't we rent panels in four tube lifts? Most of them wouldn't be worth bothering about, but if we had a panel in the lifts at Piccadilly, Leicester Square, Earls Court and Hampstead we should cover the reading public."

"Why not South Kensington and Oxford Circus?" Secker suggested.

"No. The South Kensington lift is down and up almost as soon as you get into it, and people are always in such a state of fuss at Oxford Circus about whether they'll catch the right bus or find their way to the right tube that they've no time to read advertisements."

So for the rest of that year *The Passionate Elopement*, and for most of the following year *Carnival*, was the only book advertised in a tube lift. Then some eighteen months later other publishers began to think it was a good idea, after which there were so many publishers' advertisements in tube lifts that it was no longer worth advertising books. Most of them, too, wasted their money by advertising in lifts at stations like Goodge Street whose passengers hardly ever read a book, let alone bought one.

"Your publisher must have a lot of money to spend," people used to say to me. "I can't get away from your name; it's all over London."

On April 15th Sampson, Low, Marston and Co. took nearly a page in the *Publishers' Circular* to proclaim *The Broad Highway* by Jeffery Farnol as the best reviewed first novel for years, with forty-eight quotes, half of which were taken from papers of purely local appeal like the *Camberwell Times* or the *Stoke Newington Gazette*.

We responded in the *Publishers' Circular* of April 22nd:

A CHALLENGE

The Publisher claims that "The Passionate Elopement" is the best reviewed first novel which has appeared for years, and he challenges any recently advertised work of fiction to produce from papers of equal standing a selection of criticisms which can compare in the slightest degree with the following necessarily small excerpts.

Then followed 41 quotes, every one from a paper of standing.

On May 5th we took half a page in *Punch*, which as I remember cost 40 guineas. The effect on the sales of *The Passionate Elopement* did not pay for that half-page; I realized then, what I fear few authors realize even to-day, that a publisher's advertisement of their books must be paid for by the sales it stimulates. Young authors, and all too many older ones, are inclined to blame their publishers' failure to advertise their books for the failure of their own pens to attract the public. It was important for a new publisher to advertise not so much to sell his books as to attract authors to his list. Victor Gollancz knew this when he was with Ernest Benn and used to have black processions a column long down the *Observer* and the *Sunday Times* in the early 'twenties. These remarks of mine apply only to publishing before the Second World War: I am not qualified to express an opinion about contemporary advertisement, which has made our morning papers and even more our Sunday papers almost unreadable to-day, not by the strain upon the mind so much as the strain upon the wrists.

With the need to prepare a new Folly show in that January Pélissier shook off the depression and doubt about himself caused by the failure at the Alhambra. The success of my book gave him tremendous pleasure. On the Apollo stage he was always introducing gags about passionate elopements to the complete mystification of the audience. Their obvious bewilderment would have been a good lesson to me if I had been in danger of supposing that good reviews and skilful advertisement had already made me and my work famous.

Every Saturday night during that winter Pélissier would drive down after the performance to Ramsgate or Brighton accompanied always by Morris Harvey, Dan Everard and myself, sometimes by a couple of Gaiety girls, sometimes by his brother Freddy. Pélissier wanted only one person in the car with him; we drove in two Daimlers, and the privileges of the road were taken advantage of with a kind of Dickensian relish. On the way to the Granville Hotel in Ramsgate we used to reach a public-house sometime before Blackheath in the Old Kent Road and suitably called the *Marquis of Granby*. It would then be almost ten minutes to twelve, so that it was a pious duty to alight and take advantage of the fact that there were still ten minutes to closing time in order to fortify ourselves with Dickensian drinks for the drive ahead. This hostelry had a museum of oddities collected by the landlord; we drank amid a compendium of the late Victorian era. The next stop was about one a.m. at a roadside inn, where, duly advised of our arrival, the landlady had prepared her speciality—the dish called toad-in-the-hole.

Pélissier knew how to get the best out of motoring; although he liked to be driven much too fast for my taste, he made up for that by getting the best out of any inn. When motoring with other people one was fobbed off with a dull ordinary; with Pélissier even in unfamiliar country one never failed to eat and drink magnificently. The best of our Saturday night emigrations from London were those to the Albion in Brighton. We never wasted a moment on that road over so much as a gin and bitters. Nothing was allowed to take the edge off Sir Harry Preston's reception—he was not yet Sir Harry—as the almost solitary hair upon his bald head seemed to bow in greeting. Once more I see Pélissier as Gargantua, when I recall him to my mind's eye, striding into the sitting-room and inspecting the bottles of every drink imaginable arranged on the large sideboard.

"Coronation Cuvée?" he asks, eyeing the 1902 champagne, and in response to the waiter's reverent nod of assent he beams like a schoolboy at the Christmas pudding. It was at Brighton that we used to sit up all night—Pélissier, Morris Harvey and myself—working at the new show for the Follies; it was at Brighton that after getting to bed at about seven o'clock we would be woken by Pélissier an hour later and invited to be ready to drive with him as far as Shoreham by nine.

A feature of the Follies show were the skits of plays running at the time. These were called "potted plays", one of the first of which had been the successful skit of *The Whip*, the Drury Lane melodrama. We always had difficulty in finding enough successful plays that lent themselves to being potted. We used to sit through a matinée, hoping to strike a rich deposit of potter's clay, while Pélissier would look more and more like a tired baby in the darkest corner of the box, and the performers, having heard he was in front and longing to be potted, acted for him with all their might and main. The only play at that time which really took his fancy was a Charles Hawtrey production called *Inconstant George* with a bedroom scene, as in one or two other plays then running in London. Pélissier decided to have an enormous bed which covered the whole stage, and on this all the action was to take place. I used to argue that it was really absurd to parody a farce, but Pélissier was so anxious to go bounding about in a dressing-gown on the springs of that huge bed that he insisted on potting *Inconstant George*. Another farce we potted was *Baby Mine* by Margaret Mayo. At that date the telephone was becoming more and more indispensable to the dramatist's dialogue and action, almost as indispensable as it is to the writers of television plays. Enchanting Iris Hoey in bed had a telephone on each of the four bed-posts.

We did not stop at potting plays; we potted a performance of Maud Allan's dancing in which Pélissier clad in scanty classical draperies made the reverence accorded to her posturing by earnest intellectuals look ridiculous. I was anxious to try my hand at the solemnities of the Court Theatre where, lulled to sleep by Granville Barker's voice in one of Tanner's[1] endless speeches, I once upset the chair in the box on which I was tilting and woke up not only myself but the audience as well.

Granville Barker's great theory, in which he had the loyal support of the *avant garde*, was that the actors must always imagine the audience was the fourth wall of the scene in which they were playing; in other words that they must not mind turning their backs on the audience in order to rid their performance of the least touch of theatricality. So we decided to encourage this devotion to the fourth wall by having a gauze in front of the stage with the backs of drainpipes and the back of a fireplace from which the back of a chimney rose. I wrote a play called *Self-consciousness or The Fourth Wall* of which the principal character was William Pare, president of the society for the prevention of cruelty to vegetables. Ibsen appeared at one point and then George Bernard Shaw. One afternoon Shaw came round to Pélissier's dressing-room after the matinée and I was introduced to him.

"Tell me," said Shaw, "why do you young writers imagine that I speak with an Irish brogue? If you had the faintest ear for human

---

[1] In *Man and Superman*.

speech you'd know that I haven't the faintest sign of an Irish accent."

I thought when listening to this rebuke delivered in a rich Dublin accent that Shaw was joking. Not at all, he really did believe that he spoke without a trace of an Irish accent. This self-delusion may account for his belief that he could write Cockney with phonetic accuracy, and for the B.B.C.'s inviting him many years later to serve on that committee to decide on the pronunciation of English which gave us "Eeros" for "Eros", "omminous" for "ōminous" and other barbarisms, though they can be acquitted of "eego" for "ego", which was an American importation.

I used often to argue with Pélissier that he was being too elaborate with the Follies, but he would not listen. I used to tell him they were at their best in the old years before the Apollo, when they were doing a thirty minutes' turn at one of the music-halls. If Pélissier, without expansion, could have kept that first fine careless rapture and made all the money his temperament required, it would have been better for him and better for his audience. Unfortunately no artist can crystallize himself at the moment of his nearest approach to perfection. The real reason why toward the end Pélissier began to lose some of his hold over the public was his own boredom with the development of his Follies. He became exasperated by his own creation. He was like the father of a grown-up family who resents his children's dependence on him, but who at the same time resents equally their daring to suppose themselves capable of the least independence. Without the breath of his life the Follies were dolls. Even Morris Harvey overweighted them; not being a doll brought to life by Pélissier, he always seemed like a professional introduced from town to strengthen the resources of local talent. Lewis Sidney, who combined with Pélissier to make as great a comic pair as years later Hancock and Sidney James would make on television, was ineffective without him. He did once break away to star alone, but he very soon shot back to Pélissier.

The Folly with most natural talent was Lewis Sidney's wife, Ethel Allendale. It was she who was always given the most difficult bits to do, and she alone in my experience added anything of herself without ever for a moment ceasing to be a perfect Folly. The rest of them were always themselves, and they only succeeded in being that so long as the Arch Folly was blowing life into them. Ethel Allendale was Pélissier's incarnate whim, such a perfect Folly indeed that for the public at large she remained only a shadow cast by the Pierrot moon, and they attributed many of the impersonations they had enjoyed and remembered best to Gwennie Mars.

I realized that for the Follies the end was already in sight. I knew they were beginning to expire of sophistication in the attempt to keep pace with the public's enjoyment of them and to develop as their creator himself was developing. The unfortunate Alhambra revue began to seem only a temporary setback to Pélissier's ambitions. The mortification of that had been forgotten at last, and he was for ever contemplating different ways to expand. He became preoccupied with the notion of writing a play in which I was to collaborate with him.

The fundamental idea of this play was a situation handled at the critical moment without humour, and then after a tragic dénouement the same situation repeated but handled at the critical moment with humour. Pélissier was becoming so much obsessed by the importance of humour that his own humour took on a kind of grim seriousness. He had often been asked to take the Follies to America and he had always refused because his instinct warned him that the Americans would not understand his methods. It would be Dickens and *Martin Chuzzlewit* all over again. He was probably right; indeed, for many years his instinct had been nearly always infallible; now even his sense of an audience was beginning to desert him. He would occasionally indulge himself in a kind of savage insolence toward the public; when I remonstrated with him he would declare his contempt for them because they had no humour. To the very end he remained an amateur; and, though this amateurishness was the essential charm of the Follies so long as their entertainment retained its original simplicity and ingenuousness, as soon as they fell victims to elaboration this very amateurishness struck the public as the contemptuous indifference of a too successful man. Pélissier himself did often make the amateur's mistake of supposing himself superior to his audience and his frequent failures to appear without notifying the public beforehand were typical of this unfortunate attitude. He would telephone from Brighton or Ramsgate on a Monday morning to tell his brother Freddy to go on for him that night; I would protest in vain. I who had inherited a long tradition handed on by people who were servants of the public was shocked by Pélissier's inability to grasp his responsibility to that public.

I have tried throughout a long life to do my professional duty. I have tried my hardest to keep faith with a publisher or an editor, and I have always been able to see their point of view about a book or an article as clearly as I could see my own. Therefore I have never had a row with either. Nor have I ever made the mistake too many successful authors have made of believing myself superior to the Press. I have always avoided making any concessions to critics, because if I did I should be suspicious of anything they should ever say in my favour. On the other hand I have always made every concession I could to reporters and paragraphists. With them I always do my best to be talkative. In doing so I am actuated partly by the knowledge that all legitimate publicity has a definite value, but even more by the knowledge that the reporter is earning his livelihood in the same way as I am, that is, by trying to entertain the public and myself at the same time. Why should I grudge a reporter what he can make out of me any more than I should expect him to grudge what I can make out of him? It is a reasonable piece of barter. I am a chatterbox and I have often talked with a great deal of indiscretion to reporters, but when I have added "that's not for print" no reporter in fifty years has ever let me down.

To-day the average critic believes that he ought to regard the professional author with condescension tinged with contempt; the comfort of being a professional is that one is not worried by the attitude of an amateur critic. He is impelled to denigrate professionalism in all the arts partly because it is the fashion at the moment to do so and partly because he knows in his heart that he will never be able to become a professional himself. Continuously by the speeding up of everything the mayfly existence both of contemporary critics and of most of those whom they are judging is more and more apparent. As I am writing this fourth Octave sex is seeming so much of a new discovery to authors that we may regret Adam did not sit down and dictate a novel to Eve when it really was a discovery.

I had been elected a member of the Authors' Club in the autumn of 1910 and felt quite like an old-established author when the secretary wrote to say how many members he had heard expressing admiration for *The Passionate Elopement* and asking me to present a copy to the Club library. I had also been encouraged by a letter from Anthony Hope to congratulate me upon that first novel of mine. There was a dinner in February to celebrate the centenary of Charles Dickens, which in fact was a year too soon. This I attended and was rather taken aback when at the end of the speeches the Chairman invited "our youngest novelist" to say a few words. Next day I was reading a leader on Dickens in the *Pall Mall Gazette* with which I was in complete agreement and reflecting that this was exactly what I felt about Dickens myself when I read that those were the words of our youngest novelist, Mr Compton Mackenzie, speaking last night at a dinner of the Authors' Club. I must have made well over a thousand impromptu speeches, not to

mention broadcasts, since then, but not even yet have I learnt to remember a word of what I had said as soon as I sat down. When I have
been giving what is called a "lecture" I have sometimes burdened myself with notes but I have hardly ever looked at them once I was upon
my feet.

Some thirty years ago after a speech at a Nationalist meeting in the
Usher Hall, Edinburgh, Cunninghame Graham said to me,

"Yes, you'll be able to do that till you're sixty. After that you'll
have to know beforehand exactly what you are going to say as I have
to nowadays. Otherwise you'll have a black-out one day."

The possibility of such a black-out has hung over me like the sword
of Damocles ever since. So far it has happened only once. That was
during the last war when after a week of speech-making I was going
to talk about Robert Louis Stevenson to servicemen at the Churchill
Club somewhere in Westminster. The room was packed and I could
hardly see the audience for tobacco smoke. I was talking from a small
dais which was just large enough to hold my chairman, "Shakes"
Morrison,[1] and myself. Suddenly in the middle of a parenthesis I found
myself completely at a loss to find out where I was when I got into it.
After what seemed eternity but was really only a few seconds I heard
behind me the voice of "Shakes" Morrison,

"You were talking about George Meredith."

When I sat down at the end of the hour's talk I had been asked for,
I turned to thank my chairman.

"You're the most wonderful chairman I ever had. When I'm in the
chair like that I go into a dwam until the speaker shuts up."

"So do I usually," said "Shakes" Morrison. "But I was agreeing all
the time with what you were saying about Stevenson and so I was
listening."

When Morrison became Speaker a few years later I thought what a
first-rate Speaker he would be, as indeed he was.

In that February I added to the Authors' Club the Oxford and
Cambridge Musical Club, which was housed in what had been Sir
Joshua Reynolds' old studio in Leicester Square. Here with double
windows excluding the noise of the traffic one could listen at least once
a week to a programme of chamber music, a restful experience for me
after the fever of getting ready a new Follies programme. All too soon
Joshua Reynolds' old studio was pulled down and the Club, whose
agreeable telegraphic address was "Harpsichord, London", moved to
a part of the Duke of Bedford's former house in Bedford Square.

[1] The late Rt. Hon. Viscount Dunrossil.

When *The Passionate Elopement* was published, I felt that it was imperative I should follow it up with another novel. I wrote a first chapter of another and abandoned it. Then just after the Dickens dinner at the Authors' Club I went back to that afternoon soon after we went to Cury three and a half years ago when I was taken to tea by that farmer who had married a barmaid from the Leicester Lounge. Why not write a novel about that story which I should be able to make credible because it was true? I sat down at my desk on that February evening and was granted the third of three transcendent experiences. Of the first I wrote in my second Octave; that was what we call conversion. Of the second I wrote in my third Octave; that was love at first sight. Now I enjoyed the experience of conceiving the whole of a long book in a few seconds of time. Upon the personality of Christine Maude I would build a story that would make Jenny Pearl marry Zachary Trewhella, the Cornish farmer who would kill her in the last chapter.

The Alhambra became the Orient Palace of Varieties. The stories told me about life in the ballet would be made the most of. At the same time, apart from what might be called authentic decoration, the story itself would be completely a product of my own imagination as it was revealed to me in what I can call without exaggeration a moment of ecstasy.

I wrote on all through that night at the first chapter and woke Faith about five o'clock in the morning to read it to her. That she was able to declare in such circumstances that it was wonderful convinced me that the novel of which I was dreaming ought not to be abandoned, like the previous two attempts to start a second novel, with only one chapter written.

On the afternoon of the following day I went down from Hampstead to John Street in order to read that chapter to Martin Secker. In the office was Arthur Ransome, up from Wiltshire in breeches and Norfolk jacket to discuss a study of Oscar Wilde he was proposing to write for Secker. In outward appearance at that date Arthur Ransome could have been suspected of being the first of the professional bucolics (without the Mummerset accent) with whom we have long been familiar on radio and television. He was within a day of being exactly a year younger than myself. His father, Professor Cyril Ransome, wrote a very dull history of England which was used by almost every school in the country and appropriately bound in grey. Never mind, whatever boredom his father had made schoolboys endure in the 'nineties was obliterated by the joy Arthur Ransome gave to children from *Swallows and Amazons* onwards.

I was hesitant about reading that first chapter of *Carnival*, for which I had no title yet, but Arthur Ransome seemed so genuinely anxious to hear it that I read away.

When I finished, Ransome jumped up and almost shouted, "This is genius."

Martin Secker and I shared an acute sense of the ridiculous; Secker indeed was often so much overcome by it that he wept tears of laughter. At that moment he and I were both overcome by the sight of dear Arthur Ransome capering about the office and waving an enormous pipe in his enthusiasm.

We pulled ourselves together when P. P. Howe said, with a hint of reproach in his tones,

"Ransome may be right."

Percy Presland Howe was already devoted to the memory of Hazlitt as early as this and, remembering as I do with gratitude so much encouragement and sympathy, I regret he is not still alive to read this declaration of how much I owe him; he was a great loss to sane and really well-read criticism. It was Howe who introduced me to Frank Swinnerton. The latter had not yet grown that beard with which so much of his self-consciousness was to grow away, and with which his sense of humour was to sprout. At this date he believed it was his grave duty to disapprove of what he felt was my lack of seriousness and theatrical background. When I think of the laughter we have enjoyed together for so many years I can hardly believe that he was ever the young puritan prig he was then.

I went back to Church Row that afternoon, elated by Ransome's and Howe's approval of that first chapter, and even more by Secker's murmuring to me as I left the office,

"I think it's going to be wonderful."

I was still searching for a title for the book and finally decided on *London Pride*. This was presently knocked out by the production of a play with that title by my distant cousin E. M. Symonds, "George Paston", who like so many women writers took George as a name to disguise her femininity. Indeed, half a dozen provisional titles were given to *Carnival* before it went to press that November.

One day I was looking through a pile of Muirhead Bone's discarded engravings and came across one of an evil-looking set of houses under which was the title: *Sinister Street, S.W.* When I sat down to write *Sinister Street* a year and a half later that was the title I gave it, before I wrote a word. Indeed, never since *Carnival* have I set out to write a novel of which I did not know the title before I began it.

I pressed on as hard as I could with my second novel but the interruptions of work for the Follies were constant. Moreover, I was finding
things more and more difficult financially. Pélissier would not give me
a proper salary: I had given up any money for royalties on *The Passionate Elopement* by the agreement Secker and I had made to advertize
the book: my father had just been let in by one of his business associates
for a bill he had backed for £2000 and said he could not afford to
continue my allowance. Somebody told me that a horse called Mercutio
was a good tip for the Lincolnshire Handicap. I had never backed a
horse before, but I was given an introduction to a firm of bookmakers.
I put a pound on Mercutio. He won by a neck at 33 to 1. I decided to
take up betting seriously on a capital of £33. By an agreeable coincidence after I wrote these words yesterday I took up the morning paper
to read that Mighty Gurkha won the Lincolnshire Handicap by a neck
at 33 to 1, on March 17, 1964. I have never betted since that difficult
year for me of 1911, but I like to think that a few Gurkha officers now
in rural seclusion had something on Mighty Gurkha. As I start upon
the tale of my short but arduous betting life I am again at the mercy
of omens.

At the same time as with everything I had taken up seriously during
my life I devoted myself to betting with passion. I used to spend at
least three hours every morning in the study of Ruff's *Guide*, the *Sports-
man*, *Sporting Life*, the *Racing Specialist*, and two or three other racing
papers, of which I recall most vividly the four pages of *Wiltshire Opinion*
printed on blue paper. This was produced by William Maisy, who
lived at Ogbourne in the middle of some of the finest gallops in
England, where he could keep an eye on the horses in the charge of
famous trainers like Taylor and Darling.

Our tenancy of 28 Church Row finished at the end of March; Faith
and I went back to Rivière, where I spent most of the morning with
the racing papers before sending my telegrams to the two bookmakers
with whom I was betting, my limit being £20 each way. Not that I
was betting that kind of sum. A pound each was was as much as I was
venturing then. In the afternoon I worked hard in the garden and
every night I wrote away at my novel to the accompaniment of Faith's
music.

By the beginning of May I had reached the chapter in which Jenny
and her friend Irene are driving with Maurice Avery on a rainy night
along Tottenham Court Road. I was searching for a simile to convey
the effect of rain falling on the road in front of the hansom under the
light of arc lamps. It reminded me of something, but of what? The

simile refused to come. After an hour of racking my brain I gave it up and went to bed. On the next night I looked at the unfinished sentence —"as the horse trotted along Tottenham Court Road with the rain . . ." What did rain look like? After waiting another couple of hours I was still without the simile I wanted, gave it up, crossed out "with the rain" and substituted "shining with puddles in the lamplight".

Fifteen years later when I was writing a novel called *Rogues and Vagabonds* on the island of Jethou I dreamed one night that I was standing at the corner of Bear Street close to the old Alhambra and looking northward along Charing Cross Road to watch the French army under Napoleon marching into London, their bayonets flashing under the arc lamps.

"That's what rain looks like when it falls heavily in a London street under the light of arc lamps," I exclaimed to myself. "That's the simile I wanted."

Waking at this moment with that simile in my mind I introduced a scene in *Rogues and Vagabonds* where I could use it.

I had long ago come to the conclusion that all my novels were constructed in deep sleep, and this waking dream confirmed my belief. I have always refused when I was writing to encourage my brain to suppose it could indulge in moods. When I am stuck I say to my brain, "Well, the sooner you do what I want the sooner you will be able to leave this chair and enjoy leaning back." If I have ever thought that perhaps a drink would inspire me I have never indulged that wish. If after sitting for three or four hours I am still in doubt what a character is going to do or say next I surrender, get up, sit back and enjoy a whisky, but I never put pen to paper even if I think after a drink that after all I might solve the problem. In the course of writing almost a hundred books I have never once allowed my brain to be indulged with optimistic alcohol. I have relied on sleep, and sleep has never let me down.

In mid-May Pélissier was wanting me with him in London to prepare another Follies show and announced that he had decided to take a flat in town so that when he felt disinclined for the long drive back to Finchley after the evening performance he could have somewhere more close at hand. He had found just the flat at 45 Pall Mall and suggested that Faith and I should share it with him. He would pay the rent and contribute to the housekeeping expenses when he stayed there. The flat was to be furnished and decorated by him. For his own bedroom he chose a wallpaper with large peacocks all over it. I warned him this would be unlucky, but he would not listen.

The news that Faith and I were going to share a flat with Pélissier upset Faith's family. Her sisters and brothers all wrote to protest and Faith answered them with some acrimony. Even dear old E.D.S. wrote to me from Radley, where he was living now with his son Frank, Helensbourne having been given up.

Radley College
Abingdon
May 21, 1911

My dear Monty,

I have just heard from Eton what I had not the least notion of before that this move to Pall Mall means that you and Faith are going to set up a joint establishment with Pélissier. Now Pélissier may be a good sort as you would say, and Faith would concur. She seems to be immensely smitten by his social qualities, but I should doubt very much whether he is the sort of person you would care to be stuck with. I learn too that he makes Faith presents which in a small way and in due measure may be unobjectionable but might be construed awkwardly. Christopher and Alyce think as Ned and Laura think and I am quite sure this scheme ought to be abandoned. Please let me know without further delay. Faith lost too early in life a mother who would have been the last person to approve and of whom for various reasons she saw comparatively little when she was of a pliable age. Her education was irregular and rather hap-hazard. I am very anxious about her and feel guilty in no small degree that it was so. But as she has her mother's blood in her, so I can't think that this is more than a passing fancy and I know you, I hope, well enough to be sure that you will watch over her. I wish I could help you with money to make you entirely independent but you have made a good start with the novel and I hope its successor will not be any less a success. . . . Please relieve my mind on this matter.

Yours affectionately
E. D. Stone

I do not remember what I told the dear old man, but I can feel sure that whatever I wrote I wrote pleasantly.

Faith wrote in *As Much As I Dare*:

"My outraged family sent in an ultimatum through E.D.S. as the only person who had a right to interfere. The project of a joint flat with Pélissier must be abandoned. In such an inappropriate part of London for a woman, surrounded by *men's* clubs, and what would look like a *ménage à trois*, even if it wasn't! . . . It had never occurred to me that the ménage would be considered anything except slightly crazy. . . . My family's sudden attack of conscience on my behalf surprised and irritated me. I replied to E.D.S. indignantly, stressing dirty minds and snobbery which brought from him a reply of touching humility.

"I have absolute faith in you and Monty, always have had, and that being so I ought not to have given you even a suspicion that I have not. I was thinking merely of a possible scandal if I ever gave the subject a proper amount of thinking. . . . My physical deafness is constantly shutting me out from information on various matters. . . . I live in a circumscribed world."

I *was* rather indignant at Christopher's joining in the foolish cackle because I thought he was young enough to know better. However, he was still slightly dazed by the luxury of life at The Hill, Witley, where Alice was too near the wealth left by her first husband to feel she could face the world without a butler and a footman. Christopher's marriage had enabled him to take over Lady Ham, for which I was grateful. The problem of money was for me becoming acute. However, I was doing fairly well with the horses.

In that blazing June Pélissier agreed to drive down to Cornwall one Saturday. My father's tour was finished; he and my mother were both at Rivière. So was Fay, of whom I had spoken to Pélissier and who was to meet him now for the first time. Working over the horses at 45 Pall Mall on the Friday, I backed an "aged" gelding called Pillo for the Northumberland Plate. He was a nine-year-old who I thought would start at a good price and who I felt was certain enough of a place to make him worth a bet of five pounds each way for what was known as the Pitman's Derby run at Newcastle. I had a bad night of pain and when I got out of bed in the morning two pills rolled on to the floor from under my pillow. With £5 each way on Pillo already I felt this was too impressive an omen to be ignored and I wired to put another £15 each way on Pillo. For some reason Pélissier was determined to drive west by way of Southampton and instead of starting at six it was eleven before we left London. The lunch at a Southampton hotel was bad, and as too often happened on such occasions Pélissier made himself unpleasant to the waiters.

"It's not the waiter's fault that the lunch was bad," I protested. "If you want to have a row go and have a row with the manager." In the end I began to lose my own temper and told Pélissier I would go back to London by train if he went on snarling at the waiter.

We came out from the hotel at about a quarter-past three. A newspaper boy was shouting "Northumberland Plate winner! Three o'clock race winner!"

"Good lord!" I gasped when I looked at the stop press.

"What's the matter?" Pélissier asked. "Has your leg started jumping again?"

"No, it's my heart this time. I've won . . . wait a minute—£20 at 9 to 1 that's £180 and £20 for a place—that's three into nine—that's £240 altogether. Phew!"

It was later that night when we reached the hotel in Penzance where we were staying. Luckily Heidsieck's Coronation Cuvée was available and to Pélissier's relief a really good '65 cognac.

We drove along to Rivière next morning. My father and Pélissier got on well together; Pélissier obviously took a fancy to Fay, who at sixteen and a half had suddenly decided to leave her finishing school in Paris and come home.

It was soon after this that my eldest sister Viola was married to Henry Crocker at St Cuthbert's, Philbeach Gardens. She had been determined to marry him when my play was produced in 1907: he had been equally determined to remain a bachelor. Four years later her determination won. My second sister Katie was her bridesmaid and Viola was slightly piqued when she heard very soon afterwards that her bridesmaid had been secretly married for six months to the son of an Edinburgh bank-manager, John Austen, who was on the stage. Fay was now determined to get on the stage herself at the first possible moment and I persuaded Pélissier to give her a voice trial at which Faith played her accompaniments. By July she was a Folly at £3, 10s. a week. I did not forecast for her a long career as a Folly, but I thought it would give her a better chance of developing her versatility than going on tour to play Iris Hoey's part in *Baby Mine*, which she was hoping to do.

I was apparently the only man in London who had enough sense to adapt myself to that roasting summer of 1911 by wearing a white suit; I never saw anybody else in one. Mr Grammel, the cutter at Forster's and later a director, asked when I would be leaving England.

"I'm not leaving England."

"Really, sir. I thought this suit . . ."

"I'm going to put this suit on as soon as you can finish it," I told him.

"In London, sir?"

"Of course."

The cutter found silence golden.

What a cutter he was! He made me a frock-overcoat about the end of my time in Oxford which I decided to wear at the wedding of Magdalen Fraser[1] at Brompton Oratory over thirty years later. By that time my waist was not what it had been, and Mr Grammel, who

---

[1] The Countess of Eldon.

by now was getting old himself, had the job of letting out that frock-overcoat. When he looked at that garment of his and stroked the beaver cloth he seemed to be sighing to himself with Nero: *qualis artifex pereo*—what an artist dies with me.

"We shall never see cloth like that again, sir."

I told him I intended to leave that frock-overcoat to a suitable museum as a masterpiece of Edwardian tailoring.

From that summer comes back the cool memory of the Opera Arcade between the hot pavements of Charles Street and Pall Mall. The Opera Arcade is still with us, but I suppose it will be sacrificed in due course to one of those glass and concrete rectangles which affront the sky, those megahyaline ant-hills and bee-hives of the Insect State.

It was in the Opera Arcade that I was privileged to be a client of Burgess's, a barber's shop going back to the Regency. Here not a brush was made the bristles of which had not come from a Siberian hog. Here one could still buy a pot of bear's-grease. Here one walked up-stairs to be shaved and sat for the operation in a Regency chair with one's legs on a Regency stool. Here on the walls were framed prints of Gillay and Rowlandson. Here when one waited one's turn one read *The Times*, the *Morning Post*, the *Illustrated London News*, the *Graphic* or *Punch*. If a customer had brought with him a *Daily Mail* or a *Daily Express* or even a *Tatler*, he would probably have been asked to take his beard elsewhere. It was Mr Edwardes who always attended to me in one of those two Regency chairs. He was a good-looking man with a wonderfully restful voice and hands. It was to him I owe the tip of always being shaved by a French razor and so escape the tinkling and the scraping of the German hollow-ground razor. A year or two ago after some T.V. appearance I received a letter from Mr Edwardes's daughter to say that when her father was alive he had often talked about me; that letter gave me much pleasure.

Other memories of that blazing summer are all sorts of expeditions with Christine Maude and friends of hers in the Alhambra ballet. One was to the races at Alexandra Park—Ally Pally to Londoners—where I failed to find a single winner and made up my mind not to go near a racecourse again while I was hoping to save the financial situation by betting. Instead I used to sit sweltering in some club in Shaftesbury Avenue and bet on weight-for-age handicaps on a system on which I shall not bore readers by expatiating.

I recall going to tea one afternoon with one of the show girls who was married to a taxi-driver; the show girls were eight tall and hand-some young women who did not dance but looked very decorative while the front line of boys and the front line of girls were dancing. More familiarly the show-girls were known as the "ginny" eight.

The tea-party was in a little house in Ealing and I was faintly puzzled to see above the chimney shelf in the parlour an enormous head and shoulders of Colonel Baden-Powell as they were in Mafeking days: it must have been at least five feet square with a heavy frame as well.

"Where did you get that portrait of Baden-Powell?" I had to ask at last.

"Oh, that!" my hostess replied in a tone half-way between resentment and scorn. "Jack got that instead of a bad debt."

One day John Mavrogordato and I invited his future wife and the "ginny" eight to the Zoo. I can see now the exact expression on John Mavrogordato's face when four of those tall girls suddenly picked him up and put him over the railings among some antelopes.

One poignant memory I have of that hot July, and that is the summer show of the R.H.S. in Holland Park. The lovely house had not yet been attacked by the German enemy; the lovely park had not yet been fouled by the commercial enemy. The outstanding display that year was an herbaceous border by Wallace; and the outstanding group in that border was golden *Eremurus Bungei* which I saw for the first time. They are the asphodels I hope to see one day in Elysium and walk beside them with Lucian, Apuleius and Aristophanes.

The Chelsea Show may be very grand and elaborate, but it does not compensate me for losing the Temple flower-show in May and the summer show in Holland Park.

Another feature of that summer of 1911 was the ability of *Fanny's First Play* to maintain its run at the Little Theatre in the Adelphi. It had been produced anonymously with great care to be sure that everybody knew it was by George Bernard Shaw. It was then acknowledged and run at a loss before well-papered houses for several months. Until *Fanny's First Play* was performed Shaw's plays never used to run for more than a week or two. When, after those months at the Little Theatre, *Fanny's First Play* was transferred to the Kingsway Theatre it played to crowded houses; the public and the Press bleated together in happy ovine unanimity that after all Shaw really *was* a popular dramatist, which he remained ever afterwards. Dorothy Minto's performance as Fanny has never been matched by any actress I have seen in the part since.

However, the really revolutionary effect in that blazing summer was not provided by any play; that effect was produced by the Russian

Ballet at Covent Garden. Arnold Bennett had been writing in the
English Review about the Russian Ballet's appearance in Paris in 1910,
and to that extent we were prepared for something good; none of us
was prepared for a revelation of such pulsating beauty.

It is idle to attempt to convey a dance to the printed page. I must
just thank Heaven that I have seen Karsavina and Nijinsky dance, to
the air of Weber's Invitation to the Waltz, *Le Spectre de la Rose*; I must
just be grateful to have seen Nijinsky bound across the Covent Garden
stage in two leaps when in *Scheherazade* the Sultanas take advantage of
the Sultan's having gone hunting to enjoy themselves with the slaves.

I was not able to do any work on *Carnival* during that summer but I
was able to enjoy the company of its heroine, to whom in my book I
was giving a life utterly different from her own life after her childhood.

That summer came to an end for Faith and myself in a kind of
thunderstorm in the lightning of which 45 Pall Mall disappeared.
Pélissier fell in love with Fay and got into his head that Faith was
jealous of her. I have always made it a rule to avoid the emotional
tangles of other people and told Faith she was behaving as absurdly as
Pélissier. Then came the news that he had proposed to Fay and that
she was going to marry him.

I tackled my mother and told her that she must break off such a
lunatic match. Pélissier was thirty-eight, Fay was sixteen; Pélissier
would be an emotional problem for a worldly-wise widow; he was
drinking never less than a bottle of brandy a day and sometimes two.
My mother, like her own mother before her, thought that a girl could
not be married soon enough. The attitude of the old South was in her
blood. No protest or argument of mine availed; Fay and Harry
Pélissier were to be married before Fay's seventeenth birthday on
September 18th.

I persuaded Faith to go back to Rivière at once and suggested she
should take with her Nellie Baker, the daughter whom Mrs Stone had
adopted when she became a Catholic. Nellie was learning to type and
she would be able to get plenty of practice with my handwriting by
typing *Carnival*.

I tackled Pélissier, who persisted in saying that Faith's jealousy of Fay
was the reason why she had persuaded me to object to the marriage.
Then I told Pélissier all my reasons for objecting to it, apart from the
brandy; let those reasons remain in oblivion.

I said that, inasmuch as I did not feel I could attend the wedding, I
could not work any longer for the Follies.

"But you owe me £100," Pélissier said.

"You shall have that as soon as possible."

Pillo was running in the Great Ebor Handicap: that aged gelding had helped me once and I felt he would help me again. I put £20 on him each way. He won at 8 to 1. £160 plus whatever three into eight is. This time my bet was with a bookmaker calling himself W. Kingsby who had his office over a stay-shop in Bond Street. No cheque arrived from W. Kingsby. I went round to enquire why. The office was closed. Rumour said that "W. Kingsby" was the assumed name of a fashionable Mayfair doctor. He must have welshed quite a few people; it was the end of "W. Kingsby" on the turf.

Back at Rivière I had to find somehow the money to pay Pélissier that £100 which I was no longer prepared to earn.

I must sell some of my books. I must sell those hybrid nerines of Sir Charles Strickland's from which I had hoped for so much. I must get an advance on a gardening book. And *Carnival* was far from being finished.

So I sold the Fermiers-généraux edition of Lafontaine; to this day I regret those enchanting illustrations. I sold the *Works* of Max Beerbohm and his *More*, which I had bought at the sale of York Powell's library when he died. I sold what was one of my most dearly cherished books —the first edition of Mallarmé's *L'Après-midi d'un Faune* with that copperplate engraving by Félicien Rops. I sold the limited edition de luxe of Pater signed by him and the limited edition de luxe of Fitz- gerald, both published by Macmillan. I sold that edition de luxe of Boccaccio, Straparola and other Italian story-tellers. I sold a Rabelais with large coloured illustrations of great merit. I sold Gillray's glorious caricatures. Enough. This is opening an old wound.

Looking back over a long life, I can say that this was the most anxious and harassed autumn I ever spent. I felt that, inasmuch as I could not get a penny out of my father because of his liabilities incurred by buying theatres with Milton Bode, his partner, I might reasonably ask Bode to lend me £1000. My father had insured his life for that sum for each of his five children. Unfortunately all those five policies were held by his bank as security against the overdraft necessary to buy those confounded theatres. So I could not offer the policy in my favour to Bode as a security. Nevertheless, as it was his fault that my father's money was tied up, I thought he might be forthcoming; he had no children of his own. On second thoughts I could not bring myself to ask a favour; it has always been impossible for me to ask for a loan from a friend or acquaintance. Three times in my life at difficult moments friends have offered to lend me money and three times I have accepted such loans and thank God was able to repay them fairly soon. My mother's marriage settlement was exhausted: she was beginning to put a stiff brake on her generosity owing to that theatre-buying in which my father was engaged. She did, however, ask Ethel Long, the daughter of Edwin Long the painter, to lend her £100 for me. I was worried when she sent me that money and told me how she had been able to manage it. Luckily for my peace of mind, I was able to repay Ethel Long a year later and dedicated *Kensington Rhymes* to her as a "thank you".

Martin Secker had not a farthing to spare; he, with the help of Mrs Lamont, the widow of the painter who was the famous Laird in *Trilby*, had just bought Bridgefoot House at Iver, of which more presently. Martin and I by now had become intimate friends and he came down to Rivière from time to time in that difficult autumn. I can see him now asleep in an armchair in Faith's "bower", after Faith, tired out with playing the piano, has gone to bed, as I scribble on and on at *Carnival*.

As a minor irritation I was engaged in an argument with the Authors' and Playwrights' Agency. Philip Sergeant was leaving them and I wrote and notified them that they would have no commission on my next book. This was after an idiotic complaint that they could get an advance of £60 with some second-rate publisher and that Secker refused to answer their letters in which they had asked him for that advance. He and I had agreed that instead of taking an advance I would start at 20 per cent on the first 5000 copies and 25 per cent afterwards. The wrangle with the agents went on and in the end I agreed that they should be given a 10 per cent commission on the sales of *Carnival* in Great Britain and Ireland during 1912, but that this was to be all.

I was too tired when making that final effort to finish *Carnival* by the beginning of November to get up and work out the form of the various horses engaged in the day's racing; my mind was too much pre-occupied with how I was going to make Jenny Pearl's wedding to Zachary Trewhella sound true. In any case, I was so pressed for money that I was afraid to risk even a pound on any horse. I had intended to drive over to Gunwalloe every week-end and drink in the air which had inspired the Cornish part of my book, but we had had to sell the chestnut mare; Edward the pony, now too old for such a journey, had been pensioned off to spend fine days in the paddock. One day in that October I received a letter from one of my former Sunday scholars to say that a ship with a cargo of coal had been wrecked off Gunwalloe and that they would have enough coal to last for years and years. I thought this was probably being over-optimistic. Nevertheless, the village had obviously been in luck. Was it an omen that I should have luck if I did what it was at the back of my mind to do?

At Ascot I had backed for a small amount a four-year-old bay called Willonyx to win the Gold Cup, which he had duly done, beating a fine horse called Charles O'Malley into second place. Willonyx was running in the Cesarewitch, carrying the heaviest weight ever carried by a Cesarewitch runner. Yet I felt that somehow in spite of his burden he would win. At any rate, I knew I must risk £5 each way on him. On second thoughts I said to myself that if I were going to risk £10 I might just as well risk £40 and sell some more of my books if I lost. The price of Willonyx now stood at 9 to 2; at that price I backed him for £20 each way; at 9 to 2 that great-hearted horse won.

It was about a fortnight later that at 3.30 a.m. with a mind financially at rest for the moment I wrote the last sentence of *Carnival*; *The sea-birds wheeled about the mist, screaming dismay*. Then I turned back to the first page and wrote: *To Martin Secker*.

To my regret Ballantynes were shutting up shop. Their printing coupled with Secker's infallible taste had made an admirable job of *The Passionate Elopement*. When the National Book League held their exhibition two or three years ago it gave me enormous pleasure to see that *The Passionate Elopement* was the volume chosen to demonstrate the improvement brought about by Martin Secker in the format and appearance of the six-shilling novel.

Carnival was printed by Brendon and Son of Plymouth. Secker and I went down to Plymouth to preside at the stopping of the presses after 1000 copies had been printed, so that the next thousand copies could be called "second impression": I never can feel that the first edition of *Carnival* is as genuine a first edition as that of *The Passionate Elopement* with its fifteen February days before St Valentine.

Faith and I came up to Nevern Square after Christmas to await the publication of *Carnival* on my twenty-ninth birthday. I was having a lot of pain, and hardly slept at all on the night of the 16th of January until the morning of the 17th broke in heavy rain.

MARTIN SECKER rang up from John Street to wish me many happy returns of my birthday.

"Any day-of-publication reviews?" I asked without in the least expecting an affirmative.

"No, but we'll be getting the *Times Literary Supplement* to-morrow with any luck. After the notice they gave *The Passionate Elopement* I think we can feel pretty sure we won't be among the 'also rans'."

Later, before going back to Iver, Secker rang me to say there was a good notice in that evening's *Globe*.

Neither of us was yet aware on that January evening that the *Liverpool Courier* had a long and enthusiastic "published to-day" review.

The next day was even wetter; I had had another night much disturbed by pain and had just taken my sixth aspirin when Faith came into the bedroom with a cup of coffee and the *Times Literary Supplement*.

"I'm afraid you're going to be disappointed," she said.

"A bad review?"

"It's not a long one."

I turned to the "also rans", and among some two dozen other books I read,

"The talk is true, and some of the characters vividly conceived. But it hardly stands out conspicuously in the mass of conscientious work of a similar kind." Could anything be more utterly damning?

It is difficult with 81's complete indifference to reviews good or bad, long or short, to recapture 29's mortification over that "also ran" in *The Times*. I did not even have the wry satisfaction of knowing that ten years hence the *Times Literary Supplement* would damn with equally faint praise *Main Street* by Sinclair Lewis as an "also ran".

Two or three weeks after this Robbie Ross told me that Sydney Colvin had asked the editor to send him my next novel to review. I was tempted once or twice later on in that year when I was elected to the Savile Club to ask Sydney Colvin if Ross had been mistaken, but his deafness and the cold drop at the end of his nose put me off asking such a question. That other friend of Robert Louis Stevenson in the Savile Club, Edmund Gosse, was always generosity itself.

I preferred to bask in that warmth rather than shrink in the chill cast by Sydney Colvin. Moreover, the almost unanimous enthusiasm of the critics in unusually long reviews for a novel soon made that "also ran" in the *Times Literary Supplement* seem less important than the bite of a midge.

A week after my birthday came a present from one of "Mr Punch's Staff of Learned Clerks" which was more of a thrill than any birthday-present of my childhood:

"I am going to give myself a rare pleasure. I am going to praise wholeheartedly a novel by an author whose work was previously quite unknown to me. . . . After reading a couple of pages I settled myself in my chair and thenceforward the fascination of the book held me like a kind of enchantment. . . . As for the style I will only add that it gave me the same blissful feeling of security that one has in listening to a great musician—the knowledge that every tone will be exactly right. This may turn out to be extravagant praise, and may turn out to be an entirely personal impression. We shall see."

On that January 29th the *Manchester Guardian*, always on guard against praising a novel that might turn out to be a popular success, decided:

"Mr Mackenzie hardly does himself justice in the earlier part of the book. He improves as he proceeds. We shall probably hear of him again."

The *Spectator* gave *Carnival* a whole page, but apologized at the end for introducing its respectable readers to such a book:

"We have reviewed Mr Mackenzie's novel at length not because it has given us any pleasure to read or because we can recommend it without reserves. But it deserves notice for its unquestioned if undisciplined talent and occasional brilliancy of presentation, for its frank disregard of the conventional canons of taste, and for the curious hostility toward the male sex betrayed by the author."

This must have been the review which made the President of Magdalen write, in his letter of acknowledgement of the copy of *Carnival* I sent him, that, judging by some of the reviews he had read, he did not feel that he should be able to read my book. However, he did not return that complimentary copy.

Q wrote a long notice in the *English Review*. He accepted my "realism" until Jenny Pearl married the Cornish farmer; this he declared destroyed the book's unity as a work of art. I felt that Q could not bring himself to accept "realism" for his beloved Duchy.

"Quite a number of reviewers agreed, more wisely than they knew, in acclaiming 'The Passionate Elopement' as the most promising first novel of 1911, and their agreement was the more creditable because the merits of that book were referable to little or nothing in the works of Mr Arnold Bennett, of Mr Galsworthy, or of Mr H. G. Wells—three eminent writers who appear to furnish the present-day reviewer, between them, with all his touchstones of judgment and all his canons of taste."

After strong censure of various incidents in *Carnival*, he concluded:

"The whole business awakens a mental and even physical repulsion, which is certainly not appeased when the author ends on the quotation, *Lugete, O Veneres Cupidinesque*—immortal words, henceforth contaminated for what remains of one middle-aged worshipper's lifetime."

And then with typical generosity he ended:

"Mr Mackenzie is so obviously born to do fine work—he has so obviously the root of the matter in him—that one day he will certainly be able to forgive this amount of censure from a true admirer. The censure does not come from any mid- or late-Victorian sentiment, but from applying certain hard rules which at least have the merit that they were thought out in a workshop. He has, in this reviewer's opinion, one gift at least that will triumphantly carry him through. He has—if one may whisper it, and if the compositor will look out his very smallest type—the gift of all others most necessary just now—*an exquisite sense of beauty with a hunger for beautiful words to express it*. As Mr Henry James once said, more or less, of Alphonse Daudet, 'a new novel by him is among the most delightful literary events that can occur just now'."

Presumably I wrote to Q to explain the Cornish incident which had inspired the marriage. Q wrote back:

> The Haven
> Fowey
> Cornwall
> *Feb. 5th* 1912

My dear Mackenzie

I wanted to write to you to express my contrition; but didn't know where to find you. I am delighted that other critics are kindlier; I almost hope I may be wrong on the points where we differ. I am gladdest of all that you take it so sweetly—for it means that, though I'm brutal in judgment, you do see that liking and a true belief in you underly the review. There's no man, just now, that I hope better things from. There was an idea, at one time, of tearing the review up and sending it back to Harrison. "Then"—said I—"is this a weakling, to be so dealt with?" "As iron sharpeneth iron" etc.

So you must forgive me—even if your wife won't—and we'll talk over things when we meet. . . .

Such a pretty theme came to me yesterday for a short farce! I wish you could be dwelling here for a while, and we'd make something quite funny out of it before it faded quite away to join so many voices "flautis in limine primo".

The Boy writes that he has been elected to Leander and Vincent's this term: from which I gather that he is qualifying as a blood—and "Poor Pa paid", as George Robey used to sing.

I am real glad the book is selling. While you write well you must always look to be taken seriously by

Yours ever

Arthur Quiller-Couch

P.S. There are very few really fine tragedies in the novel. The Newcomes *e.g. is merely distressful to me: because the Colonel is doomed by merely mean folk. And* Le Père Goriot *is* Lear *with Cordelia left out. Because Reade hit once on a noble clash of two noble spirits he really—though a 2nd rate man—wrote one of the finest novels of his or of any time. It is the theme—the chance of hitting a really great theme—that may support any poor one of us to the end in hope.*

The Boy with whom all Q's hopes were bound up was killed in the First World War.

To-day the "realism" of *Carnival* which was distasteful to so many seems as "realistic" as *Trilby* or *Vie de Bohême* or that stupidly neglected master of Bohemia, Paul de Kock. To-day *Carnival* appears purely romantic; and that is what will happen to *Lady Chatterley's Lover* in another few years. When *Carnival* was published, the hansom-cab, though obviously doomed, was still a more familiar vehicle to the majority of readers than a taxicab. To-day the hansom-cab is even more remote from contemporary existence than the post-chaise of Georgian elopements was for myself when young. The externals of life before the First World War have been so completely obliterated that any novel written before that disaster must appear old-fashioned to contemporary youth. What once seemed a painful realism that offended against the canons of good taste appears beside the novels being published to-day as a timid retreat from frankness.

Some ten years ago a critic on the Third Programme of the B.B.C. asked who now remembered *Carnival*. The answer to his question was provided by the fact that almost at the very moment he was asking that question *Carnival* was being read every evening to a Light Programme audience. Why was it possible to broadcast a reading of *Carnival* forty years after it was first read as a book? It may be the answer was given in the *Illustrated London News* of March 21, 1964, in a note below a portrait of myself. "He has written over 90 books; is at once romantic and classicist and outstanding among novelists of this century for the *audibility* of his characters."

Exactly fifty-two years before, in an earlier March, the *Illustrated London News* had written:

"We suppose some people will call 'Carnival' an unpleasant book. That is not the way it strikes us. It is very tender, very sympathetic to one of the most touching and pitiful things in the world—the opening heart of a woman in unworthy surroundings. . . . Mr Compton Mackenzie has caught and transmingled in her history the spirit of youth and the spirit of London. . . . In her adorable adolescence how the carnival of light and sound and motion swings on its way! Not many authors have given us the attractive side of Cockneyism. Jenny's quick slang and pavement humour are not least among her charms."

Martin Secker and I purred at each other over those reviews like a pair of cats. In a February list of best sellers *Carnival* was first in Glasgow and Manchester, second in London, third in Liverpool, Bristol and Newcastle; alas, it was unplaced either in Edinburgh or Oxford. Throughout Great Britain and Ireland *Carnival* was second, between novels by Baroness Orczy and Mrs Florence Barclay. It amuses me to remember that presently Mrs Barclay, when asked what was her inspiration for that next best seller of hers, *The Rosary*, would reply, "To undo some of the harm done by books like *Carnival*."

A Covent Garden Ball is one of the scenes in the novel. Covent Garden Balls were still being held in January 1912, although costumes and masks were by now becoming rare. I felt that we must celebrate the success of *Carnival* by such a party. John Mavrogordato and I took rooms at the Aldwych Hotel where some of the girls could come immediately after the ballet was over and get dressed and where we could all have supper at about 4 a.m. when the ball was over. Ragtime was beginning to reduce the number of waltzes. The fox-trot had been invented, but the fox-trot of 1912 had no resemblance to the fox-trot of 1964. There was also a dance called the bunny-hug, at which neither John Mavrogordato nor I excelled. I did not copy my characters in *Carnival* by persuading them to drive to the Ship Inn at Greenwich for breakfast.

I was much pleased to get a letter from J. M. Barrie congratulating me upon *Carnival*, all the more pleased because he did not realize who I was and wrote to me as to a young Scot who like himself once upon a time had embarked upon the great adventure of London.

3, Adelphi Terrace House
Strand, W.C.
19 *April* 1912

Dear Mr Mackenzie
May a brother-author write and tell you that he read "Carnival" with an
appetite and sees a new hand among the tribe whom he is proud to welcome. I am
wondering whether you are all right about American rights and have written
Scribners to ask them if they publish for you, and if not why not.
With all hearty good wishes
Yours sincerely
J. M. Barrie

Another letter that gave me pleasure came from Gustav Holst, who
sent me some of his music and suggested my sending him *Carnival* in
exchange:

10 The Terrace
Barnes
March 10
Many many thanks for the "Carnival" . . . during the short time that I was at
home I fell under its fascination and neglected my correspondence disgracefully.
As I had a heap of work to do to-day I hit on the simple expedient of passing the
book on to my wife. The results have been most satisfactory. She has fallen a
victim to it and therefore put me out of the way of temptation.
I have thus been able to get my job done. Curiously enough it has consisted in
preparing another "Carnival" for the press—an old orchestral work of mine that
was revived last year at Queen's Hall. I send you my Rig Veda hymns . . . also
an old ballad "King Estmere." It is quite unpretentious—merely a string of tunes
with a rowdy battle in the middle.

Some time in that February I met Captain Gerard Tharp, an ex-
Guardsman and secretary of Lord Astor. He was giving up his house
in Westminster to go and live in Albany, and asked me if I would like
to look at 6 North Street. I went along and was captivated by the most
attractive house in London I had ever seen, or am ever likely to see for
that matter. It had previously been lived in by Hilaire Belloc and
Maurice Baring. The rent was £100 a year, but the London County
Council, who were the landlords, were entitled to give the tenant six
months' notice to quit before the house was demolished, should such
demolition be decided upon.

The front door was in North Street (now called Lord North Street),
at which one rang or knocked as at the other doors in North Street,
which was then emerging from slumdom like Smith Square and various

Westminster streets at this date. To-day it is expensively fashionable throughout. In 1912 one might see Beerbohm Tree coming out of one house and as likely as not a bunch of ragged children from the house next door.

When the bell of 6 North Street was rung and the door was opened the visitor, instead of stepping into an eighteenth-century hall, entered a paved corridor under the house next door from which he emerged into a paved courtyard. This courtyard was bounded on the left by a high wall against which was growing a large fig tree. Opposite were three Elizabethan cottages one storey high; on the right was a cottage' of later date joined by a miniature Rialto bridge to the other three; under this bridge one passed to another courtyard overshadowed by the back of a large house recently built by the *Punch* Bradburys in Smith Square. The Elizabethan cottages had been made into one house by Lord North, the windows looking out over a high wall to the back of North Street.

Each of the three cottages still had its front door of three centuries ago, from which one walked to the upper floor by a steep little staircase. On the left of the first staircase was a tiny room with a black wallpaper covered with a golden Chinese landscape of willow trees and mandarins and rivulets. On the other side was a much larger room lined with glass, which made it seem even larger. Beyond were two bedrooms from which one walked into a passage leading across the Rialto bridge to a large bathroom and lavatory in the fourth cottage. On the ground floor there was a kitchen, a maids' bedroom and a dining-room. And what a dining-room! The ceiling was a representation of the arts in the shape of the heads and shoulders of Handel, Pope, Garrick and Hogarth. There were no windows in the back of the house. If there had been the view would have shown a stretch of damp wasteland running down to the Thames with old Lambeth Bridge rust-red and Lambeth Palace on the other side. The cottages had been lived in long ago by shepherds of the ancient Grosvenor estate.

Miss Spencer, for whom Lord North had made this love-nest out of those old cottages, must have had a greater interest in the arts and classics than most young women living under the protection of men of rank. In addition to that wonderful ceiling Lord North had given her two masks of bearded Greeks against the outside of her house. I liked to think that one was Sophocles, the other Socrates. One could suppose that Lord North after some difficult night in the Commons over the American colonies was carried in a sedan chair to this retreat where

Miss Spencer soothed him by playing restful melodies upon her harp.

The London County Council has committed many grave crimes against antiquity and architecture, but when they demolished 6 North Street and buried it beneath one of those soulless blocks of offices that to-day affront Horseferry Road they committed the most nefarious crime in that crowded register of vandalism. They did not even spare that ceiling: it was broken up. I was in Italy when the news of the County Council's outrage upon the London they were supposed to serve reached me. I telegraphed to Henry Lygon who was chairman of the fire-brigade committee to save the knocker on the front-door if possible. This was the brass dolphin from the door of Worcester House, which was given to me by the Provost for the door at Lady Ham, whence I had brought it to North Street. Even that knocker disappeared.

Whether the London County Council felt a shame and sense of guilt that municipal councillors rarely feel I do not know; perhaps they did. At any rate, after obliterating all signs of Lord North's love-nest they changed the name of North Street to Lord North Street in a burst of degraded sentimentality. Pah!

6 North Street was said to be haunted by the ghost of a harlequin. Maurice Baring claimed to have seen it; would that some of those County Councillors, inflated with "progress", could have been haunted by the portly ghost of Lord North.

Before we saw 6 North Street Faith and I had been tempted by a house in the middle of Church Row on the opposite side from the Muirhead Bones' apartment. This was an early Georgian house panelled almost throughout, the outstanding feature of which was a finely proportioned drawing-room with five tall windows looking out on Church Row. What was more tempting was the garden, which ran the whole length of Church Row beyond the tiny back gardens of the other houses. On one side of it was a studio with living accommodation and a gate out to Holly Walk; on the other side was another studio in the same style with a gate into Heath Street. The rent asked for the last eleven years of a 14-years lease was £150, and we reckoned we could let each of the two studios for £50 a year. Nevertheless, the problem of furnishing and running such a house had seemed, in spite of *Carnival's* success, too heavy a commitment for the future; regretfully we resisted the opportunity.

We were glad we had not succumbed when we saw 6 North Street. We felt that this *must* be ours. The house in Church Row would have needed a gardener as well as a cook and two maids; 6 North Street would need only two maids and no gardener. At the same time money must be found for furniture and for the valuation of what Gerard Tharp would be leaving, like those linen curtains of exactly the right shade of orange; the valuation would amount to nearly £200.

Then Faith had a bold idea. She would inherit one day £3000 as her share of her father's estate. If she could have that £3000 now and pay him interest on it at 5 per cent for as long as he lived E.D.S. would not be embarrassed monetarily; indeed, he would be better off because he would no longer have to pay Faith the annual allowance of £50 he was making to her. She had already borrowed £500 from that patrimony of £3000 for which she was paying £25 a year in interest instead of getting an allowance of £75. E.D.S. himself, as one might have expected of the dear old man, was perfectly amenable, but Ned Stone rightly felt bound to protect his father against a rash expenditure of his capital.

Faith wrote passionate letters to Ned about my financial prospects after the success of *Carnival*, and in the end he withdrew his opposition. Perhaps what turned the scales in our favour was the suggestion that Nellie Baker should come with us to North Street and learn professional typing and shorthand at Pitman's. We secured 6 North Street and moved in upon the First of April. Faith had a marvellous time buying Samarkand rugs, the portrait of some grave Elizabethan to look down on our dining-table, a chandelier to hang from the middle of its noble ceiling, six trimmed bay-trees in tubs for the courtyard, a Blüthner boudoir grand piano, old sconces of Dutch brass, and for herself a grey squirrel fur-coat. All my life I have been incredibly fortunate in having delightful people to look after my household whether it was in Scotland, England, Italy, Greece, the Channel Islands or France. In sixty years I have never had to puzzle over the solution of what used to be called the "servant problem". In spite of the severe handicap of a late Victorian childhood and youth I was never afflicted by class-consciousness. Those who have read my earlier Octaves will know how much I have owed to the companionship and intimacy of simple people, and as I write these words at 81 I am warmly conscious of the debt I have owed them all my life and *Deo gratias* still owe them.

We were lucky to find in Emily Seagrove the perfect cook. She would then have been in her late twenties, trim, intelligent, bright-eyed as a bird, with a sense of humour and a light hand for pastry. Alice, the house-parlourmaid, was a more conventional product of domestic service; Emily never allowed her to suppose that conventions were the rule at 6 North Street.

I hear Alice now as she comes into the sitting-room to announce, "The astrologer is here, sir. I've shown him into the dining-room." The astrologer was Courtenay Arundel, from whom I was taking lessons three times a week. I had heard that old Dr Richard Garnett had amused himself in his spare-time at the British Museum by casting the horoscopes of many figures of the past the time and place of whose birth were accurately known. After a large number of such horoscopes he had come to the conclusion that there was something in astrology.

After studying astrology for some years I came to the same conclusion. It is an inexact science, of course, and has been too much at the mercy of charlatans. Of recent years it has been abused by the popular Press with the daily nonsense they publish. The sign of the zodiac that rules one's life is the sign in the ascendant at one's birth, not the sign of the zodiac where the sun is. So-called Capricornians appear in the daily Press from December 23 to January 20. I was born when the 22nd degree of Pisces was in the ascendant at the hour of my birth. Those born under Pisces are held to be liable to ills from the legs and eyes: every sign is supposed to rule a particular part of the body. I have certainly been a good witness for Pisces over this.

Prophecy based on astrology can do no more than indicate what may happen; it should never presume to make the influence of the stars superior to man's free will. I have never paid the least attention to any astrologer who ventured to declare that in such or such a year something definite would happen to me. I have merely been interested to note that almost always prognostication has been accurate about what may be called a tendency for something to happen.

I was not a good enough mathematician to do more than cast a simple horoscope: but what I learnt from the astrologer who gave me lessons was enough to convince me that, however rash, however extravagant, however presumptuous astrological prophecy can be, there really was something in it.

We had hardly been settled in North Street for a fortnight when I had a letter from Gerald du Maurier asking me to come and see him. He had read Carnival and wondered if I had considered dramatizing it. There was nobody whose favourable verdict on my book could have been more welcome than that from the son of the author of Trilby. He was in management with Frank Curzon at Wyndham's Theatre and wanted a play for the autumn.

"This is all my London," he said to me as he talked about his enjoyment of the book.

I said I would have a shot at turning Carnival into a play, and two

K

or three weeks later I went one Sunday to spend the day with him at Cobham. I enjoyed an absorbing afternoon wandering along beside a stream with du Maurier's two small daughters, Daphne and Angela, both of whom were conversationalists of the first order, with a remarkably objective view of life.

I set to work on the play at once and some time toward the end of May I must have cast a clout before May was out; after coming back on the top of a bus from a visit to du Maurier at Hampstead on a cold East wind evening the sciatic nerve asserted itself as it has continued to assert itself at intervals ever since. I was in such agony for two nights that Frank Wallace had to give me morphia. Then although my leg was still pretty sore I settled down to my play again after investing in one of Foote's invalid chairs, which we bought in Bond Street for £74, an alarming price for those days. I write these words in that invalid chair and I shall be writing my fifth Octave in another invalid chair in France.

It may have been a visit to the Temple Show that sent me down to see how my tulips and irises were flourishing at Rivière. At Paddington I ran into Q, who had just arrived from Oxford to catch the Limited Cornish Riviera Express. Q was in a rage. He had been invited to stand for the Professorship of Poetry for which the President of Magdalen was going to put him up.

"So I went up to Oxford and spent £40 getting an M.A. What do you think your damned President said?" Q asked, his cheeks flushing more angrily.

I waited.

"Your damned President with that oily smile of his said, 'I'm sorry, Sir Arthur, I shan't be able to put you up for the Professorship after all because friends of mine are anxious for me to stand myself'."

Academic politics managed to get the President of Magdalen elected to the Professorship. Q declined to stand; it was a blow to him. The Liberal Government for whom he had worked so hard offered him later on in this year the new King Edward VII professorship at Cambridge with which he would be associated for the rest of his life, and which he adorned so well. It was ironical that one of Oxford's most devoted sons should have been deprived of serving her. To George Saintsbury at Edinburgh, Macneile Dixon at Glasgow, Walter Raleigh at Oxford, Quiller-Couch at Cambridge, how much has been owed! I shall abstain from mentioning professors of literature to whom young men are in debt to-day: the number of professors is larger than it has ever been but the number of those to whom anything is owed by youth is too exiguous for me to risk offending so many by mentioning the names of one or two. Those professors of Eng. Lit. cannot be blamed if their job is to get their pupils through examinations, not to cultivate their taste.

On another occasion when I went down to Cornwall that summer I had a ludicrous experience. I was sitting in the corner of a crowded third-class carriage of the Limited when a smallish man with an aggressive chin suddenly nudged me. "Do you ever do any boxing?" he asked.

"I used to box at school," I replied, "but I haven't done any boxing since."

"You wouldn't like to come out in the corridor and do a bit of boxing with me?"

"I think it might surprise the other passengers if we suddenly went out into the corridor and started boxing."

"I'm very handy with my fives. I've done a lot of boxing. I could give you some good tips," he insisted.

"Yes, I dare say, but I don't think the corridor of a train is a suitable ring."

"My wife boxes," the aggressive little man added.

I looked across at a woman sitting in the corner opposite; she was a fairly hefty blonde with a rich bosom.

"Open your bodice, dear," her husband told her.

At this she ran her fingers quickly down about a dozen buttons and pulled back her unbottoned bodice on each side of a steel breastplate.

"See what she's wearing?" the aggressive little man asked, his eyes glowering.

"I do indeed."

"Do you know why she wears that steel plate?"

"I'm afraid I don't."

"Any man looks at her in a train and insults her, she hits him and he can't hit her back and hurt her. See what I mean?" he demanded, giving me a fierce nudge with his elbow.

After this I buried my head in the paper I was reading until the aggressive little man and his large blonde wife got out at Frome.

The summer of 1912 blows in my memory like a flower of time that was; it is for me the last rose of a London that vanished during the First World War, and as I look back it returns in a series of isolated incidents.

I am seeing Reginald McKenna walking along North Street without a cane in top-hat and frockcoat and, almost to my consternation, smoking a large curved pipe. This seemed more than eccentric behaviour for the First Lord of the Admiralty on his way to the House. With him was his wife, a sister of Timmy Jekyll, an Oxford contemporary and niece of the great gardener Miss Jekyll whose boots were immortalized by Sir William Nicholson in paint.

I am at a dinner of the Poets' Club given in honour of Marinetti, the Italian futurist. Maurice Hewlett is presiding, and to my astonishment is wearing sandals over bare feet below tails and white tie. After dinner Marinetti gave an impassioned address on the revolution of the arts against the past. When I was called upon to speak I improvised a futuristic poem on the glories of the new Piccadilly Tube, extolling the symbolism of the coloured tiles of the various stations—the true blue of Down Street, the orange of Covent Garden, and so on: Maurice Hewlett thought I was insulting the guest of the evening and sent word for me to stop, but when I did stop Marinetti rushed across and kissed me on each cheek, hailing me as another apostle of futurism; he was far from feeling insulted.

I am at a gathering of the *avant garde* somewhere, listening to Ezra Pound recite or rather shout a poem to a white poppy. Unfortunately for my appreciation of that poem I thought Ezra Pound was addressing a white puppy and felt his passionate utterance would have frightened a puppy of any colour out of the room with its tail between its legs.

I recall an invitation to address the Whitefriars Club at Anderson's Hotel in Fleet Street, Clement Shorter being the presiding Prior. He was editor of the *Sphere* and had caused some amusement by writing that *Carnival* had carried him on wings; it was difficult to imagine Clement Shorter on wings. He founded both the *Sketch* and the *Tatler* and had much influence in Fleet Street. I had been to see him at his invitation to meet Dr Robertson Nicholl, editor of the great nonconformist organ, the *British Weekly*. Nicholl was as complimentary about *Carnival* as Clement Shorter.

"But you mustn't expect me to say so in the *British Weekly*. It's not a book I can recommend to *my* readers."

I thought that was a pity; the *British Weekly* was the oracle of many thousands.

I forget what I talked about at that Whitefriars lunch. What I do remember is Clement Shorter's asking me what I should like to drink and when I hesitated his saying,

"They have quite a good Bedoc here." His M's were always B's.

The price of that bottle of Medoc was eighteenpence, and it provided a discouraging liquid on which to float a speech.

Martin Secker and I were encouraged soon after this when *Who's Who* invited me to give the details of my brief career. In those days *Who's Who* was less inclusive than it is to-day and an invitation to join its columns gave one an assurance of "arrival".

Hugh Walpole managed to get into *Who's Who* in the following year and entered himself as having been educated at King's School and Cambridge. In fact Hugh Walpole after a term and a bit at King's School, Canterbury, went to Durham Grammar School. When with later eminence he felt he could say Emmanuel College, Cambridge, without feeling that what was then one of the less fashionable colleges at Cambridge was a social handicap he put it in *Who's Who*. He never admitted to being educated at Durham Grammar School in print, but out of that term and a bit at King's School, Canterbury, he built the legend of a grateful alumnus.

Finally I recall a visit with John Mavrogordato to the Post Impressionist Exhibition at the Grafton Galleries. Mavro, who was susceptible to the *avant garde* in art, enjoyed the pictures more than I did.

"But, Johnnie," I said, "pictures must represent something."

"These do," he insisted.

"Do you mean to tell me that picture over there of a dogfight looks anything like a dogfight?"

"Yes, it evokes for me a dogfight."

"It does? Well, that's very clever of it because in the catalogue it's called 'Study of a Woman Swimming'."

Toward the end of that June I was sitting to Kathleen Scott[1] for a statuette at her studio in Buckingham Palace Road. It had been with her when she was Kathleen Bruce that Ruth Daniel had stayed in Paris before our engagement was broken off. Kathleen Scott's other sitter in that June was Gustav Hamel, the handsome young Swedish aeronaut who was the first to fly across the Mediterranean, in which within a year he would lose his life.

Those sittings to Kathleen Scott are intensely vivid to me still. She talked much about her husband then away in the Antarctic.

"I somehow feel that Robert won't be successful in reaching the Pole. He has always been unlucky. If he has an important engagement the train or the bus breaks down, and he misses something that might have made all the difference. I try to put away this doubt, but it's no use. I cannot somehow believe Robert will reach the Pole, and if you knew how much his heart is set upon doing so and what a wonderful

---

[1] The late Lady Kennet.

man he is . . . next year you'll meet him and I know how much you'll admire him."

To this day I feel a kind of guilt when I think of myself in my white suit sitting there in that fine June weather and talking about Captain Scott deep in the white Antarctic who in that moment was already dead.

I recall two interruptions to those sittings. One was of Mr Asquith putting his head round the door and saying, "Kathleen, I want to talk to you about something," and of her coming back to say that the Prime Minister was getting more and more worried about the suffragettes. The other interruption was Peter Scott, on the edge of three, coming in with his nurse and demanding that he should go for his walk in exactly the opposite direction from that in which his nurse was proposing to take him.

For my future the most important event of that summer of 1912 was my election to the Savile Club, which has been my—well, really "home" is the only word that expresses what the Savile has meant to me for fifty-two years. At this date the Savile was housed in that beautiful house with the big bow-windows looking over Green Park which had once belonged to Lord Rosebery. The ghost of 107 Piccadilly now haunts the Park Lane Hotel which rose above it when 107 Piccadilly was demolished.

Sodalitas Convivium was the motto of the Savile, and it lived and still lives up to the spirit of that motto.

Orlo Williams put me up for the Club and one of the members of the Committee at my election was Reeve Wallace,[1] who at ninety-one is still with us. So too is Ralph Furse,[2] a cousin of Faith's, who was elected at the same time as myself. At this date the annual subscription was six guineas and the entrance fee the same amount.

From the moment the new member was elected he was expected to take part in the club life. This was made easier by the members' dining at two long tables and thereby making conversation general; there were also three tables for four apiece in the bow window. The great day was Saturday when the Club was crowded for lunch. Immediately afterwards most of the lunchers adjourned to the billiards-room either to take coffee or play Savile volunteer snooker. The coffee drinkers went off soon after lunch; the billiards-players stayed on in that recess, the warmth and friendliness of which I still miss. It had a comfortable

---

[1] William Reeve Wallace, C.B.E.
[2] Sir Ralph Furse, K.C.M.G., D.S.O.

settee two steps up along one side of the recess; there was no room for any seating accommodation opposite. The frequenters of that settee were a sodality within a sodality. Sometimes a couple of the coffee-drinkers would linger, talking to one another on one of the seats in the front part of the room. I recall an exquisite moment when a late Astronomer-Royal, a superb tippler who must have detected several double stars as yet undetected, was talking to the historian Stanley Lane-Poole. We on the bench watching a stroke in a tense game in the billiards handicap between Freddie Maugham[1] and Billy Orpen[2] were for a moment hushed. The silence was broken by the voice of Stanley Lane-Poole saying to the Astronomer-Royal, "And they take them to places I'm told they call cinemas."

"Cinemas, really?" said the Astronomer-Royal in puzzled tones. "Cinemas, you say? I've never heard of such places."

"Damn it," exclaimed Bill Orpen, his long upper lip seeming an inch longer than usual. "I've missed the pocket."

And then we all laughed, while the medieval historian and the Astronomer-Royal went on inaudibly to discuss the temptation of cinemas to the fair and frail. Terry's Theatre in the Strand was a particular temptation. Here at the back of a box lovers could sit making love without anybody in the audience seeing what they were at. Finally the London County Council, more zealous for the morals of London than its architecture or antiquities, compelled the management of Terry's Theatre to close those boxes to its audience, and ensure their looking at Mary Pickford, still anonymous, being made love to instead of making love in a box themselves.

Back to the Savile. The "drawing-room" on the first floor was used by members more for reading than for conversation, but in the recess at the back it was the custom of various senior members to sit and talk until tea-time after that Saturday lunch. Edmund Gosse used to ask me to come up with him to the drawing-room and I was privileged to sit and listen to the conversation of those seniors. I recall a story told by Gosse about Swinburne. One afternoon Swinburne had come into the drawing-room and balancing himself on the brass fender was holding forth in his high voice, slipping from time to time off the fender with a clang. In a corner of the drawing-room Herbert Spencer was reading the *Quarterly Review*. At last in order to exclude the sound of the poet's voice and the clang of the fender he took a pair of silencers out of his pocket and with a sigh put them over his ears.

[1] The late Lord Maugham.
[2] Sir William Orpen, R.A.

Another story of Gosse's about Herbert Spencer told of how as a boy young Monkton-Milne had been taken by his father to see Carlyle in Cheyne Row.

"You're the second famous man my father has taken me to visit to-day," the boy exclaimed with enthusiasm.

"Is that so, laddie?" said Carlyle.

"Yes, Mr Carlyle. I went to see Mr Herbert Spencer this morning."

"Oh, you've met Mr Herbert Spencer, have you, laddie? Ay, ay, then you can boast to your young companions that you've met the most unending ass in Christendom."

In those days two decanters of port, vintage and wood, and a horn of snuff were passed round the dining-tables at the end of the meal; nobody was allowed to smoke until he left the dining-room. It was a breach of Savile etiquette to offer another member a drink; one always ordered one's own drink and paid for it oneself. Frank, the wine waiter, who had memories of great Savilians like R. L. Stevenson which he occasionally let out, as it were, with a kind of casual meiosis, was now middle-aged, and Godfrey, Frank's number two, shed a kind of venerable geniality over every glass of whisky he served.

The card-room was a small room on the second floor which remained sacred to whist longer than any club card-room in England but had surrendered completely to bridge by the time I became a member of the Savile.

I seek for a phrase to express the peculiar quality of what may be called the process of Savilization which the club has been able to exercise over its members and still exercises, *Deo gratias*, to-day at 69 Brook Street. Perhaps it is the conviction that, although all men may not yet be equal, all Savilians are equal. We have members renowned for academic, scientific, literary and artistic achievement; inside the Savile nobody would suspect it. We have had members who left us because they did not find their eminence was appreciated by their clubfellows: such unsavilized members were not missed.

Carnival was published in the United States by Appletons and was given as generous a welcome by the American reviewers as it had been given in Great Britain. It is amusing to recall that "tart" and "bitch" both had to be cut out in order to avoid offending the American reader. The protracted and excessive prudery of American readers at this date is being heavily paid for by the ever-increasingly wearisome exploitation of sex by the freshmen of the University of Carnal Knowledge. Enquiries about the dramatic rights came as early as May from an American agent through J. B. Pinker, to whom I had given the handling of the play. It was finished and sent off to du Maurier some time in June. Du Maurier liked it but felt that he could not afford to be off for the whole of the third act. I could not see how to make an audience realize the effect of the absence of Maurice Avery when the curtain came down on the second act if Maurice appeared again early in the third act; he must wait for the fourth act. Du Maurier was so pleased with the second act that he clung on for a while to the hope that I should find a way out. However, it was no use. He wrote to me:

> Mullion Cove
> Cornwall
> *Aug. 16th*
>
> *My dear Mackenzie,*
> *Ceaseless rain and a merciless wind have turned your beloved and beautiful Cornwall into a Slough of Despond.*
> *Lumbago and rheumatism, a cold sea, falls from precipices, and lifting the car out of a marsh into which I had driven it, no fish (four pollack and a scab), no caddies are driving me to France next week. Farewell, Cornwall.*
> *Your version of Carnival is not to the liking of our united great minds at Wyndhams—so you can now make it Jenny's play, which it ought to be. They all think the last act impossible. I am inclined to think they are right. Can a delightful book full of literary charm, with dozens of carefully drawn characters, be boiled down into a satisfactory well balanced play? Damn.*
> *However, good luck to it and may it be well played.*
> *None of the Cornish people here have the right accent, or at Porth Leven, and they seem to have the same fondness for money that they have for pilchards.*
> *There have been several cries of Havim [?] but none of Hever.*
> *The rain is a bit warmer to-day. Greetings to you.*
> *Yours ever*
> *Gerald du Maurier*

I completely understood du Maurier's point of view; in any case *Carnival* had by now receded in the preoccupation of *Sinister Street*.

At this date in the reaction against what the younger generation were considering the novel in which life as they thought was trimmed down to serve a slick story, there was a growing tendency to depend upon autobiographical material. H. G. Wells and Arnold Bennett had set them a conspicuous example. I felt that it was time an attempt was made to present in detail the youth of somebody handicapped by a public school and university education instead of poverty or more humble circumstances. I have already in my three previous Octaves indicated how much fiction was imposed upon fact in *Sinister Street*;

the failure to survive of the many novels that would be inspired by *Sinister Street* was due to the excessive reliance of their authors upon the facts of their early lives through lack of imagination to create out of them fiction. Another feature of the current literary fashion was the trilogy, of which Arnold Bennett's *Clayhanger* was the leading example. I was determined to have nothing to do with trilogies which told the same story over again through the eyes of a different character. Even Oliver Onions made the mistake of extending that great story *In Accordance with the Evidence* into a trilogy. In *Carnival* I had tried to follow Flaubert's method with *Madame Bovary* of avoiding any incident that was not within his principal character's ken. Jenny Pearl remained throughout the centre round which the whole tale revolved.

In constructing *Sinister Street*, besides avoiding anything outside the ken of my chief figure, Michael Fane, I was more successful in avoiding psychologizing about his thoughts and behaviour than I had been over Jenny Pearl, and also in keeping out any suggestion of comment, direct or implied by myself as author. I wanted Michael Fane's attitude to life to remain what it was at the time. When I finished *Carnival*, I had a moment of exhilaration; I felt I had accomplished something significant. That I killed my heroine on the last page did not affect me with the kind of emotion in which Dickens indulged when he removed somebody like Little Nell or Paul Dombey from the world. My heroine was dead in the pages of a book but in fact she was as much her vital self as she had been all through the book until that last page. With her father and lame sister she had just moved from Harringay to live in a flat in Golders Green, which at this date was emerging in red brick from the country. I had given her a bob-tailed sheepdog called Fuz after one of the characters in *Carnival*.

When I began *Sinister Street* I was oppressed by the size of the task I had set myself and with continuous doubts about my ability to carry it through either to my own satisfaction or that of anybody else. As a preliminary to starting *Sinister Street* I had written a number of children's verses called *Kensington Rhymes*. They were illustrated by Jack Monsell, a distant cousin of Faith's and later the husband of Margaret Irwin; they were published that autumn.

Kensington Rhymes was a kind of board on which I sharpened the knife of my memory to write the opening chapters of *Sinister Street*.

I had already begun to write at night, but when I look back to myself at work on the first chapters of *Sinister Street* I am always sitting in the invalid chair beside the window of the little room in North Street in the morning. I suppose my earnest study of racing form every morning when I was betting in the previous year had accustomed my brain to concentrating in the morning. It was only the beginning of *Sinister Street* I should write by daylight; I went back to the night time for the next forty years until I transferred from night to afternoon. I have written only one book in the morning and that was due to the equatorial conditions of the Seychelles Islands. I used to call that little room at 6 North Street the "tea caddy". The black paper on the wall with its golden willow-pattern scenes, the woodwork painted the colour of red lacquer and the smallness of the room made me feel I was writing in a box.

A letter from Martin Secker just before I started the writing of *Sinister Street* in that July says:

I'm still thinking about the title and scheme of the book, and wondering even at this 11th hour whether you wouldn't be wise to consider the trilogy idea. It only means a half title before Chapter I called "I: Youth's Encounter," and it leaves you free to do a second and third volume (or a second only) in the future. Only, of course, I quite see that if this book is to be the beginning and the end of "Sinister Street", you will make more of his adventures when he meets the girl in pre-Oxford days. The thing is that it seems to me as though pressure of time and space look like cutting short your original scheme, which would be a pity. Wouldn't it be better to leave the door open to continue it when you feel like it?

The uncertainty of time to which Secker alludes refers to the play I had made of *Carnival*.

William Morris, an American agent in London, had received the play at the end of May and had expressed great hopes for it. He had sent one of his people with the promising name of Spingold to negotiate the production of the play in the U.S.A. It appeared that William A. Brady was interested in it for his wife Grace George. I had asked Spingold to tell Brady that I was anxious to get my brother from Australia to play the part of one of the "second juveniles"; and suggested at the same time that the atmosphere of the play would be helped if two of the girls in the Alhambra ballet were in the cast. My notion was for Chrissie Maude to go with one of her friends.

In the end Brady paid my brother Frank's passage from Australia to America but he would not accede to my request about the girls. Grace George told me later that she had put a firm foot on that suggestion.

A letter written by me on Saturday September 28th from the Hotel Knickerbocker in 42nd Street has survived:

Here I am and I think New York is just the most wonderful event. I leave at 12.40 to-morrow morning and arrive at French Lick, Indiana, at 6.30 on Monday evening—what apparently is called going a little bit West! I am to stay with Brady and his wife for ten days or a fortnight and make a few alterations in the play, or rather rewrite it! . . .

Well, I think I've been invited to stay in every city in America from Pittsburgh to Phoenix, Arizona, from Chicago to San Antonio, Mexico. A Mrs McCormick of Chicago—one of the six richest women in the U.S.A. I was reverently informed —was the only owner of a copy of Carnival *I could see on board.*

I was very fit the first two days. In fact I think I ate too much. Anyway on Sunday night I woke up an hour after I was in my bunk with acute rheumatism and bloody sea-sickness. What a night! I felt that nothing was worth while and spent all my time planning which State you and I should settle in to avoid re-crossing the Atlantic ever again.

I was ill all Monday. On Tuesday I began to feel better . . . but even yet the rheumatism hasn't quite gone. I was bandaged up with lint and lead and lauda-num all the time. It was hell. However, everybody on board was perfectly charm-ing and I made nearly a dozen very delightful friends. A mahogany grower in British Honduras, a young blood of New York, a Virginian company promoter, a Tennessee judge, a Chicago doctor, a Toledo doctor, a Washington banker, four funny fat women from Pittsburgh, a Jewish grocer in Arizona, and a very nice young Englishman who is going to play the lead with Kitty Gordon. He's only 26 and is getting £50 a week out here. Not so bad. I believe he has a lovely voice. . . .

Spingold came post haste from Montreal in order to meet me. He's a good chap, and Sears (of Appleton's) had sent his secretary to do anything I wanted. They had arranged a dinner in my honour for next Thursday but of course that must be postponed.

New York seems to me like living in a set-piece at a Brock's Benefit. It is amazingly romantic. Good God, why haven't they produced a great poet here during the last twenty years? The inspiration should be tremendous.

This hotel is astonishing. My bedroom has a bathroom, a lavatory, and a luggage room. There is a kitchen on my floor. In fact there are no *hotels in England.*

That letter brings back memories. The smoking-room of the *St Louis* was intimate and comfortable with a "George" at the bar who remains a personality among all the "Georges" I have met since. Are the bar-tenders of the two Queens still called George? Many good stories were told every night. At the end of the voyage a story told by a well-known American comic writer whose name I have forgotten was voted the best American story and one told by me I had heard from Gerald du Maurier was voted the best Cockney story. Neither story is printable;

in any case, even if my old-fashioned reticence allowed me to print them, they are stories to be told and heard, not read. I put the American story into my own repertoire of five *really* first-class ribald tales and was gratified when over twenty years later, after I had told it in the smoking-room of a liner bound from Monte Video to Rio, an American fellow-traveller said,

"Well, I have heard that story three times but I never heard it told so well before."

Although I am half American I am always a bit nervous about telling stories in which an American accent has to be assumed.

I recall from that smoking-room in the *St Louis* an earnest doctor from Toledo, Ohio, who kept pressing upon me the necessity of visiting Toledo before I could claim to have seen anything of the real America. He turned to a young New Yorker to confirm his advice.

"Would you not agree with me, Mr —?" he asked.

"I don't know," the young New Yorker replied. "I've never been fifty goddam miles out of little old New York and I hope I never shall be."

In those days before the films had made the sky-line of New York familiar the first sight of it from the deck of the *St Louis* was a staggering experience of an utterly new beauty.

Spingold had an engagement on the September evening of my arrival, and tried to make me promise not to go out of the Hotel Knickerbocker until he came to put me on the train for Indianapolis next morning. I told him I intended to take a walk along Broadway.

"Well, if you do go out don't get into conversation with any strangers. If anybody accosts you don't pay any attention."

I decided I would eat out, and having heard my mother speak of soft-shelled crabs as a delicacy, I found a fish restaurant—it was not Jack's in Sixth Avenue I hasten to say—and ordered soft-shelled crabs. The season for them was just over but I was served with some which must have been in store for some time. They were not merely past their best; they were bad.

I do not suppose that to-day anybody would be as excited as I was by the lighted advertisements in Broadway. At that date even in Piccadilly Circus there were not half a dozen comparatively dim displays of coloured lights. Nevertheless, I expect that Broadway to-day would still make the Piccadilly show look tame.

I saw only one sizable cinema theatre, which was hardly half full with an audience watching a flickering travel film in which jerky lions walked about to the tune of a tinkling piano. Even as late as this autumn of 1912 the American theatrical managers considered the flicks a novelty that would not last.

Next morning I went down to the barber's shop in the Knickerbocker and for the first time experienced a barber's chair that swung back to present the customer in a horizontal position. For an instant I thought I was in the hands of Sweeney Tod, the murderous barber of Fleet Street. On top of that I experienced for the first time the application of a hot towel after being shaved; it gave me such a shock that to this day I wave away the offer of a hot towel.

When the train passed the frontier of Indiana next day the conductor came along to see that anybody smoking a cigarette extinguished it immediately. At Indianapolis I had to change trains for a place called Bedford, the new train seeming old-fashioned after the one I had left. Then at Bedford I changed into a much more old-fashioned train that reminded me of the London, Chatham and Dover line in the days of my childhood. A cavalry regiment was touring Indiana, and an old gentleman who got into the carriage at Bedford told the rest of us that he had not seen so many soldiers since the War. That cavalry regiment paid a visit to French Lick a day or two later and I see now the Colonel taking off his hat and waving it with ceremonious politeness to applauding ladies.

On October 2nd I was writing in the hotel garden:

Here I am with Brady and his wife.

This is rather a delightful American Carlsbad with a casino for roulette and all sorts of other gambling games. I have already re-written the first act which is greatly improved. Brady could not get over the speed with which I did it but the puzzle was solved for him when I told him I was half American. I think that decided him to pay Frank's fare from Australia to play in "Carnival". I've just cabled to him at a cost of 12 dollars! Brady expects to produce the play in November, either in Chicago, Buffalo or Albany, after which it will have a fortnight's trial on the road before the proper first night at the Playhouse in New York. He hopes to get John Barrymore for Maurice. So if I think it may be a success you will be able to come over for the real first night.

Grace George is absolutely charming, and you could not find anywhere anybody so well suited to play Jenny. She has a very pretty and slight accent. Brady is a great nut and an awfully good sort. He bites his nails. So we make a good pair. He's a tremendous gambler. We go back to New York in about a week. I'm writing all day. The play is now:

Act I. The brilliant end of the ballet and gradual darkening of the stage. Symbolic of the play.

Act II. Scene i. *Very much as at present. Except that we go back to my original opening with Jenny in practice dress of tarlatan being sculpted.*

Scene ii. Three months later. *The dreary dusty studio all empty with the scene between Jenny and Castleton as in the book.*

Act III. *The arrival in Cornwall. Practically in fact the chapter called " The Tragic Loading".*

Act IV. *The quarrel between Jenny and Trewhella as in the book over Castleton's letter. Maurice's arrival and the death of Jenny.*

If we find that the audience cannot stand that I may have to surrender to a happy ending.

Brady and his wife think it is going to be the *play and he told me he antici- pated a two years' run through America. I want Miss George to play the part in London but she says she won't dare. However, I think she will for a season, when her place can be taken by somebody else.*

Tell Mother that I am reminded by Miss George of the pictures of her long ago.

I'm taking the waters here, which taste like puddles flavoured with bad eggs.

I wrote three completely new acts during those ten days at French Lick, but I seemed to have plenty of time for amusement. We went one day to another spa called Baden on the Kentucky border to see a baseball match between the waiters of the two hotels who were all coloured. I did not gamble at roulette or any of the other games, but one could not buy a cigar without throwing dice to decide whether one had it for nothing or paid twice as much. On one occasion after dicing for a box of chocolates to give Grace George I found I had won a first-rate suit-case. Little remains in my memory of the natural scene except the enormous beds of cannas in front of the hotel round which bonfires were kept burning all night to ward off the frost.

Brady himself was a continuous entertainment. He had started life as callboy in a San Francisco theatre and later he had carried the purse when Gentleman Jim Corbett was boxing around the States. He was of Irish Catholic origins. He had been married before and was the father of attractive Alice Brady, who three years hence would play Jenny Pearl in a film of *Carnival*. Grace George and he had one son of about ten years old who might have been a model for Buster Brown. Brady drank pretty heavily but he was on the wagon at French Lick, hoping in the company of other American men of business to get rid of the effect of alcohol with the sulphurated water and be able to drink again.

When I got back to New York from French Lick I stayed at the Flanders Hotel on W. 47th Street between Sixth Avenue and Broadway. This was only ten storeys high and was a kind of family hotel for British actors in New York.

A letter of October 20, 1912, to Faith has survived and expresses the kind of whirl I was in:

New York becomes more adorable every moment. I meet nobody who is not completely charming, and even my interviewers are kind to me. I enclose the first two. I may explain for vanity's sake that the column and a half in the "Sun" is some compliment . . . Brady was quite thrilled when he saw it. . . .

On the business side I have sold three short stories to "McClure's" at 400 dollars apiece. Not bad! Especially as they are not yet written and they have given me an advance of 250 dollars. I have a fat roll of dollar bills in my hip pocket. Very comfortable padding. If Cameron Mackenzie, the editor, likes them he will commission nine more i.e. 4800 dollars (£960) a nest egg for 1913. They are to be called the early adventures of Jenny Pearl, and Cameron Mackenzie talks about doing a moving picture series of them.

I have made good friends with Robert Loraine who is staying at the Flanders. To-night I had supper with Maurice Baring. He leaves for the Balkans to-morrow with Hamilton Fyffe. Baring tells me there are three ghosts at 6 North Street. One is the particularly pleasant ghost of a harlequin. There are also a singing lady and a masked belle of Vauxhall. The singing lady is occasionally unpleasant in her choice of songs.

What have I done? What haven't I done? The Flat Iron Building whose height impressed you so much when you were with Hawtrey in New York eight years ago is now a mere cottage beside the new buildings erected latterly. They are glorious.

I drove to Brooklyn to-day and coming home over Williamsburgh Bridge I saw the city against an orange sky. An amazingly beautiful experience. On Sunday Grace George and I drove out to spend the day with the Selwyns (Mrs Selwyn is Margaret Mayo who wrote "Baby Mine") down the Hudson in divine weather through country as beautiful as anything in the Tyrol and yet only 33 miles from New York.

I can't get over the delights of this city. It enthralls me. I must spend several months here every year. If it is a success we might buy a house on the Hudson.

It's half-past two. I never get to bed before five! Not a trace of neuritis or rheumatism and a glorious energy all the time. I'm frightfully well. There's to be a dinner in my honour by the literary nuts on Thursday, and on Tuesday I'm being lunched by the Press Club.

I really am having the T.O.M.L. (time of my life). Pray God it's not disrupted by a damned failure with Carnival.

I remember well that day in the Selwyns' country house. As early as this motor traffic was already becoming a problem for New York. It took us an hour and a half that evening to get into the centre of New York from the outskirts. Nobody in the United Kingdom would experience anything like that jam of motor-traffic for a long time. Yet our police had a great reputation in the States for the calm skill with which they managed the London traffic, and that autumn some of the New York City police who had been visiting London to study that calm skill on the spot came back with the "know how". At 42nd Street and Broadway where the traffic was at its thickest a cop was stationed on a kind of rostrum to direct it. New Yorkers, not being used to being ordered about, paid no attention to the upraised arm calling on them to stop. The cop stood this disregard of his arm for a while. Then he drew a revolver and put a shot into a car to make it stop. Realizing he meant business, motorists began to pay attention.

Hospitality was continuous. Rutger Jewett of Appletons introduced me to what I called in that letter above some of the literary nuts who liked *Carnival*. I recall particularly Franklin P. Adams, already a popular columnist, Julian Street, a great friend of Booth Tarkington, who had the longest eyelashes I ever saw on a man, and James Montgomery Flagg, who had stepped into Charles Dana Gibson's place as an illustrator. The latter married a sister of the late Nancy Lady Astor and I enjoyed a delightful lunch with them. Robin Buxton and one of the banking Bensons were fellow-guests and I remember thinking how damned casual our British manners were when Robin Buxton, whom I had not seen for a couple of years greeted me with "Hullo, Monty", without stepping away from the fireplace to shake the hand which I, already Americanized, offered. He and Benson were in New York studying the banking methods of the United States. We had a marvellous chicken Maryland at lunch; Mrs Dana Gibson kept heaping tit-bits on my plate until I could hardly manage to swallow another mouthful. I was reminded of my mother's similar behaviour at home and our guests trying to prevent her from pressing any more of a dish on them.

At this date women were allowed to smoke publicly only in two places. One was at Rector's down town, but not at Rector's up town (both restaurants frequented by Upper Bohemia). The other place where smoking was permitted to ladies was at the Plaza Hotel overlooking Central Park. Even here, smoking was only allowed between four and six in the afternoon, at what was called a *thé dansant*. The moment the *thé dansant* was over every cigarette had to be extinguished at once. Smoking was not allowed in theatre, cinema, subway or on the clattering elevated railway. Noise was becoming a problem. When

L

the lovely Metropolitan Tower was built, and rose to 750 feet, for a brief time the tallest building in New York, it was considered a fine example of civic consideration that the great clock with glowing green hands and numerals did not add to the noise by striking the hour; instead the hands and numbers glowed red at every quarter.

In that autumn of 1912 a green horse-bus used to take its dignified course up and down Fifth Avenue every hour, and one or two of the streets crossing the avenues still had horse-drawn trams or trolley-cars as they were called. I used to ask my American friends why they always had longer names than we had for all forms of transport—elevator for lift, subway for tube, locomotive for engine, automobile for motor, trolley-car for tram.

One afternoon I went to tea with Violet Asquith,[1] who was staying in one of the great houses in Fifth Avenue overlooking Central Park. Tea was a solemn business in New York; a couple of powder and plush footmen waited on us ceremoniously throughout. After tea was over the footmen reappeared, each carrying a silver ewer, and stood gravely in front of Violet Asquith. She looked up with a question in her eyes.

"The temperature of your bath, Miss Asquith," one of them gravely explained. She was supposed to dip a finger in each ewer and choose between the two specimens of heat preferred.

One of my problems was how to stand up to the drinking in the Flanders bar; finally I decided to ask for a kümmel every time a round was on the next person in the line, and I got quite a reputation for the way I could drink as much as a dozen kümmels without a sign of having done so. The explanation was that I had made an arrangement with the barman always to have a kümmel bottle filled with water from which he would replenish my glass.

One evening the manicurist, a pretty auburn-haired girl who had her little room just beyond the bar, asked me if I would take her out to dinner.

"X— keeps on and on pestering me to go out with him and I don't want to."

X— was a good-looking young leading man in an English musical comedy then running.

When we reached the corner of 47th Street and Broadway I was going to hail a taxi when Margaret stopped me.

"Why do you want to waste your money on taxis? We'll take a trolley-car."

---

[1] Later Lady Violet Bonham-Carter and now Baroness Asquith.

At a Hundred and something Street where the trolley-car stopped there was a small square with shops along one side of it.

"Will you buy me a dress?" Margaret asked. I told her to go ahead and choose one, hoping she would not decide on too expensive a dress, but grateful that the roll of dollar bills given me by *McClure's* was still fairly plump.

It was just before closing time; the girl serving her looked a little apprehensive when Margaret said she wanted a dress. She need not have worried; Margaret knew the very dress she wanted, nor did she bother to try it on. She turned to me,

"Ten dollars," she told me.

£2, 10s. for a pretty frock. I had expected it would cost at least fifty dollars.

We walked across the square to a restaurant and had not *too* bad a dinner and did not have to wait *much* more than twenty minutes between each course. When we got up to go back I found Margaret was living in a large hostel for girls called by a famous American name; it was not Vanderbilt but on that level. This had been endowed to house about a couple of hundred girls and was under the patronage of the Good Shepherd.

I tried to persuade Margaret to let me call a taxi. Nothing doing. I had bought her a dress and given her dinner; I had spent enough. The trolley-car passed the door of the hostel and that was the way she was going home.

When we reached the hostel she said I could come in with her.

"Give the janitor a dollar when we go in and give him another dollar when he lets you out."

There was no elevator and Margaret's room was about five floors up. At the head of each landing a picture of the Good Shepherd was hanging on the wall.

An hour later I walked down those stone stairs and asked the janitor if he could get me a taxi. I did not have to wait long and when I gave him two dollars he cordially opened the door of the taxi for me.

On another night I had an amusing experience. Just around the corner from 47th Street on Sixth Avenue there was a small bar which presumably by some financial arrangement with the police was open all night. Two of the British actors in the Flanders had heard about this bar and about three in the morning we decided to investigate. When we arrived we were shown into a small room at the back of the bar and sat at a table to drink our lagers. Presently a man with a heavy drooping moustache came in, his arms round two girls, and took his seat at the table.

"You're British, aren't you?" he asked us. We admitted this.

"Can you recite Portia's speech in *The Merchant of Venice?*"

We thought we could manage some of the lines.

"Gee, that's no good. I can recite the whole speech," and away he went with "the quality of mercy is not strained".

"Can it, you old tank," one of the girls protested. "You're dippy."

The man with the drooping moustache waved aside the interruption and continued to declaim the speech.

"I'm Sheriff Harburger of New York City," he announced, pulling a blackjack from his pocket and putting it down on the table with a thump. "Do you know why I recited that speech?"

We shook our heads.

"At nine o'clock this morning it will be my sad duty to arrest the one-legged hero of Gettysburg at his house on Fifth Avenue. I gotta keep on reciting that speech or I'd never be able to do what I gotta do at nine o'clock this morning."

Whereupon Sheriff Harburger of New York City started off again to boom out "The quality of mercy is not strained" in spite of the efforts of the two girls to stop him.

A few hours later that morning the Sheriff set out in a carriage to arrest the one-legged hero of Gettysburg, followed by a stream of reporters. A shortage had been discovered in the accounts of the New York State Monuments Commission, of which General Sickles was Chairman. The Attorney General, against his will, had had to give orders for his arrest. The General's negro valet had hung three silk Stars and Stripes out of the window of 23 Fifth Avenue, and the one-legged hero, now ninety-three years old, had received the Sheriff in a room at the back of the house. By this time the General had found guarantees to pay the deficit of 28,000 dollars, and so when Sheriff Harburger said,

"I'm glad to see you, General;" the one-legged hero could reply with a smile that he was glad to see the Sheriff, who was much relieved to find that he should not have to arrest the General after all.

I had fancied my meeting with the Sheriff happened in the autumn, but on checking the date I find it was at the end of January 1913.

New York continued to fascinate me more and more all the time. I was almost ready to give up wearing a wrist-watch when I was told that watches on the wrists of men were considered "sissy". However, I

did not surrender over that; I wonder how many New Yorkers to-day
recall a time when wrist-watches were considered "sissy".

I was elected to the Players Club and attended a couple of pipe-
nights when members with a rather self-conscious Bohemianism that
reminded me of the Savage Club in Adelphi Terrace days used to puff
away at Prince Albert Mixture in obviously new pipes until with
equally obvious relief they felt they could get back to cigarettes. I was
unaware at the time that there was a self-portrait of my great-grand-
father Joseph Cowell hanging in one of the rooms. I went to many
theatres, usually with Grace George and Alice Brady. I recall Caruso
singing in Massenet's *Manon* at the Metropolitan Opera House, but
most vividly of all I recall Mrs Fiske in a play by Edward Sheldon.
She was then over sixty and in the first act she played behind a gauze
a girl of sixteen, as consummate a piece of acting as I ever witnessed.
Mrs Fiske never came to Great Britain, more's the pity; she would
have had a triumphant success.

Sherry's and Delmonico's were the two most fashionable restaurants
at this date; the service was so dilatory that I have always supposed
the American habit of smoking cigarettes between courses was due to
those long waits between them. After the play we usually went to
supper at Shanley's where there was a good cabaret of which the stars
were the Vernon Castles, the forerunners of Fred Astaire and Ginger
Rogers. *Alexander's Ragtime Band* was a year old; the new and tremendously popular tunes were *Waiting for the Robert E. Lee* and *Row, Row,
Row*. The evening always ended by the orchestra's playing *Dixie*, the
strains of which were always greeted by what seemed slightly patroniz-
ing applause to show that whatever the North may have felt once upon
a time about the South all was now forgiven by the tolerant victors.

The Bradys lived on Riverside Drive not far from the Grant Memorial, and I never went to see them without being completely bewitched
by the colour of the autumnal trees across the Hudson. I recall a
beautiful October afternoon when I went to West Point to watch the
football match against Harvard: I cannot say I enjoyed watching
American football as much as baseball. On the way back across the
Hudson I was introduced to the referee, who told me the origins of
American football. Soon after the Rugby Union was formed some
British residents in California thought they would like to start the
game over there and sent for a book of the rules. Their attempt to
understand those innumerable rules was the basis on which American
football was built up: it sounded to me a plausible explanation.

Some time in that October Kathleen Scott passed through New

York on her way to meet Captain Scott in New Zealand, where she would hear the tragic news of his death. We lunched together and she was so full of that meeting, which alas, was never to be hers.

Rehearsals for *Carnival* began almost as soon as we returned from French Lick. A rhymed review of *Carnival* in *Life* may help people who have not read the book to know what it's about:

> *A baby reared in London whirl*
> *'Mid fogs that chill the gay romancer,*
> *Grew up to fame as Jenny Pearl,*
> *A graceful tip-toe ballet dancer.*
>
> *She fell in love with one Maurice,*
> *A critic chap; he wooed her nightly*
> *But felt her hold upon him cease*
> *And dropped her, awful impolitely.*
>
> *That one lost love should be her last*
> *She vowed; averse to vain regretting,*
> *She tried the life that's known as "fast",*
> *She tried a little Suffragetting.*
>
> *And then,—oh, unpropitious fate*
> *For any lively footlight charmer!—*
> *She took a grim, ascetic mate,*
> *A crazy prayerful Cornish farmer.*
>
> *Upon the Cornish coast forlorn*
> *She dwelt with alien faces round her,*
> *Yet, when her little boy was born*
> *She dreamed a ray of joy had found her.*
>
> *For baby fingers soft and small*
> *Can soothe all woe, the novels tell us;*
> *But when a friend dropped in to call*
> *Jane's husband grew absurdly jealous.*
>
> *And next, to blast her hope of peace,*
> *Who else should seek her, uninvited,*
> *But he, her traitor-lover Maurice,*
> *Presuming that she'd be delighted.*

But Jenny scoffed, "How like you men!
Don't talk to me of sweet forgiving!
You'll win a lady's love and then
Run off and spoil her joy in living?

"You're selfish, cruel, weak and blind;
Away, away, you silly rotter."
And when she thus had freed her mind
Her crazy husband up and shot her.

O, Ballet-dancers, airy band,
Attend our Author analytic:
Don't marry Cornish Farmers, and
Don't ever stoop to kiss a Critic!
                              ARTHUR GUITERMAN

Having seen John Barrymore give a perfect performance in Schnitzler's play *Anatol* at the Little Theatre, I was anxious for him to play Maurice. Grace George agreed with me, and her husband promised to get Barrymore if possible.

Then there was some trivial domestic quarrel; I seem to remember Brady forgot their wedding anniversary. Next day he showed me four diamonds he had penitently bought, from which Grace was to choose. Grace knocked up his hand; the diamonds fell on to the floor; Brady had to go round on hands and knees, looking for them. He declared he couldn't afford to pay John Barrymore's salary, and engaged an actor who would have been more suitable to play a prizefighter than Maurice. He had a pug nose, padded shoulders, and shoes with knobs on the toes. The trouble between Maurice and Jenny is his inability to marry a Cockney ballet-girl because parental gentility would be hurt; here was Jenny so much better bred than her "gentleman" lover that the play would be ridiculous. Grace George and I both protested; Brady would not give way. At last Grace George asked me if I would play the part for the month's try out before the play came to New York, when, if it promised to be a success, "Bill" would provide a suitable Maurice. Finally I agreed to do this. I refused to accept more than 125 dollars a week because Brady had been so generous to me; he had not only paid my brother's fare from Australia but also his wife's fare. So in the end it was settled that I should play Maurice when we opened at the Alexandra Theatre, Toronto, to be followed by Detroit, Ottawa, Montreal and six one-night stands through Vermont and the state of New York. We were to open at Toronto on November 18th.

The first week of that November was pretty hectic, being the week of the Presidential election. Brady was supporting Woodrow Wilson openly, but confided in me that he had sent a handsome cheque to Theodore Roosevelt. I went to the Bull Moose rally in Madison Square on October 30th and was amazed at Theodore Roosevelt's ability to hold that great audience; he had been shot in the chest at Milwaukee only a fortnight before by a mad socialist called Shrank. Roosevelt beat the official Republican candidate Taft, but the election was an overwhelming victory for the Democrats.

The *Carnival* company was forty-five strong when we left New York on the night of November 15th: it was more like a musical comedy company because we were taking twenty-five ballet-girls for the opening of the final scene.

One of the dancing girls had her little girl of five with her and I heard her asking Mr Early the manager if he could not give her a lower sleeping-berth because she found it difficult to manage in an upper berth with her little girl.

"Sorry, Miss —. There's no lower berth vacant," Early told her.

"She can have mine," I said.

Early looked at me with something like consternation in his eyes.

"Mr Mackenzie, you're the most god-damned democratic Britisher I ever met, but you must remember you're now Miss George's leading man and you cannot give up your berth to one of the ballet-girls."

"But I happen to prefer an upper berth, Mr Early, and I'll be much obliged to Miss — if she lets me have hers."

Poor Early went off, shaking his head at my breach of theatrical etiquette.

I recall from that night journey the train clanging through Syracuse and thinking what a ludicrously inappropriate name it was for such a place; I recall being woken up to see Niagara visible through the windows on the other side of the sleeping-compartment and saying it wasn't worth while waking me up to see something that looked exactly like what I knew it would look like. I should have a similar experience many years later when I saw the Pyramids for the first time, for me an unimpressive sight.

We were given Saturday to rest and told the dress-rehearsal in the Alexandra Theatre was to be on Sunday, only to find that we could not start the dress-rehearsal until midnight because a Bible conference was being held on Sunday and the religious feelings of those attending it would be upset if the Sabbath evening was profaned by a theatrical company.

A regulation had just been passed making it illegal to serve any alcoholic drink from seven o'clock on Saturday evening until Monday morning, and the elevators of the King Edward VII hotel were kept busy with commercial travellers, or drummers as they were called in American, carrying bottles of Canadian Club whisky up to their bed-rooms to sustain them over the week-end.

The dress-rehearsal finished about 5 a.m. Brady had not come up to Toronto with us, being busy with the last rehearsals of *The Whip*, a Drury Lane melodrama which was being produced at Hammerstein's Opera House. Half way through the dress-rehearsal a tooth began to ache violently, and I detected signs of swelling. I was not on in the third act and asked if the fourth act could be taken first. I was worried about the effect on Grace George if she saw my cheek beginning to puff out. I sat at the back of the circle in pain while the third act was on and got away from the theatre without seeing my leading lady.

By the time I reached the hotel my cheek was enormous. My brother Frank came back with me and we left word with the night-porter to have me called at eight o'clock to get in touch with a dentist. The appointment was made for nine o'clock; Frank and I set off in an open taxi-cab on a foul morning of sleet.

"I want you to lance this abscess," I told the dentist.

He shook his head.

"That's not possible."

"But I must get the swelling down before to-night. I am appearing in the first performance of a play of mine, and there is no understudy available. If I can't appear it means that the first night of my play will have to be postponed."

I continued to beg him to lance the abscess and he continued to refuse. At last he said,

"Well, there's one thing I might do; I might burn it out, but I don't think you'd be able to stand the pain."

"I'll have to if that's the only way."

I was seated in that dentist's chair for over an hour, holding on to Frank's hand with one of mine and clutching the arm of the chair with the other while the dentist puffed white-hot sparks on that infernal abscess.

"Now you'll have to poultice all day long to get the swelling down. And don't take this wad out," he added as he put a wad covered with antiseptic between my cheek and the upper row of my molars.

All through that long day four of the girls in the company took it in turns to poultice my cheek, which by the time I left for the theatre was so raw that I could not use any make-up on it.

My first entrance was to a darkened stage after the ballet for Maurice's first meeting with Jenny Pearl.

"Were you very nervous?" Grace George asked when the curtain had come down on that first act.

"Not particularly. Why?"

"You weren't talking quite so distinctly at first as you usually do."

"You wouldn't talk quite so distinctly if you had a wad of lint between your cheek and your gum."

I then told her about the abscess.

Guy Stone, a brother-in-law I had never met, came round to my dressing-room during the third act. He was growing fruit near London, Ontario, and had been very good to my brother Frank during his adventures in Canada; this was the only time I met a most lovable man.

The notices in the Toronto papers next morning were dull; it was obvious that their dramatic critics had hardly emerged yet from the 'eighties of the previous century. P. P. Howe, who had managed to get commissioned by the *Globe* to give some impressions of the American stage, wrote an enthusiastic notice. He was an admirer of the achievements of Granville Barker and Vedrenne at the Court Theatre, about which he had written a little volume of intelligent criticism.

Brady came up from New York, where *The Whip* had had a tremendous success, to travel with us to Detroit; we were to give nine performances at the Garrick Theatre during Thanksgiving week. In those days there was, and for all I know still is, what was called a smoke-room at the end of the sleeping-car with four wash-basins along one side opposite the window and fairly comfortable seats on the other two sides. Here I found myself sitting at about 1 a.m. with Brady, Early and Ernest Glendinning, who played the Cornish farmer with a Yorkshire accent. Brady was exhilarated by the success of *The Whip* but announced with a large blue pencil in one hand and the typewritten script of *The Whip* in the other that somehow or other before we reached Detroit next morning he must cut half an hour out of that melodrama.

"It was great," he declared to me. "Say, you remember that scene at the flower-show? The Temple flower-show they call it. All the dudes are walking about in tail-coats. Well, I saw a Klaw and Erlanger spy sitting in the front row of the fauteuils. So I made one of the dudes give me his coat and high hat and I went on and went down to the footlights and put my tongue out at that Klaw and Erlanger spy. 'How do you like it?' I said."

Klaw and Erlanger and Charles Frohmann of the Syndicate were at war with the Shubert Brothers and William A. Brady of the Anti-Syndicate, a theatrical war that was being waged from coast to coast of the United States.

After relating his triumph over the Klaw and Erlanger spy Brady turned to cutting *The Whip* with that blue pencil. Presently the licking of that pencil induced a thirst.

"Say, hasn't anybody got a bottle of something?" he asked.

"I have quite a nice bottle of wine, Mr Brady," said Glendinning.

"Wine!" Brady ejaculated. "I can't cut half an hour out of *The Whip* with wine. Hasn't anybody a bottle of whisky?"

I saw a sad resigned look pass over Early's face.

"I have a bottle of Canadian Club, Mr Brady," he admitted with obvious unwillingness, taking out of his pocket a bottle of whisky given to him by the manager of the Alexandra Theatre.

Brady accepted the bottle of Canadian Club, and Early went sadly off to his berth. By the time I left there were one or two blue streaks across Brady's face from the pencil.

When we reached Detroit on a morning so cold that it was almost painful to breathe Grace George hurried up to me.

"Where's Bill?" she asked.

"I don't know. I left him in the smoke-room last night but he wasn't there this morning when I went along to wash and shave."

Brady was discovered about two hours later in a siding to which the train had been shunted after reaching Detroit. He was fast asleep beneath the bench in the smoke-room, his face by now blue all over under the copy of *The Whip* he had been cutting.

That was a tiring week in Detroit. We gave nine performances to crowded houses, but the audiences did not seem to understand what the play was about. Brady was worried and made some rapid economies. Ricciardi, the jovial Neapolitan, who had played the ballet-master, left and my brother Frank doubled the part with the "second juvenile" he was playing. The ballet itself was thinned to hardly more than half a dozen girls. Grace George, who had played Jenny perfectly when she started, began to overact in the hope of stirring the dull audience.

I said, perhaps a little irritably, that I wished she would make up her mind on what part of the stage she was going to die after she had been shot by her husband.

"I have to run across and catch you in my arms when you fall and I must know whether it's going to be downstage or upstage, left, right or centre. One night I shan't reach you in time and you'll bump your head."

Grace George said that none of her leading men had ever dared tell her what she was to do.

"I can well believe it, but I shall continue to tell you what to do because I know just as much about the theatre as you do and I *am* the author."

Brady felt the third act was too strong for an American audience. So I offered to write a new third act. On top of that I had to write a 6000-word story for *McClure's*. This meant sitting up writing after the show, and when one had played a matinée and an evening performance this was no fun.

My two rooms high up in the Hotel Ponchartrain looking down over a large square were comfortable enough but they were always infernally overheated. A cold supper used to be waiting for me when I got back from the theatre; lukewarm ham was distasteful, and I told a young man in the company who was acting as a very inadequate secretary to put the supper tray on the outside window-sill and keep it from falling by shutting down the window; he was only on in the first act and was able to give my supper plenty of time to cool off before I got back from the theatre.

On the Friday night, St Andrew's eve, I returned even more tired than usual and revolted by the blast of hot air which met me when I entered the room. I rushed across and flung open the window, forgetting that it was keeping my supper-tray on the sill.

The crash of that large electro-plated tray with its dishes from the 14th storey into the square below was really terrific. The bonneted and kilted members of the Detroit Highland Club, who were practising their parade for St Andrew's day on the morrow, thought it was a bomb and fled in every direction.

From Detroit we went to Ottawa, where we were to play a single performance on Monday, December 2nd, graced by the presence of the Governor-General, H.R.H. the Duke of Connaught, and H.R.H. the Duchess. We stayed at the Château Laurier Hotel, which had just been opened and indeed was not completely decorated. It was much the best hotel I had stayed in so far, and I made the acquaintance of two deliciously scented liqueurs called Crême de Violet and Crême de Rose. I suspect I should find them pretty sickly to-day, but I was so much taken by them then that I sent a bottle of each to Faith.

The cold was intense. The manager of the theatre used my dressing-room to don his tuxedo and black tie every evening. Something had gone wrong with the central heating during the day and when he came in to change he found his tuxedo and black trousers frozen stiff.

In the last scene the wadding, or whatever it is called, of the blank cartridge which her husband fires at Jenny Pearl came out of the gun and just missed hitting the Duke in the box where he was sitting; this amused my brother Frank. When he was with the Inniskilling Fusiliers in Malta, the Duke of Connaught as Governor and Commander-in-Chief had been keen on combined naval and military operations. At one of these Frank was steering the boat in which was the Duke and changed course too abruptly, with the result that the Duke was swept overboard by the sail into the harbour.

"We seem unlucky for the Duke," Frank said.

The audience in Ottawa was the best we had had so far and I wished we could have played on through the week; next day we went to Montreal.

The notices in the English papers were as far away from the present as they had been in Toronto. One of them was written by Sandy Macpherson at the age of sixteen; he had been sent along by his father, the dramatic critic of whatever paper it was, because his father was in no mood for the theatre that night. Sandy Macpherson told me this himself when seated at the cinema organ on which he has been delighting B.B.C. listeners for so many years.

On the other hand, I was much reassured by the notices in the French papers, all of them showing a grasp of what the play was about and all favourable.

On Friday, December 6th, I celebrated the new third act's being rehearsed and ready for performing next week, by giving a party to the men of the company at Krausmann's Café, 80 St James Street, after the show. We did not break up until the small hours. Next day there was a matinée, after which I went back to the Windsor Hotel and told them at the desk to have me woken at six with a dozen Lynnhaven oysters. I went up to my room, threw myself down on the bed and fell instantly fast asleep.

I was wakened by the telephone.

"What is it?" I yawned into the machine.

"This is Mr Early speaking, Mr Mackenzie. The overture is just starting."

"What!" I exclaimed. "Well, keep the overture playing. I'll be down at the theatre as soon as I can. I won't have to make up for my first entrance."

I hurried down and secured a sleigh. It was a nighmare of a journey

because there was a thaw and the melting snow made the streets difficult for a sleigh. It was the eve of the feast of the Immaculate Conception and as we drove along I could see the churches glimmering as
people pressed through the west doors to their prayers.

The overture had been played four times when I arrived.

When I got back to the Windsor I asked at the desk why I had not
been called at six.

"Oh, were you wanting to be called at six o'clock this evening? I
thought it was for a morning call," said the girl behind the desk.

"At six o'clock in the morning with a dozen Lynnhaven oysters!"
Words failed me and I walked along the wide corridors of the Windsor
Hotel, marvelling at human stupidity.

The week of one-night stands began at Burlington, Vermont. I was
completely captivated by Burlington and see now the azure water of
Lake Champlain on a cloudless December day with the Adirondacks
all around. I see still the eighteenth-century houses in their little quiet
streets lightly dusted with snow; I see still the charming eighteenth-
century church. The theatre was full that night and the audience was
much the most intelligent we had played to so far.

Hudson was a sad come-down next day. As I remember, we crossed
the river. The place itself was full of yokels chewing straws; the audience had not a notion what the play was about; the hotel was terrible,
with more cockroaches running about it than I had seen anywhere.

Schenectady filled me with gloom. I took a long walk on a grey
afternoon along an endless and uninteresting street of small bungalows.
At last I came to a large square house where a lot of little boys were
playing about in the muddy garden in front flanked by leafless melancholy trees. Over the entrance I saw a plaque on the wall and, crossing
over to read what I supposed would be the name of some school, I read
that here lived once upon a time John Howard Payne, the author of
Home Sweet Home. Thirty-six years later I should see the grave of John
Howard Payne, in Tunis, and feel inclined to congratulate the author
of *Home Sweet Home* on his last resting place more cordially than I could
congratulate him upon his first.

Albany came next. We had a full house in a large theatre, but as so
many of the audience were of German origin they were obviously
puzzled by *Carnival*. I recall the Ten Eyck Hotel full of pseudo-
Jacobean oak furniture and one armchair in particular with four rejected lumps of pink chewing-gum stuck to it.

Next day we were in White Plains, where Harry Thaw was lodged
in the big lunatic asylum. I was tired out and lay down for a couple of

hours in a squalid bed in a squalid room. Feeling I ought to have
something to eat before I went to the theatre, I asked for a sausage
to be sent up to me. I lifted the cover and a cockroach hurried off the
dish.

We finished those one-night stands at Poughkeepsie, where we had
to play a matinée. The scenery did not arrive until after the curtain
was due to rise; the orchestra had only three tunes, which it played
over and over again for an hour and three-quarters to a patient audience full of charming girls from Vassar. When the curtain came down
on the matinée it went up again half an hour later for the evening
performance.

By this time I was sick to death of tinkering with the play and even
more sick of acting; I told Brady he really must get another Maurice
for the fortnight he was proposing to play *Carnival* in Philadelphia.

By now it was clear to me that my personality was too strong for
Grace George. She was still admirable in the scenes with Castleton but
was overacting in the scenes with Maurice. By this time I realized that
John Barrymore would equally have too strong a personality for her
and I urged her to get another actor rather than try to persuade her
husband to engage Barrymore. Fortunately from my point of view
there was another domestic tiff. The fortnight at Philadelphia was cancelled and Brady bought a Philadelphia baseball team instead. Finally
he decided that the New York production must be indefinitely postponed. I was not in the least disappointed, for I felt that success in
New York was a toss up. I realized what a bitter disappointment it was
to Grace George herself, and I volunteered to make a translation of a
French play in which she saw a possible part for herself. I cannot
remember what it was called and do not know if it was ever produced.

By this time I had signed up with the *Metropolitan* to do twelve
stories called the "Metropolitan Nights Entertainment", which were
to begin in February 1913 with London, Paris, Madrid and New York
as the cities for their setting. For these I was to receive 400 dollars a
story for the American nights only.

On December 19th I was writing to Faith:

*I do love New York. I'm so glad to be back that I never want to leave it. It
makes me extraordinarily fertile with ideas and fills me with renewed energy. I
intend to live in America for eight months out of twelve and visit every State in
turn. I'm at present in a quandary whether to take the forty-first storey of the
Metropolitan Tower (786 feet high—three rooms South, West and North) or
whether to buy an electric brougham and live in a cheaper apartment. Perhaps I'll*

be able to do both, as I may get my rent from a newspaper for writing from time to time "How I live in the Metropolitan Tower".

I've got 1200 dollars from Hearst's Magazine for two stories, and if they like them 2400 more for another four.

Now about your coming to New York. You must get the necessary money in England because my income won't begin till early spring. I've sent you the money for my first McClures story by cable. Everybody wants to meet you.

But give up the idea that you're coming out for a first night of Carnival. I don't see my way to altering the play to make a sentimental appeal. Frankly I'm bored with it and anxious to get on with Sinister Street. I get fearfully fed up with acting. Never again! Not even for £1000 a week. It really is a rotten way of wasting a pleasant evening. Those one night stands with the exception of Burlington, Vermont, were bloody. Oh, how tired I get of chickens' bony backs and those birds' bath-tubs full of uneatable cereals.

Three incidents stand out from those days before Christmas: I was invited to go up to the top of the Woolworth Tower, which was over a hundred feet higher than my beloved Metropolitan Tower. None of the floors was yet built and we went up on a wooden platform holding on to ropes; it was an alarming experience, but the view at the top was inspiring enough to make me forget the prospect of the even more alarming descent. I thought it was a mistake to build a Gothic skyscraper; the severe design of the Metropolitan Tower, utterly modern though it was, had a comparatively classical quality.

The next incident was seeing a dead body lying at the edge of the sidewalk on the opposite side of 47th Street where it touched Broadway. Everybody carefully crossed over to our side of 47th Street in order to avoid passing it. The corpse of somebody who had been shot in the night lay there for half the morning before the police removed it.

The final incident was the first night of *Peg o' My Heart* at the opening of the Court Theatre, a block or two beyond 47th Street. People used to wonder whether a theatre so far up town could be successful. It was much advertised beforehand as the most beautiful theatre in the world. Certainly it had an agreeable exterior, but in order to be different the proscenium was a blaze of lights in the intervals, which was tiring to the eyes. However, they lit up the stones in Diamond Jim Brady's white "bosom".

The play was sentimental twaddle, but Laurette Taylor's performance redeemed it and it was a great success on both sides of the Atlantic. A young Englishman called Peter Bassett played the butler. He was an Old Etonian, the son of a Hertfordshire squire, who was hard up and unable to extract any paternal cash. I lent him 125 dollars,

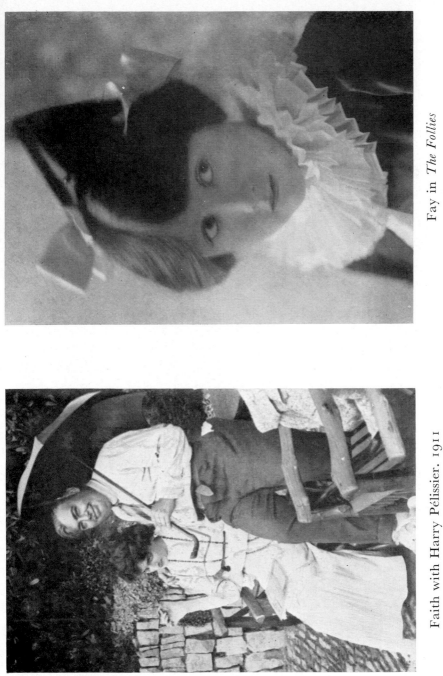

Fay in *The Follies*

Faith with Harry Pélissier. 1911

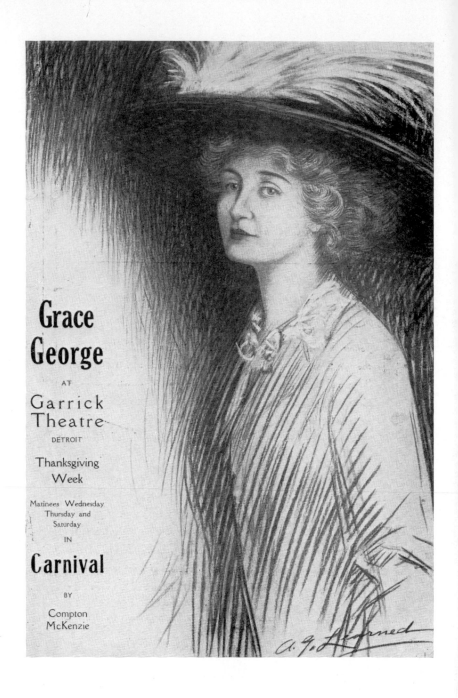

Grace
George

AT

Garrick
Theatre

DETROIT

Thanksgiving
Week

Matinees Wednesday
Thursday and
Saturday

IN

Carnival

BY

Compton
McKenzie

and as always when I lend money I made a point of forgetting it. To my amazement fourteen years later when I was in the Channel Islands I received a letter from dear Peter Bassett with a cheque for £25. He had come into the family estate, and was remembering money he owed. Alas, he died soon after this and I never had the pleasure of thanking him for a gesture so very rare in my experience.

I spent Christmas Day with the Bradys on Riverside Drive; on New Year's Eve I went to a party at the Plaza. Suzanne Sheldon was one of the guests and after the usual merry-making at midnight I offered to drive her back to her hotel. When we got into the taxi she asked me if we might drive round Central Park because she wanted to talk to me about the break up of her marriage. I told in my third Octave about Suzanne Sheldon's making a really good actor out of Henry Ainley. He was now living with Baroness von Hutten, whose novel *Pam* had been a memorable best-seller. Pam von Hutten was a woman of classic beauty and, unlike most women of classic beauty, brilliantly and continuously witty and amusing. Ainley and she decided that it was the duty of two such handsome people to give the world handsome children, which they successfully achieved.

Henry Ainley and Suzanne Sheldon had spent some days of their honeymoon at the invitation of Bobbie Whitworth Jones in the house he shared with George Montagu at Burford, of which I wrote in my third Octave. As we sat driving round Central Park in that damp taxi on that dank New Year's morning I was seeing them both at breakfast, Ainley dressed in Norfolk jacket and breeches, in which somehow he gave the impression that he was acting in a costume play. Suddenly he jumped up, and going across to Suzanne, seized her hand and exclaimed in the rich voice of Paolo making love to Francesca,

"Oh, I am so happy!"

After this outburst he returned to his bacon and eggs with renewed appetite.

I listened as sympathetically to Suzanne Sheldon's long account of that broken marriage as I should listen a year or two later to Pam von Hutten's equally long account of her love-affair with Henry Ainley.

It was nearly two o'clock when I got back to the Flanders Hotel.

A few hours later I woke in agony with the most violent attack of sciatica I had yet endured.

M

THIRTY YEARS OLD: 1913

I CALL it sciatica because the pain is centred in the sciatic nerve and its tributaries and because, as in sciatica, the pain is never in both legs at once. It is different from most of the sciatica of which I hear or read because it is spasmodic and unrelieved by lying down and resting the leg. It has nothing to do with rheumatism. I suffer from rheumatism occasionally, but the usual aspirin compound can alleviate that. The original salicylate came from the willow tree and I have wondered whether its effect on rheumatism was due to the willow-tree's developing it to counteract the effect of the damp surroundings in which the willow flourishes. Salicylate is powerless to mitigate one of those sciatic seizures of mine, which are apparently the result of nervous exhaustion. By such I can be laid out after the concentrated effort of constructing a book in my mind, with sometimes a few brief notes, in the same way as I can be laid out in the course of writing a book. These attacks seize me as other nervous subjects are seized by migraine or asthma.

I have been subject to these bouts of violent pain ever since the time of which I am writing and thank God they are less frequent in old age than when I was younger. Yet for all I know when I have finished writing about that New Year of 1913 I shall be laid out by one of those seizures, the only alleviation of which is given by morphine, and for me the morphine was so disgusting an alleviation that I used to have moments of nausea when peeling a pear because the smell reminded me of the smell of the spirit rubbed on before I was given an injection of the morphine, which meant for me hours of nausea. The doctor who has looked after me since I came to live in Edinburgh eleven years ago has discovered that this nausea could be averted by a dose of avomine half an hour before the injection.[1]

Notwithstanding the damnable way in which from time to time those attacks have prevented me at the last moment from keeping engagements to speak during the last fifty years and more, I am grateful for them. I believe that the continuous need to fight pain in youth is a blessing for old age, because one no longer fears pain; no pain can possibly be worse than the pain I have already suffered. Moreover, aware as I am of the fortune and happiness I have been allowed by

[1] To this day half a grain of morphine is usually enough to check the violent pain.

Providence, I have always been willing to pay for it with pain and have never felt sorry for myself.

Doctors in London, Paris, Rome, Naples, New York and elsewhere have said in turn that the kind of attack by which I am laid out at intervals was within their experience unique. In the last chapter I quoted from Faith's reminiscences an example of the suddenness of these attacks. Even as I am writing about them I keep the fingers of my left hand crossed against one of them starting when I get up from my chair.

Faith was already on board the *St Paul* when I was struck down and it was depressing for her to be met in New York by my brother Frank with the news of my condition.

In our sitting-room at the Flanders there was a picture of the Faraglioni rocks at Capri and we decided to make for Southern Italy when I was well enough for the voyage. We had met Norman Douglas last year when he had taken over from John Mavrogordato the job of sub-editing the *English Review*, which Austin Harrison had acquired from Ford Madox Hueffer. *Siren Land* had been published and I had been as much bewitched by it as any mariner of long ago by the Sirens' song. The doctors in New York had agreed that in future I must winter in a kindlier climate than either New York or London could provide.

On February 17 P. P. Howe wrote from 5 John Street:

News has come to me that you are ill. My dear old chap, I think you ought to chuck all this reputation-making and go to live somewhere nice and quiet where you can write books. *What's a success in the theatre, anyway, and what's the use of getting a thousand dollars for a short story if it bores you to write a short story? Write some of the books that want to get themselves written, and at the rate of one a year they'll keep you all right if you don't want to live in Riverside Drive or Grosvenor Square and if you don't rush yourself to death and want doctors. I hope to hear next that you're somewhere in this world where you can't do anything at all but enjoy life and write* Sinister Street.

While we were discussing our Italian project one of my American friends wrote to ask if I had considered California for the future. Some friends of his had recently acquired a small ranch called Hollywood not very far from Los Angeles where they were going to build a cinema city with scenic streets suitable for film-making for different periods. He had written to those friends and they had offered at once to give me hospitality and an opportunity to decide whether I should like to consider films for my future. When I reflect what a different career mine might have been if I had been in on the ground-floor at Hollywood, I remember that the First World War would have brought me back to Britain a year and a half later and that by the time it was over Hollywood was no longer a little ranch bought for an experiment.

Between intervals of pain I wrote two of the series I had contracted to write for the *Metropolitan*, two of the Jenny Pearl stories for *McClure's* and another one for *Hearst's*. I also did the translation of that French play for Grace George. Cameron Mackenzie wrote letters to say what he wanted me to do with the Jenny Pearl stories, which in a word was to sentimentalize them. One day when he came to see me at the Flanders I said,

"Cameron, I've thought of the perfect serial for you."

His editorial eyes gleamed hopefully.

"First of all you will buy Thomas Hardy's name, that is of course if the old boy will sell it. Then you will buy a story by Marie Corelli without her name, and you will announce a great new breath-taking, heart-throbbing, tear-jerking serial by Thomas Hardy."

I remember Paul Reynolds, my agent in America, kindest and best of men, showing me a pile of correspondence with Cameron Mackenzie.

"The trouble with our magazine editors is that unless they can show a pile of correspondence like that about a contract they've made with an author nobody thinks they are good editors," Paul Reynolds commented. "There's a growing habit now among magazine editors to think that an author's story must be rewritten in the editorial offices, and I'm sorry to say there are signs of that spreading to the offices of publishers."

Those weeks in January and February 1913 were a wearisome time. The kindness I received from the friends I had made in New York was boundless. Yet I was glad when by the middle of March I was well enough to sail for Naples in the Norddeutscher Lloyd liner *Prinzess Irene*.

The Atlantic was grey and cold but as we drew near to the Azores the weather improved and I see now those green islands as we sailed past them in the blue March dusk.

Our first port of call was Madeira, where we had a jolly day with bullock-carts and sleighs, and for me the excited recognition of so many of the shrubs I had grown in Cornwall. To my disappointment I was not able to wander far enough into that wild northern part of Madeira to see *Clethra arborea* in its native surroundings; that shrub with flowers like lilies-of-the-valley was one of my proudest exhibits in the garden of Rivière.

After we passed through the Pillars of Hercules into the Mediter-

ranean I became obsessed with a desire to see a fleet of Portuguese
men of war, or nautili. I never saw those fairy sails which can be so
unpleasant for a bather who encounters them, in spite of gazing hour
by hopeful hour at the calm pale-blue sea.

I recall passing close in to the southern shores of Sardinia and seeing
on the slopes above the *nuraghi*, those round towers built so many
centuries ago.

I recall passing close to Ischia on a silvery morning and to my shame
have to confess that in spite of living so many years in Capri I never
saw Ischia so close again. I recall passing Procida and wondering why
Virgil called it *alta Procida* because it seemed such a low island compared with Ischia or Capri. No tourists visited Ischia in those days:
the shadow of that disastrous earthquake in the 'eighties when an
hotelful of visitors were killed still lay over Ischia.

We did not stay long in Naples and went to a cheap hotel in Sorrento
while we looked for a small villa within our means. In our sitting-room
at the Lorelei beside a fire of chestnut-logs, although I still had a certain amount of pain occasionally, I started to go on with *Sinister Street*
where I had left off in North Street the previous September. It took a
tremendous effort of will; I felt such nostalgia for that little room in
North Street that I believe I should have gone back to London within
a week of reaching Sorrento if we had not received notice from the
London County Council that 6 North Street had been condemned for
demolition, and that our tenancy would be finished in six months.

I reminded myself that Ibsen had written *Ghosts* in Sorrento and
somehow compelled myself to get on with *Sinister Street*. Nevertheless,
it was a perpetual temptation to go dreaming along that sublime cor-
niche road above the Salernian gulf. I am glad I succumbed to temptation upon one day at March's end by driving to the Punta di Campanella to see the site of the famous temple of Minerva where thanksgiving was offered when the corn-ships from Egypt passed through into
the gulf of Naples, and the food of Rome was safe for another winter.
The whole promontory was covered with wild sweet-peas and the
whole air was scented by them. The sweet-pea was introduced to Great
Britain from Sicily toward the end of the eighteenth century. Shakespeare's fairy Pease-blossom in the *Midsummer Night's Dream* was the
everlasting pea. I had been regretting the increased loss of scent in the
sweet-pea owing to the craze for producing size and I was wondering
if by crossing the original sweet-pea with the new Spencer strain
that was so much the vogue I might be able to restore that wonderful
scent which had defied the synthetic scent-producers to copy: they

could fake lilac and lavender and other perfumes, but the sweet-pea was still defying them even ten years ago.

While I was gazing at those tiny, washy crimson flowers rampant over all that promontory I suddenly saw a small terra-cotta head. This was Minerva herself. Some pilgrim must have bought one as a souvenir of his visit to the famous temple and dropped it to be found by me two thousand years later. Minerva's profile was blurred by time; Minerva's helmet was slightly battered. Nevertheless, she herself it was.

Looking across from the Punta to Capri, Faith and I decided we ought to put in a week-end there and use some of the letters of introduction which Norman Douglas had sent us. So when the boat called at Sorrento next day on its way from Naples to Capri we boarded it with a couple of suitcases.

The moment we emerged from the funicular in the Piazza we felt that nothing must prevent our living in Capri. Wherever we looked there seemed to be dizzy pinnacles of rock, crowned by Gothic castles· The white columns of distant pergolas made us think of Greece. A Judas tree flamed like a great rose of solid blossom against a passionate blue sky. Round us, in a jingle of bells and laughter and cracking whips, stood so many people, natives and foreigners, who from living in Capri had achieved such a brilliance of effect as butterflies and humming-birds achieve from competing with the light and colour of the tropics. As for me, in my dull travelling suit, I felt like a clothes-moth beaten out of a Persian carpet slung between pomegranate-trees, like a piece of grey fluff in a kaleidoscope.

We stayed at the Pensione Faraglioni, looking south across the grey domed roofs of the Certosa, or Chartreuse, to the sea. Old Signor Ferraro who ran it with the help of his wife and family was "mine host" to perfection. The other residents were mostly gurgling German tourists with one or two English old maids, who came back triumphantly to lunch with the latest floral treasures they had found. Federigo, the eldest son, had learnt the hotel business somewhere in Germany and therefore spoke the language fluently.

I recall one of those Germans saying to me how sad it was that the English had been unable to appreciate the genius of Oscar "Vilda" and for that reason had persecuted him. Another of them called, as I remember, Baron Koenig, asked me one day if our new King and Queen were popular.

"Oh, yes, I think so. I don't really know."

Baron Koenig shook his benign and venerable head with a sentimental smile.

"I remember your Queen Mary so well at Stüttgart when she was a girl. I was one of the chamberlains at the Württemberg court. She was so full of spirits. We were all so glad when she came to Stüttgart; she made us all feel so cheerful. She would stand behind a pillar in the ballroom and put out her foot to trip two of the dancers, and sometimes she would run out and push one of them in the back and run back again so fast behind the pillar. She would have been sixteen years old then, or perhaps seventeen. Yes, yes, indeed she was quite the life of Stüttgart. Such a laugh as she had!"

Many years later I was taking part in a long B.B.C. programme about Queen Mary and I thought that this memory of her would present a side of her which might surprise the British public; at the same time I feared it might give offence at Marlborough House. While I was wondering what to do I found myself at a lunch in the Dorchester next to old Lady Airlie. I asked her advice. She thought Queen Mary would welcome the story but said she would make sure; a day or two later I received a message at the B.B.C. that if the story were true, as no doubt it would be, there was no reason why it should not be told.

The richest reward from those letters of introduction Norman Douglas gave us came from Miss Kate and Miss Saidee Wolcott-Perry, who lived in the Villa Torricella half way down between the Piazza and the Grande Marina. At this date Miss Kate may have been over seventy and Miss Saidee over sixty: they were two American friends who had come to Italy long ago and fallen in love with it. It was Miss Kate who was the wealthy one and it was her money that built the Villa Torricella. I do not know when Miss Wolcott and Miss Perry decided to hyphenate their names and so give the world an impression that they were sisters.

Faith wrote:

"Their villa above the Grande Marina was built for gaiety: salons and loggias blazed with fairy lamps; long pergolas were lit by coloured bunches of glass grapes among the vines. Till dawn they would speed the dancers, plying the band with wine, Kate fanning herself vigorously, her tall figure held upright in its lace dress till the last guest went.

"'Oh, my! How I hate to have folks go!'

"Saidee more sober and ten years younger went quietly among her friends seeing to food and drink, her steadfast eyes fixed often on their hero, their Count Jack, who, after a humiliating exile from Capri, was allowed back this May to his remote villa beyond the ruins of Tiberius's palace."

Count Jack was Count d'Adelswaerd-Fersen, half Swedish, half French, who had arrived in Capri a couple of years before and built himself the Villa Lysis.

At this point I must make an apology. In two books—*Vestal Fire* and *Extraordinary Women*—I painted portraits of one after another of the Capri characters I knew, and almost without exception they looked and behaved exactly as I have made them look and behave. Therefore the names I gave them and their villas have often displaced in my memory the real names, and the actual sequence of events is often blurred by the sequence of events I used for the construction of a work of fiction. I did not write *Vestal Fire* until Miss Kate and Miss Saidee and Count Jack had died. Except in those two books I have painted very few portraits in my forty novels. Jenny Pearl of *Carnival* was a portrait; her story was fiction. Sylvia Scarlett was entirely a creation of my own fancy, but much of her story was fact.

When Count Fersen came to Capri his wealth and prodigal entertainment made him as much the hero of all the residents as he was to Miss Kate and Miss Saidee. Then an uncomfortable rumour began to circulate about Fersen; it was said he had served a term of imprisonment in France for an offence against minors. The *municipio* in a fit of puritan nerves procured his banishment from Italy. This decree of banishment had just been revoked in that spring of 1913 and Fersen was to be allowed to return. Miss Kate and Miss Saidee, who had refused to believe that "Count Jack" could possibly have committed any offence, prepared to give a dinner in his honour. Those who accepted an invitation remained welcome guests at the Villa Torricella; those who declined were never allowed to enter it again.

Charles Coleman, an American painter and veteran of the Civil War, was the heart of the opposition to Fersen. He was an extremely handsome old boy who lived with three or four girls to look after him in the Villa Narcissus, where in his studio he painted occasional pictures of pretty *contadine* in picturesque attitudes, but almost day in day out he used to do charming pastels of Vesuvius in sun or shade, in mist or rain, at sunrise, at sunset, the volcano being perfectly framed in a north window of his studio.

"Uncle Charlie" was as hospitable as his former dear friends Miss Kate and Miss Saidee. I hear now an echo of his cracked voice saying "drink hearty" as he raises his glass of wine to toast his guests.

Faith and I were too much newcomers to feel that we were involved in the split. We went to the dinner in honour of Count Fersen; we went to dinner the next night with Charles Coleman.

Another visitor to Capri with a scandal attached to him was the ex-Vicar of Sandringham, who a year or two before had had to leave England over trouble with choirboys. This was a Farrar, a son of *Eric or Little by Little* Dean Farrar of Canterbury. Nobody wanted such a scandal at Sandringham, and no charges were to be made provided he left the country. As a kind of defiant gesture he had married a sister of Richard Harding Davies, the romantic American war-correspondent of Theodore Roosevelt's Rough Riders in Cuba. He was now wandering round the continent with his wife, and I have never heard a man so damnably and cruelly rude to a woman at a luncheon table. He had a pair of cold blue eyes which one felt were actually stabbing that unfortunate wife. When the war came next year he joined the forces and had a gallant career, winning a D.S.O. and an M.C., each of outstanding merit. When the war was over the Anglican authorities felt that he had retrieved his character and under another name he was given a living. In 1941 he was charged with an offence against a little girl in a railway carriage. I might have found this story hard to believe if I had not been told it by Francis Underhill, a former Bishop of Bath and Wells.

One resident of Capri I met was Maxim Gorky, whose house halfway down to the Piccola Marina was full of Russians talking incessantly and playing chess. Gorky and I used to attend the tiny little Capri cinema-theatre together. Our conversation was not up to Russian standards because I was far from being voluble yet in Italian and Gorky was equally at sea with French. Nevertheless, he seemed to enjoy those visits to the cinema; perhaps they were a restful contrast to the incessant talking of the refugees from Tsardom in his own house. For me those walks with Maxim Gorky to the cinema are a cherished memory. He was a tall lanky man, his head always out-thrust as he walked.

The great day of the year in Capri was the feast of San Costanzo on May 14th. The large silver head of bearded San Costanzo was believed to have come ashore miraculously at some time in the very early Middle Ages, having floated there from Byzantium, possibly in protest against the schism between the Western and Eastern Church. On the eve of the festival San Costanzo was carried up from his church on the Grande Marina to the *duomo* of Capri, a former cathedral and still dignified by Canons. Here due reverence was paid it by the Capresi in the hope of a good year from the olives and the grapes. At dawn on May 14th the maroons were banging away in preparation for the great procession which in the afternoon would carry San Costanzo back to the Grande Marina for another year along the winding road strewn with genista and roses all the way, showered from walls and balconies. The clergy of Capri and Anacapri would be marching on either side of the saint with lighted candles and at the end of the procession the old Archbishop of Sorrento would be blessing the spectators all the way.

It was a grievance to the people of Anacapri that their clergy were compelled to take part in the rejoicings of Capri whereas for their own feast of St Anthony of Padua on June 13th the clergy of Capri were exempt from attendance. In the previous year it had rained on June 13th and the paint had run down St Anthony's face, much to the mocking pleasure of the Capresi who had seen it happen.

On this May 14th, just as the procession of San Costanzo was half way to his resting place, across the blue sky above the bay of Naples came a grey squall which broke over Capri and drenched the procession. The candles were extinguished; the showers of broom were soggy. The silver head of the saint began to wobble as the bearers of the small platform on which it stood began to break into a trot.

Two Anacapresi were watching the disaster with a triumphant grin.

"*Ecco,*" said one of them. "*Nostro padre Sant' Antonio a dato una buona pugnalata a quello porco di San Costanzo.*" (Our father St Anthony has given a good punch to that pig St Costanzo.)

The jeers of the Capresi in the previous year about a saint whose paint had run were avenged.

The gaiety of life on Capri in that spring of 1913 was not conducive to work. Nevertheless, I managed to produce my short stories for America, and what was more important I managed to write about forty more pages of *Sinister Street*. I owed my ability to do this to the blessed hours of the siesta; while everybody else was dozing away from three until about five I worked at my novel, secure against interruption in the peace of the Pensione Faraglioni during the afternoon siesta.

By now Faith and I had made up our minds that Capri must be our home; the only thing to be settled was where.

"Why don't you make old Andrews let you Caterola?" Norman Douglas asked in a letter.

La Caterola had once belonged to Douglas himself. It was a small farmhouse in several acres of olives and vines above the steep cliffs on the north side of the island, some two hundred feet below "Timberio", the south-easterly peak of Capri on which the Emperor had built his favourite palace. A series of steps led down between the terraces to a wide level walk beneath the olives by the edge of the cliff, from which on a clear day one could see the Ponza Islands some forty miles away to the north-west; looking down over the cliff's edge almost the last of the *Chamaerops humilis* were visible. *Chamaerops humilis* is a dwarf palm and the most northerly representative of the mighty family. Norman Douglas had planted stone-pines and cypresses among the vines which were already tall enough to make an impression.

William Andrews was a hypochondriacal New Englander guarded by his wife Edith with a kind of half resentful devotion. He had been at work for many years on a translation of Goethe's *Faust* and could talk about nothing else. We used to have a game at Capri to see how long we could keep *Faust* out of William's slow speech. None of us ever succeeded in doing so for more than five minutes at the utmost, even if we enquired about William's health.

In that spring Caterola was still called a farm and in fact two cows were living there. From his tenant William received a certain amount of milk and a certain amount of olive-oil every year. The oil was always *muffo* or slightly rancid and the milk had recently become suspect. So William decided to get rid of the cows and offer Caterola to us instead. It was a small house not too adequately furnished, and William wished to reserve for himself one of the rooms as a study so that when in summer he made the long ascent on a donkey he could lie down and rest before continuing to translate *Faust*. We were to pay £6 a month and Caterola was to be ready for us by the beginning of November after some repairs had been made; our lease was for a year. At this date nearly all foreigners hurried away from the Mediterranean by the end of May at the latest for fear of the sun, returning in October when its fierce rays had abated. There was hardly a tourist to be seen or heard in Capri when, most unwillingly, we went to England. There I should have to work pretty hard to get *Sinister Street* written in time for autumn publication.

At Rivière in that June, where we were joined by Nellie Baker, I buried myself in *Sinister Street*, to be taken out of it from time to time to write those short stories for America; the money they brought in was really earned. Martin Secker came down to stay for a while, bringing with him a box of Richter's stone bricks. I told in my first Octave of the 7s. 6d. box of stone-bricks I chose as a present for my seventh birthday. Now I bought for £20 the largest collection of stone-bricks available; building with them the complicated architectural designs was my reward at the end of an afternoon and evening with *Sinister Street*. I can feel myself now eyeing Martin suspiciously when I still have half a page to write in case he should start on the next layer of whatever we were building before I was ready to join him. My other recreation was flying a large box-kite. There is nothing more soothing than to sit on the slope of a hill with a kite five hundred feet up tugging gently at one's hand.

I had a violent go of pain at the beginning of July and was laid out for ten days. Preoccupation with the past caused by *Sinister Street* suddenly sent me back to verse and I wrote a sequence of poems about Ruth Daniel. I felt that they were the best verses I had ever written, but when my brother-in-law Christopher came down to spend a couple of days with us he seemed so unimpressed that I supposed I must be deceiving myself and destroyed them. Three or four lines which remained in my head were put into my novel *Guy and Pauline*. It did not occur to me at the time, but looking back I wonder whether Christopher's judgment may not have been prejudiced by what he thought might disturb Faith's emotion.

By mid-July it became obvious I could not hope to complete the book as I had planned it, in time for autumn publication, and the decision was taken by Secker and me to publish *Sinister Street* in two volumes. Due no doubt to fatigue, I was continuously oppressed during that July by what was seeming the futility of writing a novel of such length when a great war would come presently and make novel-writing look ridiculous. Nevertheless, in the dedicatory letter to my father-in-law E. D. Stone I wrote of expecting to finish the second volume for publication in January or February; obviously the premonition of war was no more than a malaise at the back of my mind. I finished the first half of *Sinister Street* on August 3rd, little dreaming that almost to a day a year thence my premonition would come bitterly true.

Martin Secker and John Mavrogordato were both at Rivière when the first volume was finished; their two bread-and-butter letters to Faith have survived.

From 5 John Street the former wrote on August 5th:

Here is Carnival in a new dress. Isn't it amusing? Monty will soon have to start a bibliography of his various editions. The express yesterday was only a few minutes late. It lost time outside Teignmouth where Keats with wonderful prevision wrote the quotation to introduce Sinister Street.[1] *After that no more checks,*

---

[1] "The imagination of a boy is healthy, and the mature imagination of a man is healthy; but there is a space of life between, in which the soul is in a ferment, the character undecided, the way of life uncertain, the ambition thick-sighted."

but this was sufficient to make me miss my train to Uxbridge. John's pessimism at Teignmouth was terrible, but at Paddington he expressed his complete satisfaction with the journey.

I hope poor Monty didn't have a very dreadful time over that story, and that Brendon will send proofs to beguile his journey on Thursday. . . .

From 52 Queen's Gate Gardens John Mavrogordato wrote on August 6th:

Happily I lost my bet to Martin, and we had a most comfortable journey on Monday; at least I did. Martin spent most of the time in the corridor, having been turned out of his carriage at Devonport by nineteen bluejackets. . . . He tells me too (perhaps I ought not to report this) that he has hardly recovered from his late nights at Rivière. . . . I'm looking forward to seeing Monty to-morrow. Particularly, because I feel that I left him with the impression that I didn't appreciate the last chapter. I hope I'm wrong—but it's on my conscience: and I was actually very stupid that last night. I suppose every climax in life is a bit disappointing; and if I implied it, he may have thought it was the fault of the writer. I saw Norman Douglas to-day—I went to try and persuade him to play Beethoven to me but he wouldn't. He showed me a letter from old Andrews, who says with a lot more, that Capri is become this summer "a sort of debased Trouville—" but he is already rejoicing over his new tenants. . . .

What would William Andrews say about the isle of Capri in summer to-day? What happened in that summer of 1913 was that the Neapolitans suddenly discovered that the Grande Marina of Capri offered better bathing than anywhere else within easy reach.

Until I read that letter I had forgotten John Mavrogordato had come to Capri for a day or two that May on his way back from the Balkan wars. I remember now his hanging out a Greek flag on San Costanzo's day and telling me that Italian jealousy of the Greek victories had led to the disappearance of that flag. I remember, too, my little barber in the Piazza saying to me,

"Come parla bene Italiano, vostro amico! Non si capisce proprio una parola."

(How well your friend speaks Italian. One simply doesn't understand a word.)

John's throaty Florentine accent with *Ella* for *Lei* was too much for my little barber's nasal Neapolitan.

I must have waited to correct the typed copy of the last chapter of *Sinister Street* Vol. I and send it off to Brendons in Plymouth before I followed Secker and Mavrogordato to London; I remember correcting three signatures in the train.

On August 28th Pinker had written to say how much he had enjoyed *Sinister Street* but that he feared it would not be as attractive to the general reader as *Carnival*. Therefore he felt I ought to accept an offer from Methuen for the next three books, for which he would pay advances of £750, £850 and £1000 respectively on a straight 25 per cent royalty.

I wrote back on August 30th that I was not prepared to leave Martin Secker.

Harry Pélissier, with advanced cirrhosis of the liver was at 1 Nevern Square where my mother was nursing him; he would die about six weeks later. I went to stay with Secker at Bridgefoot.

Secker and I were a little apprehensive about the decision to publish *Sinister Street* in two volumes and Secker wrote to William Heinemann to ask if he and I might consult him. Heinemann had published a novel by William de Morgan in two volumes but they had appeared simultaneously. It had been Heinemann who had killed the 3-volume novel by publishing the 6s. novel, Hall Caine's successful novels having been the first to justify what was then a bold experiment.

Heinemann received us with as much stately courtesy as Sir Frederick Macmillan when the firm of Macmillan was proposing to issue *The Passionate Elopement* as one of its sevenpennies. The first firm to publish sevenpennies small enough to slip into one's pocket and bound in hard cloth was Nelson in Edinburgh. For a shilling one had a book worth putting on a shelf and fivepence change as a generous tip to a railway-porter. Sir Frederick Macmillan enquired whether *The Passionate Elopement* had ever been offered to Macmillan and on hearing that it never had gave his impressive assent to include it among his firm's sevenpennies.

Heinemann was not outwardly as grand a figure as Sir Frederick Macmillan, but one felt one was in the presence of equal authority.

I opened the conversation by congratulating him on the success of a novel he had recently published.

"Oh yes," he said, "a success with the little London clique, but of what importance is that to a publisher?"

Mayfair, Belgravia, Kensington, Hampstead, Chelsea . . . and hardly talked about at tea-tables even in the outer suburbs. Of what importance indeed?

"Well," said Heinemann, "I wish you both well, but I'm glad I am not going to publish a novel in two volumes, the first of which will appear on its own."

Then he turned to me,

"But let me add, Mr Mackenzie, that I have always regretted you did not give me the opportunity of publishing your first book."

"But I did, Mr Heinemann," I told him.

"Did you?" he asked in a tone which suggested he thought I must be making a mistake.

"Yes, I sent it to you after Mr Henry James wrote to ask you in 1909 if you would give it your attention. The typescript came back to me in three days."

One may read of a brow darkening, but I had never observed the phenomenon until that morning in William Heinemann's room in Bedford Street.

"I never saw any letter from Henry James," he said. "When was it you say he wrote to me?"

I told him as well as I could remember about the date, the summer of 1909.

"I must have been away in France," he muttered.

And as Secker and I left him I felt that somebody at Heinemann's was in for it presently.

I had always supposed that letter of Henry James must have vanished, but in February 1964 *Books and Bookmen* published it, after the house magazine of the Heinemann group had printed it:

> Lamb House
> Rye
> Sussex
> *August 18th* 1909

My dear Heinemann,

An old friend of mine, Edward Compton, the "play-actor", has written to me to say that his son ("Monty" of that ilk) has sent you a novel for consideration under the title of "Curtain Wells" in the pseudonym of Compton Mackenzie (the latter being his father's real name) and he asked me if I would "kindly speak in favour" of the composition in question. Therefore behold I do, to this extent though I have never seen the book! You won't publish it because of this, I have replied, but only, if at all, because you think on examination that it may do—but if you would have it (tenderly) examined I shall have achieved the purpose of this vain plea. I remember the young man as apparently intelligent and ambitious.

About three weeks later I received a letter from William Heinemann about *Sinister Street*. That a publisher in Heinemann's position should take the trouble to read a book written by a young novelist not in his own list astonished me: I was touched and grateful.

20-21 Bedford Street
W.C.
September 17, 1913

Dear Mr Compton Mackenzie,

  *At last I have been able to read Sinister Street, and I want to write and con-
gratulate you on a very remarkable achievement. We all of us try to throw ourselves back at times into our boyhood, but we are prevented from any complete
realization of it by a want of a proper power of projection. The details of the day
one lives seem to be microscopically accurate in one's mind as one lives them, and
yet how soon they lose their clearness of detail! That is why your story of Michael
is indeed a feat,—because one feels that one has lived with him as one reads the
book, and that you lived with him as you wrote it—projecting yourself as few of
us could into the temper and sphere of boyhood. I look forward with the pleasantest
anticipation to meeting him again.*

Yours sincerely,
William H. Heinemann

When Secker started to subscribe that first volume it was clear that
the circulating libraries did not like the idea of a novel published in
two volumes, and tried to project their anxiety about money into
anxiety about morals. During the last two or three years the libraries
had exercised a kind of semi-censorship on books. In other words they
did not display books they disapproved of, but did supply them if asked
for by customers determined to choose for themselves what they read
and not to leave it to assistant-librarians.

In the last week of August a book by Hall Caine had appeared called
The Woman Thou Gavest Me, which as usual had a great reception by
the *Daily Telegraph.* At this period for some reason or other the *Daily
Telegraph* seemed to think that Hall Caine was Great Britain's most
important novelist and the publication of one of his novels just before
the autumn rush of books was heralded by a review covering almost a
full page. It was a blow to the prestige of the *Daily Telegraph* and Mr
Hall Caine when the libraries restricted its circulation by only supply-
ing it when asked for. The head of W. H. Smith and Son's library
department was Herbert Morgan,[1] who was much more concerned to
keep down their subscription order for a popular favourite than for its
moral effect upon their respectable clients.

Hall Caine wrote an indignant letter to the Press complaining of his
treatment, but it failed to achieve news value. Smith's and Boot's were
both shy of subscribing to *Sinister Street*; Mudie's and The Times Book

---

[1] The late Sir Herbert Morgan.

Faith, Capri 1914

Il Rosaio, Anacapri

Inscribed by
Max Beerbohm
*"Colonel of
Volunteers
with Faun"*

Max Beerbohm
and C.M.

Norman Douglas

Club, which had subscribed generously after the success of *Carnival*, were somehow persuaded by Smith's and Boot's to toe the line and at once cancelled their large subscription for a very much smaller one.

Secker, who had ordered a first printing of 5,000, was worried. Then we were cheered up by a message from H. H. Bashford, the Literary Editor of the *Daily Mail*, to say they were proposing to give a column to *Sinister Street* on the day of publication.[1]

Thomas Marlowe, the greatest editor of this century, had started to read the review copy of *Sinister Street* on his way down to Brighton and had given orders accordingly. As a result Keble Howard, Chicot the Jester of the *Sketch*, a popular gossip writer, had been told to interview me and review the book. In spite of the greatest publicity that could then be given to a novel the libraries refused to supply the demand that such publicity might arouse.

Throughout that week, in spite of many enthusiastic reviews, Smith's and Boot's held out; Mudie's gave way and ordered freely. I decided to send this letter of protest to the *Daily Mail*:

"Sir, We hear on all sides tales of the new method by which the libraries restrict the circulation of authors whose works are in their opinion unfit for general reading.

"It is essential that library subscribers should grasp the fact that this method has nothing to do with the now old-fashioned 'ban'. The book of Mr W. B. Maxwell and my own new book are not 'banned'. They are just 'queered'.

"We also hear that this process of restriction is adopted by all the four great libraries. It may be so as regards some authors, but my own experience leads me to except Mudie's. I may, of course, be doing them an injustice by thus imputing greater common sense, but my evidence does not include them.

"The root of this censorship exists in the head office of W. H. Smith and Son. Here is their method. In September my new book 'Sinister Street' was published. On August 20 four copies were sent round to the four libraries. Mudie's and *The Times* Book Club subscribed generously. Smith's and Boot's declined to order: the book was still under consideration. On eight successive days my publisher's traveller called round in person at Smith's. 'Still under consideration' was the reply. The eighth day was the day of publication, and when this was pointed out to the manager of the library department he said, 'I can't help that, I've been away.' On Tuesday (Sept. 2) there was still no order

---

[1] This was done very occasionally. *Zuleika Dobson* and Conrad's *Chance* were given this rare attention. Normally a few inches only were allowed for book reviews.

N

from Boot's or Smith's, notwithstanding many long and important reviews, including a column on the leader page of the *Daily Mail*.

"On Wednesday my publisher wrote and demanded an explanation. The manager of Boot's wrote a charming letter of apology and explained that a hitch had occurred the nature of which he was not at liberty to divulge. Then he gave his order.

"The manager of Smith's said my publisher's letter was his first intimation of the book's existence! Then on Thursday, four days after publication, Smith's ordered 200 copies to supply over 1500 bookstalls and shops. This was finally increased to 750 in order to take advantage of subscription terms. Now perhaps your readers understand what restricted circulation means to an author's pocket."

[I had tried to persuade Secker to refuse the terms for an order of 750 and insist on their paying the price they would have had to pay for a smaller order. I remember trying to snatch the telephone from him, but he gave way.]

"Another book of mine 'Carnival' was subjected by Smith's to restricted circulation last year. That is to say, it was only procurable on order. Yet when the same firm had a chance to stock the shilling edition, on which they made 5¾d. a copy profit, i.e. twice as much as the author and publisher combined, they accepted on terms which allowed all unsold copies to be returned. In addition to this the 'immoral' book was given a show-card wherever my publisher chose to pay 6s. 6d. a month for the hire of it.

"This, Sir, is morality at nearly one hundred per cent.

"Compton Mackenzie

"Savile Club, September 8."

Herbert Morgan, the manager of Smith's library department, was better at judging profits than prophets. He joined Lord Leverhulme in the latter's bid to make the Western Isles pay; when Leverhulme abandoned his enterprise Morgan bought Smith's Potato Crisps and made a lot of money. He obviously knew more about potatoes than books. Some time in the 'thirties I was called upon to propose the health of the guests at some lunch. The late Lord Ampthill was in the chair and on his right was May Sinclair. I could see Ampthill's button head upon his tall trunk looking down to try to read the name of May Sinclair. Finally he gave it up and asked,

"And do *you* write?"

"A little," she squeaked in reply.

I took the opportunity of chaffing Herbert Morgan about his career as manager of a library when I came to him in my speech; he took it badly. Later I met him at some public dinner and he asked me to drive Lady — home to Kensington. He was in court dress because he had to attend a reception at Buckingham Palace for King Carol of Roumania.

About an hour later he arrived at the flat in Stamford Road in a block built over the site of my grandfather's old house. He was limping and we suggested that his breeches were too tight round his knees. I hear him now creaking as he bends over to unlatch those breeches, and I see Lady — kneeling down to assist.

Bashford sent back that letter of mine with a note to say that the *Daily Mail* could not publish it, and adding jocularly "Haven't we done enough for you already?"

That afternoon I was with Martin Secker at John Street when the telephone rang. Was I there? If I was would I speak to Mr Bashford? "Have you still got that letter I sent back to you? You have? Good. I'm sending a boy for it right away."

About half an hour later a boy arrived from Carmelite House and went off with the letter.

Secker and I were jubilant and wondered what had caused the *Daily Mail* to change its mind.

Next day Tuesday Sept. 9 were the head lines:

Two Censored Novels

—

The Libraries Again

—

Sex Problem Books

—

Mr Compton Mackenzie
and Mr W. B. Maxwell

—

There was a column and a half about the "Banned Book Feud", with my letter and a letter from W. B. Maxwell.

Maxwell had sent his letter about the banning of *The Devil's Garden* to the Press Association for circularization in the Press. It appeared in all the morning journals without headlines. The *Daily Mail*, with my letter as well, decided to make the libraries' action headline news. The evening papers were full of it and their comment was unanimously unfavourable to the attitude of the libraries. A week later, on September 16th, the *Daily Mail* announced:

"Sinister Street"

—

No Censorship

—

"Mr A. D. Acland, a partner in the firm of Messrs W. H. Smith and
Son and Chairman of the Circulating Libraries' Association, in an
interview yesterday, replied to Mr Compton Mackenzie's recent letter
in the *Daily Mail* complaining that his new novel, 'Sinister Street', has
been subjected to restricted circulation by Mr Acland's firm.

" 'The suggestion that a ban of any kind has been placed on Mr
Mackenzie's book . . . by my firm is absolutely without foundation,'
said Mr Acland. 'The book is being freely displayed on our stalls,
shops, and libraries and can be purchased or obtained on loan by a
subscription in the same way as other books. No special application is
needed. It is quite true that there was some delay in ordering copies of
the book, but this was solely due to the fact of the manager of our
library department being away at the time. . . . We do not need to be
told by an author how many copies of his book we should order'."

"Well, well," I commented. "Where does litotes end and lying
begin?"

Nobody could have been kinder or more helpful than W. B. Maxwell
during that fight with the libraries. He went out of his way to associate
himself always with me; many novelists with a junior newcomer tagged
on to him on an occasion like this might have resented such an association. Not so Maxwell. There was not the faintest hint of jealousy. He
took me out to Richmond to be presented to his mother, the famous
Miss Braddon of *Lady Audley's Secret*—that best seller of the Victorian
period.

I have always thought Maxwell never had the respect from critical
opinion that he deserved. He made his first great success in 1905 with
a novel about a shopgirl called *Vivien*. Critics seemed to think he had
never written anything else. In fact novels like *The Guarded Flame* and
In Cotton Wool were very much better than many of the novels treated
with far greater respect. However, Maxwell's novels have never been
revived and so presumably did not possess the authentic life that I for
one thought they possessed.

Sometime about 1920 I found myself sitting next to him at a Literary
Fund Dinner, and he said to me, "My family laugh at my books, but
they read you."

I like to suppose that *Sinister Street* would have made its mark as
quickly as it did without the artificial aid of prurient curiosity. After

all, prurient curiosity must have been very soon disappointed and could hardly have sent the book into its thirty-fifth thousand by the end of the year: it certainly would not have kept it in print year in year out for so long after it was first published. In due course the two volumes would be published as one, but nearly fifty years would pass before it appeared as a Penguin in a really cheap edition while still in print.

It is difficult for me to-day to believe that in 1913 this book was regarded as an instrument for the corruption of youth and the disgust of maturity: it will be even more difficult for young people to believe it.

Here is a letter from Canon Cogswell, the Rector of Wallasey, in the *Liverpool Post*:

"Sir. In your article on popular books I see with distress the high place occupied by Mr Compton Mackenzie's 'Sinister Street'. I saw it described, in a letter written about our public schools, as a magnificent book, and in duty bound bought it and read it.

"I cannot say how disappointed I am. It is not necessary to be a prude to be disgusted at it. The very title is suggestive. The hero and heroine are quite gratuitously bastards. . . ."

And the Canon continued to blather like this for another 300 words.

A more important Canon than Canon Cogswell now entered the lists in the person of the Headmaster of Eton.

From a long letter to *The Times* a few sentences reveal the schoolmaster's anxiety:

"Those who are working and hoping, however feebly, to encompass the lives of our boys and girls with wholesome atmosphere must know that in regard to sensuality two facts stand out. First, that in proportion as the adolescent mind grows absorbed in sex questions wreckage of life ensues. Secondly that sanity and upright manliness are destroyed, not only by the reading of obscene stuff, but by a premature interest in sex matters, however it be excited. . . .

"Those therefore who in responsible positions are trying to do their duty to the country are not concerned with the dispute whether a sexnovel is 'artistic' or not. They know that the more attractively it is written the more harm it will do; and they may be pardoned for thinking that, as between two parties, the librarians have the better right to the honourable title of 'sincere'. Anyhow, they have sacrificed their profits to what they conceive to be a duty to their fellowmen. Have these writers done any such thing?

"Meantime, as to the mischief done I doubt if it is to be stayed by any public action, much as we may admire the effort of the librarians. What has been its result? My bookseller tells me that directly a book is censored orders for it pour in, many of them from schoolboys. Sir, are we as a community to rest content with this state of things? . . ."

Faith wrote an angry letter to Lyttelton. Let her continue the story.[1]

"He replied suavely that he liked to see a woman defending her husband, but wasn't it as well to be sure first that he had been attacked? He declared that when he wrote the letter to *The Times*, he had not read *Sinister Street*, or only so little of it that *the thought of it never crossed his mind*. The italics are mine. . . .

"Because Sinister Street was forbidden it was voraciously read at Eton. Ned (E. W. Stone) having confiscated the book from one of the boys in his house, was faced by the awkward question:

" 'But, sir, isn't Compton Mackenzie your brother-in-law?'

"It was an uncomfortable situation. My father was apparently sponsoring a book frowned upon by all decent schoolmasters. His name was there in full, with an affectionate dedication from the author. . . . The feeling at Eton was very strong that the dedication should be withdrawn, and at last under great pressure the dear old man wrote to Martin Secker and Monty asking that his name should be removed from further editions. 'It has got me into trouble.' It was obvious that he hated doing it, and when he received my hysterical protests and realized that Monty was deeply hurt, he shut his deaf ears to any more interference.

Dec. 3rd 1913

Dear Mr Secker. On second thoughts I withdraw my prohibition. I am sure that I ought to stick to my colours and I am anxious not to cast any possible slur on the book, however I may wish that certain episodes had been less highly coloured.

I am anxious it should not on my authority be classed with some other books, whose evil tendency is undoubted.

"To Monty he wrote:

Faith must not be too hard on the genus schoolmaster or regard him as a humbug. I may have been one, but honestly I was never aware of it. I never analysed myself with sufficient care.

"To me he wrote of 'the cant which you and I abhor'. . . . He was able to appreciate the sincerity of *Sinister Street* and Monty's conviction that ideals of faith are of greater importance to a growing boy than ideals of conduct.

"The amorous school friendship is now a commonplace of fiction and public discussion but in those days it was hopefully ignored. . . .

[1] *As Much As I Dare.*

The moral effect upon an innocent schoolboy of those three pages was too horrible for the educational ostriches to contemplate."

By the time my dear old father-in-law had been dragged into the Great Book War of 1913 Faith and I were back in Capri, and I must return to that September.

I was much elated to get this letter from Ford Madox Ford (Hueffer):

I am going to write for the Outlook of which I am "assuming the literary editorship" a series of Literary Portraits similar to those I contributed to the late Tribune which you are too young to remember, but in their day those articles made the fortunes of writers. I propose to start the series with a Literary Portrait of you and Sinister Street—which, by the bye, is all right. Would you then, in return for this attempt on my part to honour you, write for me . . . a short article on any Literary topic you like—from the metres of Horace to the methods of Literary Agents. . . . Your article would then appear side by side with the Portrait and . . . if Secker would advertise in the same number you would get a pretty good show. I am trying, really, to awaken the dying public interest in Literature and there is nothing, for that, like treating a set of writers to a boom. It acts in a sort of contagious way, because other papers have to take it up in self-defence. . . .

Yours,

Ford Madox Hueffer

Ford began his Literary Portrait by mentioning two young writers:

"Mr D. H. Lawrence, on whom I at least pin the most enormous hopes. . . . Mr Ezra Pound, who, with his humorous appearance, is seriously enough undertaking the considerable job of starting a new movement in poetry."

He ended that article,

"Possibly *Sinister Street* is a work of real genius—one of those books that really exist otherwise than as the decorations of a publishing season—exist along with *L'Education Sentimentale, Fathers and Children, Heart of Darkness*, and the *Purple Land*. One is too cautious—and with all the desire to be generous in the world, too ungenerous—to say anything like that, dogmatically, of a quite young writer. But I shouldn't wonder."

In his generous foreword to a French translation of *Sinister Street* called *L'Impasse* published in 1953, André Maurois wrote:

"Ford Madox Ford ne s'était pas trompé. Le livre a duré. . . . Quand un roman montre cette vitalité, après quarante années, on peut penser qu'il est en train de devenir un classique et de prendre sa place, avec la modestie qui convient, à côté de *L'Education Sentimentale*, de *Pères et Enfants*, de *David Copperfield*, peut-être de *Swann*, ce qui amène le lecteur à se demander pourquoi cet ouvrage a, plutôt que tel autre, gagné sa niche au porche de nos cathédrales littéraires."

André Maurois went on in two or three pages of masterly criticism to explain what he believed to be the reason.

In a foreword to a new edition of *Sinister Street* published by Macdonald in 1949 I wrote:

"My original plan was to take the subsidiary characters of *Sinister Street*, one after another, and make them principals in other books. I stuck to this idea . . . until I was compelled to recognize that the First World War had smashed the series of listed novels I intended to call *The Theatre of Youth* because I should never be able to escape from it. The First World War as a *deus ex machinâ* would soon have become intolerable to myself and to my readers. Moreover, my own experience in that war had left me at the end of it as impatient of the mood of *Sinister Street* as any man in his mid-thirties should be of his 'teens. That I have been able, so many years later, to read this old book of mine with interest may be a sign of my own senescence or it may be a tribute to the vitality of the book itself. I really do not know."

André Maurois, after quoting that last sentence in French, added, '*Nous* savons'.

In the course of his criticism I was pleased to find him coupling me with Maurice Baring, whose two novels *C.* and *Cat's Cradle* are so stupidly neglected by the young people of the moment because they find themselves so much more at home with Lady Chatterley's lover than with her husband.

I had met Maurice Baring briefly in New York, but a letter from him in Russia that September was a most encouraging surprise:

Sosnofka,
Govt. of Tambov

Dear Mr Mackenzie,

I met you once in New York and I used to live in the house where you live if you still live in North Cottage. I have just read Sinister Street and when I finished it I began it again. The first time I read it I was so much interested in the story that I hurried—I wonder whether Michael's view on the Ten Commandments is a reminiscence of life. When I was a child I used to puzzle over them too, but I hadn't the faintest idea what to "take in vain" meant. I thought adultery was something to do with selling bad milk and I never asked. Michael appears to have known. Perhaps he asked his mother. This was before Miss Carthew came. In spite of what people say to the contrary I don't think authors mind being told someone has read their book with immense interest and pleasure and twice running. I am looking forward impatiently for the sequel. It is all living to me as if it was a part of my own experience. Sinister Street is as real to me as North Street. I don't feel this often and dislike most modern novels, but this seems to me the real thing. If you think this is impertinent on my part please forgive me. I wonder if you are as fond of North Cottage as I was. I think of it perpetually and I wonder if you ever saw the ghosts and whether Ray the night watchman plays a part in your life. Michael's schoollife seems to me marvellously described—and as a rule books about school seem written by people who have entirely forgotten what school and boys are like. I was at a crammer's once at Bournemouth and one of the boys used to take me to the church you describe, only I didn't take the slightest interest in ritual or in the Anglo-Catholic Movement and was then a very militant "freethinker"—in full reaction against long years of having been dreadfully bored in church and have made up my mind at the age of 18 that if ever I believed in Christianity again I would become R.C.—which I did many years after.

Yours very truly,
Maurice Baring

I wonder what I wrote in reply. Anyway it brought me another letter:

Govt. of Tambov,
Russia
30.10.1913.

Dear Mackenzie,

Thank you very much indeed for your letter. What you tell me about the genesis of Sinister Street interests me enormously. It is just what I supposed. The characters which are now indistinguishable to you from the shades that haunt the limbo of your real life are now likewise indistinguishable to me from the shades that haunt the limbo of my real life. I know very few authors who achieve this for me. I am awaiting part 2 with impatience and it is hard to have to wait a whole year! I shall also take advantage of your kind invitation if the winds blow me to Capri —who knows? I gave Sinister Street to a Russian to read and he tells me he thinks it one of the most remarkable novels he has ever read.

I hope you are well—now—and I hope we may meet. I shall probably have to go south for the winter as I'm pursued by malaria. I had read and immensely enjoyed Carnival before Sinister Street but I don't know your earlier work and am looking forward to getting to know it. I have never in my life read a whole novel twice through running, beginning it again from the beginning the moment I had finished it the first time—as I did with Sinister Street. By the way what was the school? St James's. Was it St Paul's or Westminster? The book is brimful of intangible poetry.

G. M. B.

Looking back on the September of 1913 I am grateful to a background which made it impossible for me to lose my head. I was naturally pleased with the success of my book; the knowledge that it would be in its 35th thousand by the end of the year was reassuring to my pocket; I recognized that the banning of it by the libraries was largely responsible for its sales. Nevertheless, I was worried by the "Great Book War" because I was afraid the second half of the book would be more "shocking" to the libraries than the first. I realized fully that *Sinister Street* Volume I was only half a book and I was anxious to get back to Capri as soon as possible to start on Volume 2. Moreover, in London I was acutely aware of the jealousy I had aroused in most of my contemporaries. Thanks to a kindly liver I have never experienced the emotion of jealousy in my life. When I have made that statement and been asked in return what I have ever had any reason to be jealous about, pursued as I have been by good fortune, I have urged the questioner not to confuse jealousy with envy. I am convinced that jealousy is caused by insufficiently controlled bile and that in men it is a mental and emotional state stimulated by the liver. I know at least two writers at the top who cannot bear to hear about somebody else's success. I have noticed the curious yellowish-green tinge flooding their pupils when somebody else's success is mentioned. I feel sure that Shakespeare observed that movement of bile when he called jealousy "the green-eyed monster".

Hugh Walpole was the prey of jealousy, but his was not caused by a bad liver. His was on a par with feminine jealousy, for which if any physical cause is to be sought it must be sought for in the uterus, and is frequently noticeable in homosexuals whether they be soldiers or authors.

I recall going to lunch with Hugh in Hallam Street, accompanied by Martin Secker, and feeling compelled to tell Hugh that his new novel *Fortitude* might have been written by a schoolgirl; Martin swallowed a fish-bone in his embarrassment and nearly choked. In self-excuse I must plead that I only said this after reading in Hugh's weekly letter to some American paper that in spite of all the fuss being made about it he refused to look at *Sinister Street*. In his last volume of reminiscences Frank Swinnerton writes of a quarrel between Hugh Walpole and myself lasting some years and of his achieving a reconciliation. It was the first I had ever heard of such a quarrel, for I was merely amused by Hugh Walpole's social and literary gymnastics. After his three-book contract with Martin Secker was complete he went to Macmillan, telling Secker that he could not "afford to be in the same list as Monty". I merely regarded this as one of Hugh's naïve admissions on a par with his cutting a dinner with the Marriotts because Lady Lovelace was more important to his social future. I have never been able to feel anything but affection for those who have made me laugh.

It could have been Reggie Turner, who on hearing I was going back to Italy that September, suggested that Max Beerbohm would like me to stay with him at Rapallo on the way to Capri; Faith was remaining in London, where Harry Pélissier was now on the edge of death. Anyway to Rapallo I went. I see now Max Beerbohm at the railway station; to my surprise he had grown a heavy moustache a dragoon-guard of the '80s might have envied. I was to sleep in the *albergo* he patronized but spend all day with him and the wife from Tennessee he had recently married. Florence Beerbohm had a mass of golden-red hair and a rose-red complexion; she was looking after Max with devotion. I am again at lunch with them in the tiny dining-room of the Villino Chiaro and from the wall the picture of a harlequin looks down at us.

Max Beerbohm's own exquisite aquatints in prose of the visits he had paid to various great men might induce in the most confident writer a sense of presumption in venturing to record a visit to him. I remember with a qualm of self-reproach that on this very visit Max told me that his last hours would be haunted by the fancy of the good story that would be fathered on him by the paragraph gossips on the morning of his obituary notice. "Mr Max Beerbohm, whose regrettable demise is chronicled this morning, will perhaps always be best remembered for the following story . . ." he antequoted with an urbane shudder. And then would be set down, for ever indisputable, some horribly pointless anecdote for which the wretched author was never responsible and never could have been responsible, or some base coin of wit he would have scorned to pass. And I, who have now lived long enough as a speck of dust in the public eye to read such anecdotes about myself, can appreciate that macabre anticipation in which Max indulged fifty-one years ago. Shall all my labours end in finding myself best remembered for a bad pun I never made? I dare to console myself with the thought that television may provide a more authentic memory.

I have already told about Max's breakfast at 43 High in 1904 with

myself and other undergraduates and about those cuffs like Hall
Caine's. When I reminded Max of the breakfast he said he had been
as much frightened as he always was when meeting undergraduates.
"They terrify me into silence." He was no longer wearing such cuffs,
and it may have been the shock of discovering that he and Hall Caine
wore the same kind of cuffs which made Max grow that moustache.
Max was aware of its military character. Toward the end of that visit
he told me he could not caricature me and must have noticed the disappointment in my eyes. Anyway, Florence Beerbohm took some snap-
shots of him and me together on that white terrace, above, even in
1913, the noisy main road.

Photography was occupying much of Max's attention in that September; it had just enabled him to invent and carry through with the
most scrupulous ingenuity an enchanting trick at the expense of
Bernard Shaw. There had recently appeared a number of the *Bookman*
devoted to Shaw; such special numbers were illustrated with photographs of the hero at different periods of his life. Max had cut out each
reproduction of an early aspect of Shaw and with a fine nib had slightly
altered every one of them. Thus if there was a photograph of Shaw in
knickerbockers, Max would slightly prolong those knickerbockers till
the wearer looked more than merely absurd. He would exaggerate
Shaw's eyebrows in one, bulbify his nose in another, give him spots in
a third, and thus turn every single portrait not into a caricature but
into a very slight distortion of the original which was more ludicrous
than any caricature.

This was only the beginning of Max's elaborate joke. After the
portraits in the magazine had been thus treated they were cut out,
pasted on cardboard and sent to a photographer in Genoa who re-
photographed them and printed them off with the faded appearance
of portraits in an album of thirty or forty years ago. No sign was any
longer perceptible of Max's elfin pen. The effect was of genuine photographs in which Shaw's clothes were even uglier than the clothes of
anybody else when he was a young man, that Shaw's nose at the age
of twenty-four testified to many hours spent in tap-rooms, that in fact,
Shaw if he ever intended to be a famous man should never have
allowed himself to approach within a hundred yards of a camera.

Not even yet was the joke finished. These apparently genuine contemporary photographs were now sent one by one at intervals to various friends in America and Great Britain with a request to mail them
back to Shaw himself in Adelphi Terrace, accompanied by a letter
from some mythical devotee saying he had come across the enclosed

photograph of Mr Bernard Shaw in an antique shop in Buffalo or had discovered it on a boarding-house chimney shelf in Bloomsbury and begging the original to be so kind as to sign it and return it to the sender in the stamped addressed envelope enclosed.

I do not know if Shaw ever discovered who was responsible for those goblin photographs of himself, but his life must have been a nightmare after the first of them reached him.

Max played a joke of the same kind on Herbert Trench, who took himself and his talent even more seriously than most poets. Indeed, I ought not to use the word talent, for Trench himself when describing to me on one occasion a play of his about Napoleon lowered his voice reverently as he always did when he was talking about his own work and, leaning across, whispered, "Well, the effect . . . well, you won't misunderstand me, my dear fellow, when I say it is genius."

Max put into my hands a volume of Trench's poem *Apollo and the Seaman*, saying, "You know this, don't you?" or something like that, and I murmured something vaguely and, as one does when one has been well brought up and books are put into one's hands, I turned over the pages and read a line here and there. The poem is a longish one—a duologue in verse between the god Apollo and a seaman who talks rather like Coleridge's Ancient Mariner, indeed rather like all sailormen in poetry. Then I looked harder at the page. I had not remembered that Trench had made his seaman talk like one of W. W. Jacobs's bargees.

> *Apollo*
> *What shipwrights' hammers rang on her,*
> *The stout ship and the leal?*
> *In what green forest inlet lay*
> *Her cradle and her keel?*

> *Seaman*
> *I think some arm of the sea-gods*
> *Framed us 'er stormy frame,*
> *And ribbed and beamed and stanchioned 'er,*
> *And gave 'er strength a name.*

> *Never, Sir Traveller, 'ave you seen*
> *A sight the 'alf as fine*
> *As when she 'ove up from the East*
> *On our 'orizon-line!*

I turned more pages.

By no man's 'and unfurled was 'eaven!
... That was the pit of 'ell!

"Curious," I said, "I hadn't remembered Trench made the seaman drop all his aitches."

Max smiled.

"I took them out myself with a penknife very carefully, put in an apostrophe, and then sent the book to Trench."

"He must have thought he'd gone mad."

"He was a little offended about it," Max admitted, in that tone whose gentle suavity of utterance no pen can hope to convey.

I may have taken this occasion to ask him if the victims of the *Christmas Garland* were hurt by his parodies. Anyway, I remember his telling me that all of them had written to assure him of the deep enjoyment they had derived, with the exception of A. C. Benson who had written to say that he was pained by Max's opinion of him as a writer. Was A. C. Benson more sensitive or more honest than the others? Who shall say? And then, as if to let me know that he enjoyed playing jokes on himself quite as much as he did on other people, he showed me a copy of *Zuleika Dobson* on the fly-leaf of which was pasted the following extract from a review in the *Daily Express*. "Mr Max Beerbohm may be able to draw, but he certainly cannot write."

It should be borne in mind that the *Daily Mail* had given *Zuleika Dobson* leader-page treatment.

As we sat down to lunch I thought how appropriate it was that the only picture in the room should be of a harlequin, and that indeed almost the only other painting in the villa should be of another harlequin.

Most of the two or three days I spent in Rapallo were passed on that big white terrace, the roof, I seem to remember, of a large garage. Behind, the hills sloped up in boscages of olives and cypresses to some remote hills beyond in that dear and familiar landscape which welcomes us to the *riviera di levante*. Immediately in front, though hidden unless one chose to gaze directly over the parapet of the terrace, ran the dusty white road on which from time to time we could hear the horn of a passing automobile, and beyond the road lower down the cliff was the railway-line on which the trains puff in and out of tunnels along the Mediterranean strand. It struck me then that the noise of invisible cars and trains was perhaps necessary to this Horatian withdrawal of one who had written so exquisitely of cities. However, I have outlived that kind of pathetic fallacy; I take it that Max probably chose his Villino Chiaro because it was the kind of house which suited him and because he would have been far too indolent to look for another merely to avoid the noise of passing automobiles.

In one angle of the terrace was a diminutive room which could just hold Max standing up to draw on a sloping desk his illustrations of the pretensions, follies, and absurdities of our epoch. That it should somehow resemble a sentry-box was symbolical; perhaps it was working in this sentry-box which suggested the idea of that military moustache. Above the door was a pale blue porcelain tile on which was enamelled in white THE STUDY. When perhaps I was looking a little awed by what was to me a sacred place and was perhaps wearing that expression of devout enthusiasm which sometimes my own visitors assume when they look at the chair in which I reluctantly embed myself every afternoon to work, I remember that Max dismissed his drawing with a kind of impatience, blew as it were the diminutive sentry-box off the terrace like a plume of thistledown, and said that if only he could write with as little effort as he could draw . . . after which we returned to our chairs on the terrace and to drinking those sweet Sicilian wines which were brought at intervals by Florence Beerbohm all through those sunny September days. I remember we talked a great deal about words; what between the wine and the compliment I felt very "heady" when Max told me he would one day use some word I had invented and that if two recognized writers of English used a word the compilers of the Oxford Dictionary were bound to accept their authority and incorporate that word in the language.

Another topic was a letter I had just had from the Secretary of the Simplified Speling Sosieti congratulating me upon Sinister Street.

We notis that you spel "surprise" with a "Z" . . . it would be a very great pleasure to hav you in membership.

Max and I were shocked to find that Professor Gilbert Murray was "Prezident of the Sosieti" and among the "Vies Prezidents" were the "Riet on. James Bryce", Miss Burstaff, Manchester Hie Scuul for Gurls, R. W. Macan, Maaster of Yunivursiti Colej, Oxford, Michael Sadler, Vies-Chaanselor ov the Yunivursiti ov Leeds, and other distinguished and scholarly cranks. William Archer was on. secretari of the Comiti and Walter Kippmaan on. trezherer. Most disgracefully of all Sir James Murray of the New Oxford Dictionary was a Vies-

Prezident. I felt that no Murrays had been more fatal advisers since Lord George Murray advised Prince Charles Edward to turn back at Derby.

The motto of the Sosieti was,

"Simplified Speling iz the Children's Magna Charta."

"I'm afraid I shan't be at Runnymede with William Archer," said Max gently.

The visit came to an end like so many other jolly things in 1913, and soon I was travelling southward down through the dusky Maremma with an agreeable sense of security about art and with nothing to worry over in the world except some twinges in my little toe bequeathed by those sweet Sicilian wines.

From that visit of over fifty years ago survives a letter from Max Beerbohm:

> Villino Chiaro, Rapallo
> *October* 13, 1913
>
> *Dear Mackenzie,*
>
> *Your works are having here, as everywhere else, a great vogue: my wife is sunning herself in Curtain Wells, as she will have told you: and I am in the thick of Sinister Street—a truly fine work, as well you know, and don't need to be told by me. In spite of the needlessness I should like to write my reasons for admiration, but I refrain because I am no letter-writer and no critic: no critic, in the sense that in praising I am so deadly dull that I dishearten my praise's object and myself into the bargain: In writing that is. By word of mouth I can praise all right. So to our next meeting. Here meanwhile is that ballade. Also here are some photographs of you—including one of myself—myself a choleric Colonel of Volunteers, entertaining a Faun. . . . But haven't the Volunteers ceased to exist? I dwell in the past. . . . Fauns, too—worn down by the persistency of Maurice Hewlett in writing them up, they have in self-defence abolished themselves, I believe. It was a great delight to us both, your coming here, and we hope the same sort of thing will recur soon.*
>
> *Yours very sincerely*
> *Max Beerbohm*

We stayed at the Faraglioni for a week or two before we moved in at La Caterola, where I superintended the planting of some hundreds of Darwin and Cottage tulips on either side of the steps going down between the terraces to that level walk under the olives by the edge of that 600-feet cliff.

I knew that I ought to settle down at once to writing the second part of *Sinister Street,* but the enjoyment of Capri company was too much for my resolve and I appeased my conscience by telling myself that I had been overworking and that I ought to rest until Christmas. Long walks in the benign autumnal weather followed by two hours' gossip in Morgano's Café were not conducive to work. One of the villas I most enjoyed visiting was the Villa Wordsworth which had been built by William Wordsworth, the great-nephew of the poet, when he retired from the Indian Civil Service in 1890.

William Wordsworth was now nearing eighty and was being looked after by Miss Kennedy, whose brother, calling himself Robert Sherard, had written that emotional account of Oscar Wilde. I forget the relationship between Wordsworth and Miss Kennedy, whose pungent commentary on Capri society was always a delight; I was glad to be able to feel that she approved of Faith and myself.

William Wordsworth the Second was exactly like William Wordsworth the First in appearance, and when he read to me from his great-uncle's poems I knew that I was hearing the very accents of the poet himself. He had managed to have a window made above his fireplace, so that he could sit by the fire and look out at the Capri sky. His companions were two black poodles, one extremely lively, the other growing decrepit. I recall my astonishment when I was told that the lively dog was the father and that the decrepit dog was the son.

William Wordsworth had been at Rydal Mount when the poet died and as a boy of fourteen had stayed on there with his Aunt "Durrothy" as he called her and as no doubt the famous Dorothy had been called by her brother.

His Aunt "Durrothy" liked to sit out in a wheeled chair on the sweep of the gravelled drive up to the house and it was William's job to order away inquisitive visitors who had made their way up the drive to stare at the poet's house.

"On one occasion two middle-aged women had found their way up and when me aunt Durrothy called to me I supposed it was to send them off down the drive. To my surprise me aunt Durrothy told me to bring them to speak to her.

" 'Would you like to hear me read to you some of my brother's poetry?' she asked them, and I recall one of the two visitors saying to the other 'How pleasant it is to receive attentions from elderly females.' I thought it an excessively droll remark at the time."

And as he said this William Wordsworth chuckled over that memory of over sixty years ago.

"Me aunt began to read the ode on intimations of immortality," and as he said this William Wordsworth the Second began to declaim

o

the ode in what must have been the exact accents of the poet himself. So to-day I can brag of being able to read that great ode almost as the poet himself used to declaim it.

"After me aunt Durrothy had been reading for a while she noticed that the two women's glances were wandering. 'Go away, you two old cats,' me aunt said angrily, 'you don't deserve to hear me read to you.' And with this she flung the volume at them, and I hastily led them away down the drive."

The weather deteriorated after Christmas and when Martin Secker came out to stay with us the boat could not land passengers at Capri and had to put back to Sorrento two days running. He had brought out with him a telescope I had bought for ten guineas at Steward's in the Strand. The gale which had been blowing died away and left behind something we hardly ever saw in Capri—a thick sea-mist which lasted for three days and nights.

I had got into my head that I wanted to see the planet Saturn, which as far as I could work out from a stellar guide should be visible in the north-west sky. At last on the third night the mist began to clear. The telescope was placed on the parapet of the terrace and the 160-magnification glass was screwed in. I had to sit down on the damp tiles in order to gaze through the telescope at what I estimated was the right angle to start looking for Saturn. I expected it would be a difficult job because with a glass of such magnification a celestial object as soon as it was found passed out of vision. My elation can be imagined when, with the odds anything you like against it, Saturn swam into view. Keats expressed it in the sonnet he wrote after first looking into Chapman's Homer.

> Then felt I like some watcher of the skies
> When a new planet swims into his ken.

Soon after Martin Secker left us I was laid out with as bad a go of that sciatica as I had had in New York a year ago, and was beginning to wonder whether I should ever finish *Sinister Street* when I received a letter from J. B. Pinker:

Talbot House
Arundel Street
Strand
5th Jan. 1914

My dear Mackenzie,

Before I went away I was advising Henry James to read Sinister Street and I think it will interest you to hear what he says in a letter to me:—

"I have just been reading Sinister Street by young Compton Mackenzie, of which you spoke to me some time since, and am so exceedingly struck by it as a young thing that I mean at once to read its two predecessors, or at least the immediate one. I should even like to get at him. Don't I seem to remember your telling me that he had gone off to live at Capri or in some like retreat? In that case I must wait or perhaps will write to him. He affects me at any rate as, putting one or two aside (or rather as putting Wells only and Wells is not as good for Wells as Compton Mackenzie is for him) as very much the greatest talent of the new generation. And the modernity of him! It is such a happy and unexpected change to be interested! If you write to him tell him I pat him very particularly on the back."

I am so glad Henry James liked it, for in matters of art he is exacting and uncompromising.

Yours always sincerely

J. B. Pinker

The draft of the letter I wrote to Henry James has survived.

La Caterola
Isola di Capri
Italy
January 14, 14

Dear Mr James,

There has just come to me from Pinker a message about my last book which I may truly say has elated me more than all that mass of inappropriate praise and blame I call an album of press notices.

I sent it to my father for a birthday-present as it seemed to me the choicest I could give him. To my mother (your devout admirer) it will perhaps give the keenest pleasure of all.

I suppose my first realized view of a writer came when I kicked my heels in your room in De Vere Gardens, listening to you and my father discussing The American. That must have been in 1890 when I was seven. . . . At present I am banished, and I scarcely expect to be back in England until the end of next July. If you are in the mood I would like to make a pilgrimage to Rye, but I have a dread of worrying people, and if young writers bore you, please put me off.

I have always rather envied Hugh Walpole's opportunities for seeing you very often, and I have once or twice proposed to myself to go and see you. At the last moment a foolish sensitiveness always prevented me, and so I never wrote. But the real purpose of this letter was not to talk of visits paid and unpaid, but to thank you very deeply for encouragement that is to me inestimable.

The answer to that letter came a few days after my thirty-first birthday, a wonderful present.

THIRTY-ONE YEARS OLD: 1914

21 Carlyle Mansions
Cheyne Walk, S.W.
Jan. 21, 1914

My dear "Monty Compton!"

For that was, I think, as I first heard you named—by a worthy old actress of your father's company who, when we were rehearsing The American in some touring town to which I had gone for the purpose, showed me with touching elation a story-book she had provided for you on the occasion of your birthday. That story-book, weighted with my blessing on it, evidently sealed your vocation —for the sharpness of my sense that you are really a prey to the vocation was what, after reading you, I was moved to emphasize to Pinker. I am glad he let you know of this, and it gives me great pleasure that you have written to me—the only abatement of which is learning from you that you are in such prolonged exile on grounds of health. May that dizzying sun of Capri cook every peccant humour out of you. As to this untowardness I mean, frankly, to inquire of your Mother— whom I am already in communication with on the subject of going to see her to talk about you! For that, my dear young man, I feel as a need: with the force that I find and so much admire in your talent your genesis becomes, like the rest of it, interesting and remarkable to me; you are so rare a case of the kind of reaction from the theatre—and from so much theatre—and the reaction in itself is rare—as seldom taking place; and when it does it is mostly, I think, away from the arts altogether—it is violent and utter. But your pushing straight through the door into literature and then closing it so tight behind you and putting the key in your pocket, as it were—that strikes me as unusual and brilliant! However, it isn't to go into all that that I snatch these too few minutes, but to thank you for having so much arrested my attention, as by the effect of Carnival and Sinister Street, on what I confess I am for the most part (as a consequence of some thankless experiments) none too easily beguiled by, a striking exhibition by a member of the generation to which you belong. When I wrote to Pinker I had only read S.S., but I have now taken down Carnival in persistent short draughts—which is how I took S.S. and is how I take anything I take at all; and I have given myself still further up to the pleasure, quite to the emotion, of intercourse with a young talent that really moves one to hold it to an account. Yours strikes me as very living and real and sincere, making me care for it—to anxiety—care above all for what shall become of it. You ought, you know, to do only some very fine and ripe things, really solid and serious and charming ones; but your dangers are almost as many as your aspects, and as I am a mere monster of appreciation when I read—by which I mean of the critical passion—I would fain lay an

*earnest and communicative hand on you and hypnotize or otherwise bedevil you
into proceeding as I feel you most ought to, you know. The great point is that I
would so fain personally see you—that we may talk; and I do very much wish
that you had given me a chance at one of those moments when you tell me you
inclined to it, and then held off. You are so intelligent, and it's a blessing—
whereby I prefigure it as a luxury to have a go at you. I am to be in town till the
end of June—I hibernate no more at Rye; and if you were only to turn up a
little before that it would be excellent. Otherwise you must indeed come to me
there. I wish you all profit of all your experience, some of it lately, I fear, rather
harsh, and all experience of your genius—which I also wish myself. I think of
Sinister Street II, and am yours most truly,*

Henry James

On February 3rd my mother wrote from Nevern Square:

*It is delightful to hear that you feel able to start Sinister Street II. Dear old
Henry James, he has a real sort of affection for you. He was hoping you were
writing it and then when I told him you ought not to work he was so anxious that
you should take care of yourself as you were of such "vital importance to the
world". I felt almost as elated as when James Bewsher said to me "your boy is
very remarkably clever". . . . James had to see any photographs I had of you. . . .
I had the reproduction of the Bassano in the Tatler. He was very pleased with
that. "He looks as one would wish him to look." He found a certain resemblance
to my family but none to his father. I've promised to get him that photo. He
wanted to know all about Faith (she got quite a good character!) He was delighted your marriage was like it is. He understood how her playing the piano
might satisfy and soothe your nerves. He said "What a gifted young devil," this
was apropos of your knowledge of flowers. He had been greatly struck with that
in "Carnival". I mentioned your being a seven months baby as a reason for
delicacy of constitution. He said "I was a seven months baby"—quite apologetically for remembering that he had been a baby once. He is such a very nice
man. . . . Do answer his letter as fully as you can. You are evidently a source of
pleasure to him. He was so relieved that America was not entirely the cause of
your illness. He felt a sort of responsibility apparently! This will amuse you. I
told him that en masse though you were very fond of us we rather overwhelmed
you. "Certainly, I went to Europe!"*

I was in and out of pain through most of that January and February;
Sinister Street II made hardly any progress at all. The general opinion
of Capri was that Caterola was too damp.

One day in March, Edwin Cerio, the future author of *Aria di Capri*,
asked us if we should like to look over the new house he was building
on the south side of the island. The anemones were in full bloom as
Faith and I walked along the cliff path reached by steps from the end

of the Via Tragara, where most of the fashionable villas of Capri were situated. Casa Solitaria stood on the edge of the cliff three hundred feet above the sea and was protected from the north by the bulk of the Telegrafo rising another five hundred feet behind it. Cerio had cut a semicircular terrace in the side of the cliff below the house and half planted it with a row of young cypresses. At the end of this terrace a huge rock rose about a hundred feet. This was Pizzo Lungo, and to the Capresi was the name of Casa Solitaria. I knew at once that this was where we should be living next winter, and when Cerio offered us a seven-year lease at £50 a year I closed immediately.

During those bouts of pain that winter I made up my mind to be received into the Catholic Church, and the Parroco of Capri used to make that long walk along the narrow roughly paved *strade* to give me instruction. I can see him now slightly out of breath as he hurried along between the peach-trees in blossom to expound Catholic doctrine. He was surprised to find that there was nothing he could teach me about Catholic doctrine and I made it clear to him that my reception into the Church was not to be regarded as a conversion but as a submission, a logical surrender to an inevitable recognition of the fact that Jesus Christ had founded his Church upon the rock of Peter. The Parroco had the good sense to recognize this and the instruction soon developed into an attempt by me to initiate him into the mysteries of Anglicanism—of Low Church, Broad Church and High Church. I fear I was unsuccessful; he remained mystified. At the same time, I made it clear to the Parroco that I could not accept the invalidity of Anglican orders. I was completely convinced after an exhaustive study of the question that they were valid. That remains my belief to-day, and I have no doubt whatever that in due course the whole question will be re-examined and the provisional decision reversed: the terms in which it was given out allowed for that.

At this date Modernism was worrying the saintly Pope Pius X and as an "intellectual" I had to affirm my freedom from any inclination to encourage the views of the Abbé Loisy, Father Tyrrell, S. J. and the rest of the Modernist clergy, regular and secular. As I had no intention of celebrating my submission by plunging into theological arguments and equally no intention of making my future novels vehicles of propaganda I was able quite sincerely to renounce any intention of encouraging Modernism whatever I might privately feel about it.

Apropos of my submission to Rome the *Church Times* had a kindly little paragraph to say they regretted losing me but that G. K. Chesterton was still with them, which was more important. Ironically, almost the only really fatuous review of *Sinister Street* was in the *Tablet*.

The date of my reception into the Church was fixed for April 14th in the little chapel of the Sisters of St Elizabeth near the Certosa. This was a small nursing order whose members, half a dozen elderly Sisters, were doing invaluable work among the Capri *contadini*. The Superior was a handsome Prussian baroness at least twenty years younger than any of the Sisters. Teresa was her name in religion, and she was my godmother at the conditional baptism. There comes back to me from that April morning, fifty years ago almost to a day as I write these words, breakfast in the Convent parlour with the Parroco beaming at me over two boiled eggs. A week later he and I went over to Sorrento where I was confirmed by the dear old Archbishop, whose smile as he tapped my cheek I can still see.

I asked the Parocco whether there was any likelihood of my being accepted as an Oblate of Monte Cassino. He said it would be difficult for an *inglese*. However, he set to work and was able to tell me a year later that I had been accepted in the very week that I was to leave Capri for Gallipoli.

A year or two later Don Giuseppe de Nardis, that lovable Parroco, was made Bishop of Sant' Agata dei Goti, the former diocese of St Alfonso di Liguori between Naples and Capua.

When I came back to Caterola on that April morning I went down between the Darwin tulips to the walk under the olives by the edge of that high cliff on either side of which Domenico Ruggiero had planted purple irises now in full bloom. I was not as spiritually elated as I might have been if it had been a conversion instead of a submission to what I felt was a logical necessity for somebody who saw his future against a European rather than a British background.

Mimi Ruggiero, as he was always called, had a small plot of ground in the Via Tragara where he grew carnations and other flowers to sell in a tiny shop close to the Quisisana Hotel. "He ran down the steps of his garden as we came along on one of our first walks in Capri," Faith wrote, "and there was something about him, his wiry movements, the intelligence of his flashing brown eyes, and the rakish angle of his straw hat, worn at the back of his head and yet over one ear, that proclaimed him a personality not to be passed by. . . . From that moment he became a part of our life in Capri."

More of Mimi later.

It was in that April that Henry James's two articles about his junior contemporaries appeared in the *Times Literary Supplement*. He dealt with H. G. Wells, Arnold Bennett, John Galsworthy and Joseph Conrad in the first, and with Gilbert Cannan, Hugh Walpole, D. H. Lawrence and myself in the second. I was glad to be away from England, where James's article kindled a bonfire of jealousy among *les jeunes* who had not been singled out for such attention. Henry James sent me cuttings of his articles.

21 Carlyle Mansions
Cheyne Walk
S.W.
April 5th 1914

My dear Monty Compton,

I have been very backward with you, but I have to be backward with everything in these days—the hand of time being heavy upon me, and I try to make it up a little by sending you herewith the 2 morsels of an article lately contributed by me to the Times *and in the second fraction of which I have indulged in some reflections about your work which I hope you will find sympathetic and intelligible. One does things in the scant journalistic compass with a sad sense of their being but half done—but so must they try to serve. I beg you not to take my delay in acknowledging your last letter as the real measure of my hope that you are getting on without bad visitations. I earnestly desire and invoke for you and for what you are doing the most progressive alleviation. Before long I shall go to see your Mother again in the hope of some assurance of this. I had 10 days or so since a note from Martin Secker, who then appeared to be staying with you, but who alas didn't avail himself of the opportunity to give me the least personal news of you—which fact made me sigh at the perversity of things. If my admirable old friend Axel Munthe is still at Capri (which I apprehend he may not be, however) I should like to ask you to beg him for me that he kindly let me know of his next whereabouts—and whenabouts—in England: so extremely would it interest me to see him again, after much too long an interval, so do I suffer from lack of knowledge of him. If you have been in his care, as I surmise, I rejoice in the conviction of your great profit of it. But aren't you already rather grilling on your sun-scorched rock? However, it is doubtless blest to you to grill. On second thoughts I dare say you have already seen the things I rather belatedly enclose— or will have done so by the time this reaches you; yet I none the less give them this chance. Emerge and breathe at ease and labour bravely and fruitfully; also believe me all faithfully yours*

Henry James

It soon became apparent to me that if I was ever going to write the second part of *Sinister Street* I must escape from the temptation of parties at Capri, from tango teas, from the pleasure of sitting with Norman Douglas on the terrace of some restaurant and talking the hours away in his magical company. Edwin Cerio suggested that he should lend us a cottage he had in Anacapri, and we betook ourselves to Il Rosaio—a sitting-room, a bedroom and a kitchen with a domed roof, all opening into a small garden with more roses flowering at once close together than I have ever seen since. Graham Greene has Il Rosaio to-day.

We were looked after by Nannina, a woman of saintly simplicity; except for the barking of wandering packs of dogs on moonlight nights utter tranquillity reigned. The view was equally tranquil, a wide silvery green slope of olive groves stretching gently down to the lighthouse, near which in a grove close to the sea were half a dozen olives with huge gnarled trunks, at least five hundred years old.

It cost a tremendous effort of will to settle down to write those first Oxford chapters of *Sinister Street*. There is an echo of my mood in some verses I wrote for the Eights' Week number of the *Isis* in response to an editorial appeal:

Oxford in Italy

Drowsed by the aromatic wind, bewitch'd
By winking of the blue Tyrrhenian sea,
By shadows of Aleppo pines enrich'd,
A sudden thought comes waywardly to me
That I have never taken my M.A. degree.

Buried in myrtle, rosemary and thyme,
With dizzied senses steadied by a crag,
To ponder easefully the upward climb,
I call to mind one most successful rag,
Or the sedate appearance of the Oxford Mag.

Misenum, Baiae and Minerva's cape
Below me lie, and yet that trancèd coast
Can conjure back for me no classic shape;
Rather I think of undergraduate toasts
Go ringing through, alas, a J.C.R. of ghosts.

What flowers blow on these Virgilian fields
Where I am cast by unreproachèd fate,
Yet every flower that my exile yields
I would surrender might I contemplate
The scarlet and the lilies of my College Eight.

Why do my thoughts persistently incline
Towards Oxford, when the air is full of spices?
Why may I not dream on beneath this pine
Of Sirens and of earthly paradises?
Great Scott, I promised something for the Eight's Week Isis!

At the beginning of June John Mavrogordato arrived from a second visit to Greece, where in some vaguely helpful capacity he had been attached, as one might say, to the sequel of the late war in the Balkans. He stayed at the Hotel Paradiso and hired a man to escort him back every evening from Il Rosaio to the hotel to protect him against the wandering dogs.

By the end of June Il Rosaio had become steadily hotter; not a petal was left of its roses. A brief holiday appeared vital to my further progress with *Sinister Street*. Three days but not an hour more could be spared: three full days of sun and sea-water and sublime laziness. Vincenzo, my boatman at the Piccola Marina, had relations in Nerano, a village on the other side of the Sorrentine peninsula, and he knew of a house right on the beach of Cantone below, a tumble down old *palazzo* where we could spend as many nights as we liked in comfort. "*Aria sana, aria fresca,*" he urged, as if the air of Cantone would be fragrant with a further magic of health and refreshment that even Capri could not provide.

The ratcheting of the cicadas from the olive-covered slope above the crescent of that beach is in my ears now. As our boat glided over the sleek blue water of a breathless afternoon to put us ashore, we looked for some monstrous millwheel, so busy and so pervasive was the sound. The natural scene here is sacred to the pen of Norman Douglas. His are the sea-caves and the goat-trampled grottoes of the mountains, his the screaming of the swifts, the sea, the sky, the lucid air; in turning the pages of *Siren Land*, so aromatic are they, so fragrant with sun-dried wisdom and rosemary, the reader looks instinctively between them for the flowery keepsakes of a cherished summer day overpast.

We landed on the Galli islets and fed the lizards that scuffled across the relics of a Roman pavement. We planned to rescue Douglas from sub-editing *The English Review* under Austin Harrison and to enshrine him here with the roses and cedars of which he had written. We walked about the wide empty grey beach of Positano, little thinking that one day it would be one of the most crowded resorts in Bikiniland. We planned—oh, what did we not plan, supposing that the second volume of *Sinister Street* should sell in myriads and that John Mavrogordato would obtain a great price for some property of his in Constantinople?

On that evening as we walked along the beach at Cantone I told John Mavrogordato I was going to dedicate to him the second volume of *Sinister Street*. Suddenly he said to me that he was going to ask Christine Maude to marry him when he returned to London. She stood for so much in my life and I was so anxious her future should be as much assured as, thanks to her inspiration of *Carnival*, was my own that I was overjoyed by John Mavro's news and hoped she would accept him.

That night we had the parish priest to dinner—a kind of Friar Tuck exuding a rich breath of good wine and a deal of dog Latin. To-morrow he was to be in the boat with us for his favourite sport of shooting rock-pigeons. However, to my relief, in the end he spent the day in and out of the water—a hippopotamus of a man, but learned and subtle, a Thomist hippopotamus. It seemed that the *fiesta* of St Anthony of Padua might have to be celebrated at any moment. But that had been on June 13th, I observed, a fortnight since! Quite so, and every morning he had been coming down to say Mass in the little chapel by the sea's edge. It was the fishermen's *fiesta*, he explained; the celebration of it depended not upon the calendar of the Holy Roman Catholic and Apostolic Church, but upon the catch of fish. If there were no fish, there was no money to buy fireworks. It rested with the Saint to provide for his own commemoration. What a sensible way to treat a saint, we thought, especially a saint who himself had preached with such success to fishes and could not be excused through ignorance of their habits. No fish, no fireworks. It was reasonable.

That very evening the catch was made. The image of St Anthony was rowed out to meet the triumphant boat full of anchovies, in the prow of which, silver-laden, he solemnly and benignly returned. There would be fireworks two days later. Alas, we should not see them. This positively had to be our last night; and we sat on the crescent beach, with a young yellow moon hanging over Monte San Costanzo to westward and in the old *palazzo* where we slept the yellow candlelight winking under the lee of the eastward horn of the land. A boy of about thirteen called Giacinto sat on the beach beside us and played ducks and drakes with glossy pebbles. His soul was filled with the glory of fireworks. He chattered in a partially comprehensible dialect about a life that for some days would be spent in a perpetual blaze of golden rain and a rousing din of maroons. Down through the dusky olive-grove came Vincenzo with the evening's provisions and the newspaper.

"What news?" we asked.

"No news," he said. "The fireworks cannot be set off for three days and some Austrian duke has been killed somewhere. *Ecco il giornale!*"

It was too dark by now to read even the headlines; but in the candlelight of that tumbledown *palazzo* by the sea's edge we read how the Archduke Francis Ferdinand had been assassinated at Sarajevo. Whether it was to create an impression of knowledge for simple folk or because I had a moment's illumination of the future I do not know; but I declared that this murder would mean a European war.

Vincenzo smiled.

"*O signor scherza,*" he said politely.

Four months hence when we met again he would be reproaching himself for being such a fool as to think I was joking on that fateful evening in June.

The journey from Naples to Calais has remained in my memory not as the end of a jolly time in Capri but as the end of an epoch. As the train runs northwards through France the names of stations we passed like Verdun seem printed in blood. Yet the head-steward of the restaurant-car, a German with a fair Kaiserish moustache, was so courteous and attentive that on our way north I began to think we might have been premature in hurrying home so quickly. Michael Arlen came along and made himself known to us. When I told him we were hurrying home in case war was on its way he smiled indulgently at my overheated fancy.

We got back to London when the University match had started at Lords. A day or two before we arrived T. W. H. Crosland had been acquitted by a clod-pated jury of conspiring with Lord Alfred Douglas to make a false charge against Robert Ross. This was the revenge for Robbie Ross's having given evidence for Arthur Ransome in the libel action Alfred Douglas brought against him for his book about Oscar Wilde, which Martin Secker had published. I went to call on Robbie Ross at his rooms in Half Moon Street to express my indignation. He was in something like an hysterical condition and asked me if I did not realize how much I compromised myself by going to visit such a social outcast. It was a painful visit, and I went off worried by his mental state to see Oxford beat Cambridge at Lords.

Various friends asked me what had suddenly brought me back from Capri.

"I'm worried about this war," I told them.

"This Irish business? Oh, that'll be all over presently."

"No, not civil war in Ireland," I said. "I mean a European war."

"Of course, you *would* have to work out for yourself something improbable."

Nobody I met would consider a European war even a remote possibility. On the posters advertising Bottomley's infernal paper *John Bull* at the tail-end of the omnibuses was TO HELL WITH SERVIA. What had the assassination of an Archduke by Servians got to do with a Great Britain being conducted by Horatio Bottomley?

I went down to see Gilbert Cannan in his Buckinghamshire wind-mill at Cholesbury near Tring. He was as sceptical as everybody else about the likelihood of a great war. I came to the conclusion that Cannan's head had been turned by that spiral staircase leading up to his writing-room at the top of the windmill.

Mark Gertler had planted himself upon the Cannans in the subur-ban-villa attachment to the windmill, and Gilbert was finding him an interruption to his own work, although full of praise for a frieze Gertler was painting in that study of his.

Gilbert Cannan, a year younger than myself, had started with a couple of pseudo-Meredithian novels, and as the dramatic critic of the *Star* had been one of the critics laughed at by Shaw in *Fanny's First Play*. After he went down from Cambridge J. M. Barrie took him on as his secretary; he fell in love with Barrie's wife and was co-respondent in the subsequent divorce. I recall the wonder at Barrie's noble behaviour in settling £300 a year on his erring wife. In fairness to Mary Barrie it could be said that for several years before Cannan appeared on the scene all marital relations had ceased, if they had ever fully existed; Barrie's generosity was dictated, in justice to him, by his own sense of failure as a husband.

Cannan had joined Martin Secker's list with a novel called *Round the Corner* and followed it with *Old Mole*. Both were successful; his earlier Meredithian prose had simplified itself. He was an indefatigable worker and translated with skill Romain Rolland's huge novel, *Jean-Cristophe*. I never believed myself that Cannan was a novelist with a future because he was too much concerned with preaching, and became continually more and more incapable of speaking the truth. Neverthe-less, some people incapable of speaking the truth have been able to write it; Ford Madox Ford is an example of that. Then Cannan found a young woman with £300 a year of her own and deserted Mary Cannan; the young woman fell in love with the rich heir of Lord —, and for a time there was a strange *ménage à trois*. During the war and after it Cannan's behaviour became more and more eccentric, his books less and less worth reading. He went to the United States on a lecture tour in which his perversion of the truth, whether about people or politics, was steadily maintained. Finally in about 1925 he was certified and established in a private asylum at Richmond by Lord and Lady —. Cannan believed that it was a private house and that the attendants were his own servants. He spent much of his time writing letters to successive Prime Ministers and various Cabinet Ministers. These letters were posted in a private letter-box in the asylum whence

they were taken out at once and duly disposed of by the asylum attendants. For some thirty years Gilbert Cannan lived in this asylum,
dying in 1955 at the age of seventy-one.

He was a slim handsome man with eyes that always looked beyond
the person to whom he was talking into his own private world.

I was convinced that war was coming and was in a fever to finish
Sinister Street. Faith and I went to stay with Martin Secker and Mrs
Lamont at Bridgefoot, where I would often be writing and revising all
night, and going to bed at seven o'clock in the morning. The second
volume of *Sinister Street*, like the first, was being set up as I wrote it, so
that revision had to be meticulous.

Our beloved sheepdog Bob was now living at Bridgefoot and another
guest was Maurice, my green Amazon parrot. Maurice was not a good
talker like the grey West African parrots, but he had a keen sense of
humour and was a slapstick comedian in the best tradition, one of his
performances being to lie on his back at the bottom of his cage and
beat time to one of Martin Secker's performances on the pianola.

All that July I was obsessed with the fear that we were going to let
down France if things came to the worst. Meanwhile, ordinary life was
going on. Eton beat Harrow at Lords: the Players beat the Gentlemen
at the Oval. In the air race from London to Paris and back two out of
the six starters finished, taking about three and a half hours each way.
The Home Rule Conference failed. The Ulster Volunteers had obtained 35,000 rifles and 3,000,000 cartridges from Germany in the
spring without any attempt being made to stop them. Now the Irish
Volunteers landed 2,500 rifles and 125,000 rounds of ammunition.
There was an attempt by the King's Own Scottish Borderers to stop
them which ended in their firing on the people of Dublin and killing a
woman and a child.

Two days later Austria-Hungary declared war on what we were told
should be called Serbia, not Servia, and after the capture of Belgrade
Russia began to mobilize. Desperate last-minute efforts were made to
prevent the conflict's extending into a European war. It was too late.
Next day Germany declared war on France and Russia. We still abstained. The Germans were stupid enough to give an ultimatum to
Belgium; the British Government could feel that it would have the
nation behind it if it gave an ultimatum to Germany which would
expire at midnight on August 3rd.

I was writing away in Bridgefoot at *Sinister Street* all that Tuesday
evening, the countryside hushed. When midnight had struck that
hushed countryside was filled with the rumble of trains running south-

ward. All night while I was writing that rumble continued, and when I leaned out of the window to drink in the morning air before going to bed the rumble of the trains bearing equipment and munitions and stores to the south coast could still be heard.

That afternoon I went to London to consult a G.S.O.(2)[1] at the War Office who had recently married Mrs Desmond Deane, a great friend of ours. What steps should I take to obtain a commission in the Seaforth Highlanders? Louis Vaughan smiled at me indulgently.

"We don't want married subalterns of thirty-one."

"But I did hold a commission in the Volunteers fourteen years ago."

"I dare say, and if you were still eighteen I would do all I could to put you in the way of a commission to-day. But you are thirty-one. Your job is to keep us amused by writing books. You'll be much more use to your country that way than as a subaltern on active service."

That was that. I went back to Bridgefoot, determined to get into the war somehow but meanwhile to go on with the writing of *Sinister Street*. The manuscript of that second volume is now in the Bodleian at Oxford, and from time to time on the opposite sheet are the names of the cities and towns falling before the German advance—Namur, Liège, Valenciennes and the rest of them.

On the day Great Britain declared war on Austria-Hungary Faith and I went over to Eton to lunch with the Vice-Provost and Mrs Warre-Cornish. Father Martindale, S.J. was there and we had a long talk about *Sinister Street*; he was anxious to know how I was handling the second volume, but I can never give more than a shadowy outline of a book I am writing or going to write.

Presently the conversation between Martindale and myself was interrupted by the arrival of Desmond MacCarthy and Molly, who was a daughter of the Vice-Provost and Mrs Warre-Cornish. There was a great scurrying all over the place to find change for the florin which was more than Desmond needed to tip the cabman.

In the middle of the search for small silver Mrs Warre-Cornish bore down on me across the lawn and said in her deepest and most sublimely inconsequent tone:

"*We* have declared war upon Austria. Sixpence can always be found. But *we* have declared war on Austria!"

Stories about Mrs Warre-Cornish should not be told except to those who knew the sound of her voice. Aldous Huxley attempted a portrait of her in one of his books, but she is incommunicable.

---

[1] The late Lt.-General Sir Louis Vaughan, K.B.E., C.B., D.S.O.

I find it difficult to understand how I managed to concentrate upon *Sinister Street*, so much did I long to be in the war. Do not suppose that this longing was inspired by any lofty sentiments of patriotism or even by sympathy with "plucky little Belgium". No, no, it was inspired by the realization that this was the greatest moment in the history of my time and that somehow I must be sharing in the excitement of it.

Presently Lord Kitchener was appointed Minister for War and "your country needs you" appeared under his head on recruiting posters. Secker and I were playing croquet when a waggonette-load of excursionists driving past the lawn on the other side of the hedge shouted to know why Secker and I had not enlisted.

It is difficult to realize now the inability of Londoners to appreciate how utterly the Great War for Civilization was going to change their world, difficult to believe that in the shop windows there were placards with "BUSINESS AS USUAL" to which some added "though there's a War on". At the same time too many Londoners were wondering why others had not enlisted and too many idiotic young women were handing white feathers to boy-friends they were tired of.

Toward the end of that August I took another day off from *Sinister Street* to visit the Cannans at the Mill House. Gilbert suggested a visit to D. H. Lawrence, who was living not far away at Chesham. I had been much impressed by *The White Peacock*, but had not yet read *Sons and Lovers*. However, I felt pretty sure Lawrence would not have read *Sinister Street* and I agreed to the proposed call. We drove to a modern red-brick cottage in Bellingden Lane, the ugliest cottage I had ever seen. It stood in a tiny garden crowded with tall nettles, the tops of which growing above the window-sill shed a green gloom over the sparsely furnished little sitting-room out of which a curved staircase went up to a couple of rooms above. When Cannan and I arrived Lawrence was on his knees, with a pail beside him, scrubbing the floor. With his small red moustache and reddish hair and the attractive pink-and-white complexion of a redhead he looked much younger than his twenty-nine years.

"We've only just got in and the place was filthy," he told us. "We wouldn't be here at all if it wasn't for this war." Then, rising and wiping his hands, he went to the bottom of the staircase and shouted, "Frieda!" There was no answer for a moment or two; then he shouted again twice as loudly, "Frieda!" A pair of legs in ringed black and white stockings came into view at the top of the curved staircase before the body they supported appeared. "Shut that door!" he called. The legs kept on their way down. "Frieda, shut that bloody door!" he shouted angrily. She turned back to shut the door, after which she descended into the sitting-room. There was a slightly proprietary air about Lawrence, who two or three months earlier had been able to marry Frieda, her husband having divorced her after some delay. He had obviously been elated, as he wrote in a letter about this time, by marrying "the daughter of Baron von Richthoven, of the ancient and famous house of Richthoven". Now war had come with Germany, and Lawrence's rage with the war was fed by his having a German wife. I hardly exaggerate when I say that one might have supposed we had gone to war with Germany solely for the purpose of annoying Lawrence personally.

Frieda herself was shedding a warmth and geniality of welcome to us when on Lawrence's orders she went out to the kitchen to prepare tea.

In the course of conversation I told Lawrence that if I could not get into the war I should go back to Capri next month when I had finished the book I was working on.

"Why don't you become a special constable like me?" Cannan asked.

"That's not getting into the war," I said. "I can't imagine anything more depressing than spending the winter in England as a special constable. I can't face the depressing view of those flat English fields surrounded by their melancholy elms without leaves."

"You're right," Lawrence exclaimed. "Those melancholy elms. You're right. It is a terrible view. It's the saddest sight in the world. Flat fields and elms. Frieda!"

"What is it, Lorenzo?"

"We can't stay in this cottage with these elms. We must get down somewhere to the sea," Lawrence declared.

I asked him why he did not go back to Italy.

"We're moving into a new villa this autumn and you could have our cottage at Anacapri for the winter. Everybody thinks the war will be over by next spring."

"I'll remember your offer of this cottage," Lawrence said, and five years later he would still be remembering it and come to Capri.

The next attempt I made to get into the war was to try to join a Red Cross unit that was being organized by Lady Paget for work in Serbia. That failed to come off. Then I went to consult Henry Newbolt on Campden Hill. He was sympathetic and offered to write to H. J. Tennant, who was Under-Secretary for War.

"But don't be disappointed if nothing can be done about getting

P

you a commission," Newbolt said. "From what I hear the whole business will be over by February at latest. That's the general feeling among those who know."

"Kitchener doesn't seem to think that. He asks for three-year volunteers for his army."

"Ah, well, Lord K's a cautious chap," Newbolt said with a smile.

"I don't believe Winston thinks the war will be over by February," I argued.

Newbolt smiled again.

"Winston is enjoying himself too much to think that."

"I wanted to get into his Naval division, but I wouldn't have had a chance to get through a medical. I'll have to get somewhere with a fairly decent winter climate."

"I'll tell Tennant that," Newbolt promised.

An admiring and optimistic friend told me that Sir John Maxwell would welcome my services on his staff in Egypt. A day or two afterwards H. J. Tennant was having tea in the Savile and, hoping that Newbolt had spoken to him about me, I got myself introduced. Alas, the Under-Secretary of State for War was not so powerful as I had supposed he must be. All he could do was to tell me that the 42nd Division, consisting of Lancashire territorial battalions, was in Egypt, and that if I wanted to reach Egypt the only way it could be managed was by applying for a commission in one of those battalions through the Lord Lieutenant or some such Lancastrian dignitary.

I see the Under-Secretary now in our faded old drawing-room at 107 Piccadilly. We were not as a club famous for dandyism, and whether it was the comfortable shabbiness of the room or the equally comfortable bagginess of the members' trousers I do not know, but certainly as I look back to that interview I seem to fancy the impression of a slightly excessive elegance in Mr H. J. Tennant, a certain statesmanlike unreality about his high glossy collar. Perhaps I thought our Under-Secretary of State for War had no business to resemble a *Vanity Fair* cartoon of the 'nineties unless he could do something more useful and *affairé* than tell me what I knew already, unless he could in fact obtain for me a job on the Staff of Sir John Maxwell. We were most of us in a condition of elated credulity at that early stage of the war.

It was lucky that no influential star did draw me toward Sir John Maxwell, for a job on his Staff in Egypt might have led to a job on his Staff in Ireland. "Conky" Maxwell was responsible for the shooting of those young Irish patriots after the Easter Rising; I thank God I was never on his Staff, for I should either have deserted or lost my reason.

In that October I went to see Henry James at Carlyle Mansions. He received me at the flat off Cheyne Walk with a kind of ceremonious warmth and led me to his study.

"And now, my dear boy, make yourself as comfortable as, in this monstrous time of war, comfort either of body or mind is . . ." he paused to grasp at the adjective floating for a moment out of his reach, and then, just as his fingers were closing upon it, or rather (I become Jamesian myself as the memory of the scene recurs)—or rather pausing like a butterfly-hunter, net in air, to swoop upon the perfect adjective and imprison it in the reticulation of his prose—at that moment his housekeeper came into the room. Henry James looked round for the epithet now well on its way to escape, desperation in his mild and magnificent eye, and then his housekeeper said gently but most firmly,

"It's about the marmalade, Mr James."

"Marmalade?" he ejaculated.

"Marmalade from the Army and Navy Stores," she insisted.

Henry James turned to me.

"Will you, my dear boy, try to entertain—or perhaps not so much entertain as engage yourself with a book while I devote a minute or two of most unwilling attention, or rather tortured concentration upon one of these hideous encounters with domestic necessity. A vast emporium, one of those appalling achievements of our modern craving for the huge, the immense, looms between myself and this delightful company of yours, to the enjoyment of which I have been looking forward with a so lively. . . ."

"Mr James," his housekeeper interposed, with hardly concealed impatience, "the man from the Army and Navy Stores is waiting for their order."

"In one moment, Mrs Dash. I will not keep you a moment. Now, my dear boy, here is our dear H. G. Wells's last book. Full of that Wellsian quality which sometimes flows a little too. . . . Or you may rather beguile yourself for a moment while I surrender to the remorseless ritual which these domestic conveniences demand from us. . . . Yes, here is our dear Arnold Bennett's last. . . ."

While Henry James was picking up book after book on the table and bumbling round them like a great irresolute bee, his housekeeper was tapping the floor with her foot.

"Mr James, please," she protested.

The great novelist seated himself at his desk and, pen poised above the notepaper, looked anxiously up at his housekeeper.

"How would you . . . how shall I address the apex of this pyramid

. . . the . . . er . . . director of this magnificent display of . . . er . . .
co-operative energy?"

"Mr James, just write the order please and the man will take it,"
she almost pleaded.

"And what was the peculiar title of the condiment which we need
to import into this so humble corner of this vast London of ours,
Mrs Dash?"

"Mr James, we were going to order six jars of that Oxford marmalade you liked."

From the corner of my eye I watched the operation of writing that
order as Henry James's pen advanced to the paper and drew back and
then hovered above the writing-paper, making a traceless pattern upon
the air in a kind of sarabande to which the housekeeper's foot tapped
quite out of time.

At last the pen descended upon the paper and the large angular
script flowed across it. The six jars of marmalade were ordered; with a
sigh of exhaustion and relief Henry James came back to his guest,
apologizing once more for the interruption and full of solicitude for
the way I had been able to pass the time while the marmalade was
being ordered.

He went on to talk about *Carnival*.

"I feel, my dear boy, that perhaps you have . . . er . . . erected upon
your little Cockney ballet dancer a more elaborate . . . a more richly
decorated edifice of narrative than she as the central and supporting
figure of your story is capable of sustaining." Then quickly lest I should
be hurt by this judgment he said, "But let me quickly add, my dear
boy, that I should have made, had I dared, the same observation to
our dear Gustave Flaubert about *Madame Bovary*."

"Yes, I know what you mean, Mr James. There's too much analysis
of a simple mind. I think one is apt to psychologize when one is not
perfectly sure what one's character is going to do next. I realize this
now and when this war is over I shall revise and perhaps even completely re-write *Carnival*, now that I have more experience of novel
writing."

Before I could expatiate further Henry James held up his hands in a
wide gesture of dismay.

"You alarm . . . you . . . horrify me with such news," he declared,
his large smooth face momentarily puckered with genuine distress. "I
once wasted ten . . . indeed, twelve precious years in foolishly supposing that in the light of experience I could grope my way toward a
more . . . toward that always elusive . . . in short that I could add yet

something to what, when it was written, I had given all that I could
give at that time. I had failed to grasp that these dreadful English
participles condemn us to those 'ings' the monotonous tinkling of which
obtrudes on every sentence we write. And those sibilants, those remorseless English sibilants!"

He paused, staring for a moment beyond as if he were confronting
some angry cobra raising its malign head from one of his sentences.
Then he turned to me:

"Renounce this preposterous ambition of yours, my dear boy. You
have been granted the boon which above all is what a novelist should
beg for himself. You have been granted that boon with a generosity
beyond that accorded to any of your young contemporaries. You toss
the ball up against the wall and it rebounds immediately into your
hands. Whereas I . . ." he looked round the room in the Chelsea flat
from the windows of which one saw the river shimmering through a
filigree of boughs now almost bare of leaves, "whereas I toss the ball
against the wall, whence it rebounds not into my hands, but on to the
next wall and from that wall to the next." He followed with apprehensive glance the flight of that ghostly ball round the room. "Until," he
concluded,"at last it falls to the ground and dribbles very very slowly
toward my feet, when I, all my old bones aching, stoop, and very very
laboriously pick it up."

He paused for a moment while I was asking myself what I had done
to earn what was seeming a solemn benediction.

"You will be glad when you are as old as I am that you were able
to put the spirit of youth into a book of yours: like *La Vie de Bohême*,
like *La Dame aux Camélias*, all roses and sweet champagne. No, you
couldn't make your heroine die of consumption: consumption has by
now become tuberculosis. So you had to kill your heroine with a gun.
Roses and sweet champagne," he murmured to himself. "I was never
fortunate enough to write such a story of which I should have been
ashamed when I reached thirty but of which I should have been so
fond in my old age."

"Mr James," I said, "you know how tremendously grateful I was
for being mentioned by you in that article of yours in the *Times Literary
Supplement*. Yet there was something in that article which rather worried
me. You seemed to think that Hugh Walpole's novel *Fortitude* was . . .
you seemed to think it was the same kind of a book as *Sinister Street*, and
I find *Fortitude* . . . well, really I find it a ridiculous book."

Henry James held up his hands in another of those wide gestures of
dismay.

"You . . . er . . . bewilder me. All I thought I had indicated about our dear young friend Hugh as tenderly as I could was that so far in his eager . . . his eager and hopeful . . . that so far he had written absolutely nothing at all."

That October day was to be the last time I should see Henry James.

By the end of the month, still with no prospect of getting into the war, I felt it would be wise to return to Capri and take possession of Casa Solitaria. When I was saying good-bye to Edmund Gosse at the Savile he gave me a French novel to beguile the journey.

"Mind you, I'm not suggesting there is any similarity between *Sinister Street* and this book by a Frenchman. Yet they both of them seem to be expressions of a new approach to the novel on similar lines."

He put into my hands *Du Côté de Chez Swann* by Marcel Proust, which had recently been published. I must have lent that volume to somebody, or perhaps somebody just borrowed it without telling me, for that precious first edition is no longer on my shelves.

The desperate battle of Ypres was at its height when Faith and I went back to Italy. On the boat crossing the Channel I saw Louis Vaughan in khaki and told him I was going back to Capri to write a book.

"The best thing you could do. We don't want all these amateurs."

"I was hoping for some kind of obscure Staff job in Egypt."

"My dear man, the last people we want on the Staff are charming amateurs like yourself. And anyway, this business of diverting to Egypt troops we require in France will have to stop. The only place where anybody is any use at all just now is over there." He pointed to the misty outline of the French coast beyond that ashen autumnal sea.

I felt apologetically superfluous among that crowd of mixed uniforms on the quay at Boulogne. Even that little fellow with the face of a provincial comedian in a uniform between the Salvation Army and the Church Lads' Brigade, who was going to hand out tracts and toffee somehow or other behind the lines, was living life as it ought to be lived, not as I proposed to live it presently in Capri, writing one more unnecessary novel. I waved Louis Vaughan good-bye in the blusterous chill of late October and enviously watched him like a senior schoolboy greeting other important seniors at the beginning of a new term.

Over thirty years after that first Battle of Ypres I should be dining at Viceroy's House with Lord Wavell, and after one of those long silences of "guinea a word Archie" he would ask me abruptly if I had ever heard the story of the sergeant and the private at the first Battle of Ypres. After my negative he went on,

"A sergeant and a private were on their way to the front line and had been toiling along through the mud in the wind and rain for some time when the private said to the sergeant, 'Couldn't we sit down and rest for a bit, Sarge? I'm feeling shocking tired.'

" 'Rest?' the sergeant echoed sharply. 'What do you want to rest for? You'll be dead in half an hour.' "

Then the Viceroy relapsed into another long silence. I have wondered what it was that suddenly made him think of the first battle of Ypres at Delhi in November 1946.

The peace of Capri in that cloudless November made me feel even more guilty about inaction when things were so desperate in France and Flanders. I was thankful when I was asked to write an article[1] on behalf of the Commission for Relief in Belgium. The two letters below illustrate the generosity of men who, engaged upon as noble a task as men ever undertook, found time to make an author feel that he had been of some use.

3 London Wall
London
Jany. 5th 1915

Dear Sir,

On behalf of the Belgian Minister and the Commissioner please allow me to express our sincere gratitude for the magnificent *article which you were kind enough to write. It could not have been better.*

Yours gratefully
W. A. M. Goode[2]

The second letter is from Mr Hoover, who did such a superb job for the Belgian refugees, and was to become President of the United States one day.

3 London Wall
London
Jany. 7th 1915

Dear Sir,

I have had the great pleasure to-day of reading the article which you have prepared for us on the subject of Belgium.

The ordinary commercial person may feel all that you have set forth, but the gift of expressing it comes to but few. You have described the work of this Commission in a manner which reaches an absolute ideal and I wish to convey to you

---

[1] Appendix B.
[2] Sir William Goode.

our individual thanks for your interest and work. I am certain it will be the most fruitful of the statements which we have yet been able to put before the American people.

Yours faithfully

H. C. *Hoover*

Casa Solitaria seemed to us incomparably the most attractive villa in Capri. Faith wrote:

"We found Solitaria quaintly furnished by Edwin Cerio with a set of ceremonial Venetian arm-chairs of surprising discomfort, Maxim Gorky's writing-table, which was about seven feet long and covered with green baize, a divan, the size of a small room, from Gorky's Capri house . . . and an enormous baroque mirror in the salone which must have come from some Roman palace, and though it was oval in shape it covered nearly the whole of one wall.

"Such necessities as beds and chests of drawers had been supplied with an obvious lack of enthusiasm. Our own furniture and curtains were already on their way out so what did it matter? . . .

"The dining-room floor was paved with porcelain tiles of a charming yellow lily design, and the salone next door had thistle tiles. . . . Two bedrooms and a bathroom completed the ground floor. . . .

"To reach the studio it was necessary to go out of doors, up the front steps and round to the great room that held so much of our story. A huge window looked out to sea and the Faraglioni rocks. A smaller one, with a window-seat, framed a matchless view of Monte Solaro and every sunset. East was the french-window that led to the terrace which was the roof of the rest of the house. . . . From this terrace we could see the moon rise over the Sorrentine peninsula and watch the dolphins playing round the Monacone rock below us, and at night the fishermen with their torches casting giant shadows against the Faraglioni. . . . There was a half-moon terrace below the house, over the parapet of which was a sheer drop of three hundred feet to the emerald water below . . . clear as a precious stone."

We were, as almost always, immensely lucky in our *famiglia*, as in Italy the household is called. How sad it is that the English parvenus of the industrial revolution made "familiar" a word to suggest contempt! In justice to Scotland, people there never made their servants feel they belonged to an inferior caste.

Our beloved Carolina, a wisp of a woman just over fifty, would be with us until we left Capri over ten years later. She could neither read nor write. Yet she never made the mistake of a *centesimo* when she went through the *spesi* every morning after her arrival from the market-place with the day's provisions. In that autumn her nephew Antonio, aged fifteen, was our chef, and a jolly good chef too; later he was called away to serve with the Italian army, and Carolina's youngest daughter Gelsomina joined us as housemaid.

Nellie Baker, who had had an adventurous escape from Germany in the first month of the war, came out to Capri with us, and would presently be typing for me *Guy and Pauline*.

I shall leave until my next Octave portraits of some Capri characters because when one sets out on such a narrative as I have embarked upon one cannot help feeling that the reader may not have read the previous Octave and that for the reader who has it will be boring for him to have characters introduced to him all over again. However, I cannot postpone John Ellingham Brooks.

Brooks had come to Capri first during the emigration of homosexuals at the time of the Wilde case. There he had befriended a young American painter who was struggling along in poverty, and soon afterwards married her. They had not been married long when she inherited a large fortune. Now independent and a lesbian, she and Brooks had separated, and on condition that he did not intrude upon her life in Paris she made him an allowance of £300 a year. As Romaine Brooks she became a distinguished painter; her portrait of Gabriel d'Annunzio is in the Luxemburg. We shall meet her in the next Octave.

Brooks lived in the Villa Cercola, inland as far as one can be inland in Capri. Here with his piano he spent his time translating the sonnets of Hérédia. Somerset Maugham and E. F. Benson each paid a share of the rent of the Villa Cercola; they used to come regularly to Capri in the summer, usually at different times. I recall Brooks coming along one day in a great flutter to say that Maugham had got himself involved with a married woman and that he was going to have to marry her.

"I don't know what I shall do if Maugham brings a wife to the Cercola. I don't think Benson will like it at all either."

Somerset Maugham himself has told the story of that marriage; he never brought Sirie Maugham to disturb the bachelors' peace of the Villa Cercola, but he continued to come there himself after the war.

Fersen arrived back from the tour of the Far East he had made with the Wolcott-Perrys and the Villa Torricella was again the centre of those prodigal parties. Kate and Saidee Wolcott-Perry talked of Count Jack's decision to join the French forces, but the days went by and Count Jack, who had brought back from that tour a trunkful of opium, dreamed away the winter instead.

The second volume of *Sinister Street* appeared on November 11th and, without the help of being banned by the circulating libraries, sold nearly as well as the first volume. Henry James wrote in a letter which I have lost that I had emancipated the English novel.

My heart was still set on getting into the war and I paid little attention to the reviews, which were mostly favourable. I was able to pay off all my debts and could feel reasonably secure of financial stability in the future.

Down at the Piccola Marina, Vincenzo, our boatman, had secured a two-roomed cottage built on an outcrop of rock at the tip of the beach. Here in the week before Christmas I gave a dinner to the fishermen and *carozza* drivers. No motor-car had yet defiled Capri. The dinner was an uproarious success.

In that week before Christmas the Parroco had obtained Episcopal permission to say Mass at Casa Solitaria. The house was solemnly blessed beforehand and while the Parroco was sprinkling the rooms with holy water the two *zampognatori* played, one on the bagpipe the other on the chanter, some age-old tune of the mountains. The bagpipers used to arrive on the Feast of the Immaculate Conception and play at the little roadside shrines all over the island until Christmas. They played, too, at every villa in turn and after they had been complimented on their playing with a few liras they presented the donor with a wooden spoon; I never discovered what that wooden spoon signified.

Upon three halcyon days of December I was thrilled to see two swallows fly out to sea and return. In ancient Greece it was believed that the swallows, or halcyons, flew out to build their nests at sea on those calm and cloudless winter days. Hence the halcyon weather of which we speak.

There had been frequent criticism by the reviewers of the formlessness of *Sinister Street* and also of Michael Fane's future still being in the air at the end of the second volume. They did not seem to realize that everybody's future is so often still in the air at twenty-three and that the book could not have a positive ending. I was determined to show with *Guy and Pauline* that I could tackle as difficult a piece of construction as any novelist could set himself, by composing a sort of violin and piano sonata. I debated with myself all through that autumn whether I had a right to draw upon the emotion of my own engagement to Ruth Daniel. Then, still hoping to get into the war, I decided that if I were destined to be killed in that war it was my duty to put into what might be the last book I should ever write the most poignant experience of my life, while at the same time changing all the externals of the real story into a work of imagination.

So on New Year's Eve of 1914 I sat down at Maxim Gorky's great table covered with green baize to write the first sentences of *Guy and Pauline*. It was a night of breathless calm before the savage south-west gale which shrieked round the studio as the great window creaked and groaned with hardly a lull for the next twelve days, at the end of which I was laid out with an attack of neuritis as savage as the gale.

A few days earlier I had received from Henry James a letter in answer to one I had written to tell him of my decision to start *Guy and Pauline*:

> 21 Carlyle Mansions
> Cheyne Walk, S.W.
> *December 19th*, 1914

My dear Monty,

It is very good to get your news—news of such pure and unadulterated goodness not being quite all over the place just now. Forgive my resort to this impersonal manner of thanking you, a "war measure" to which I am reduced; and read between my lines—which you easily will when they are so beautifully straight—all sorts of the most insidious personalities. It's very wonderful to think of you as already bathed in that glorious aether, even though your slightly grim address makes one feel you, considering the time, a little inordinately "out of it". However, your announcement of prompt operations of your very own—how splendidly you keep them up!—fills my ear as with the scratching of your pen, which floats to me over seas and continents, mountain barriers and multitudinous slaughter and woe, with an authenticity that feeds my own still fond clutch of the arts, or at least of the art, of Peace. In that sign we shall still finally conquer—especially if your good Italian friends help us; though I don't pronounce yet as to their best way for that. You will by this time know that the great stroke off the Falkland Islands has been followed here by a hideous German shelling of three Yorkshire towns, two of them the exposed and utterly defenceless Scarborough and Whitby, where the enemy's main triumph has been the annihilation of women and small children. It is galling that their four or five ships, concerned in the grand deed, slipped away successfully, that is fled with all speed, a thick morning mist aiding, before retribution could overtake them. However, the account is piling up that I refuse to believe won't be eventually presented to them in an altogether overwhelming manner. Don't mind these things, at any rate, if you can at all manage not to; but keep the Muse hovering, irresistibly fascinated, about you, and, yes, yes, yes, as I said before, go on making all the fine life you can, as against all that's being unmade. The memory of our long good talk before you went hangs also in the most encouraged fashion, please believe, about yours all faithfully

> *Henry James*

Not less heartening was a letter from Edmund Gosse. This was held up for a week by the Censor and sent to me with a note to say I should advise my correspondents to write at less length to avoid delay. Gosse was furious and sent a letter of protest to *The Times*.

17 Hanover Terrace
Jan. 5, 1915

My dear Compton Mackenzie,

If I put off much longer the pleasant duty of thanking you for your letter, you will think me churlish. For that letter was one of the most agreeable that I ever received, and I should be ungrateful indeed if I did not let you know how much I value it. But I was anxious so far to reciprocate your generosity as to discuss with you your own latest work. In doing that, I have been confronted with many delays. . . .

But first I must thank you for your Poems. I value the book, and shall bind it and preserve it among the poets. Yet you will let me be quite frank. Your verses are highly accomplished and full of delicate grace, but they are lacking in temperament. There I miss a vocation. These are Guy Hazlewood's poems, written at Plasher's Mead, because he was determined to write poetry. It is quite different with Sinister Street, *because you have the temperament of prose. You are a most interesting and advancing prose-writer—far and away the best of your generation. Therefore, it is worth while to apply the most powerful lens to your performance. Certainly, you have written hitherto nothing so good as this second volume of* Sinister Street. *Your verbal felicities are more numerous and more sparkling than ever. Don't let them be too deliberate. . . .*

Still I notice what I ventured to suggest to you before, a sacrifice of structure to ornament. You hardly give yourself time to build a sentence, you puff out little flotillas of brilliant phrases. I wish I could induce you to submit to the charm of the periodic manner, not to be constantly used, but trotted out for purposes of reflection and the building of an argument. . . .

The Oxford part, from a more general point of view, is delightful. Far and away the best account of University life that ever was written. Though I had the ignominy—as Michael and his friends would think it—of being Cambridge, I was deeply moved.

Now what shall I say to you about "Book Four"? I should like to discuss it with you orally for hours. The separate pictures in it are incomparable. I put the fight on the stairs at Neptune Terrace quite at the top. It is really worthy of comparison with the very first descriptive things in literature. Everywhere there is abounding vision, the sharp hard light thrown on colour and form. A little too hard, sometimes? I don't know, but I might read you a sermon on "Rudyard Kipling: or, the Shocking Results of an Early Intemperance in Style". But in your case, only just a little hard sometimes. What puzzles me most, however, in this Fourth Book is the return to the picaresque manner. There had not been a picaresque romance in English for generations. Here we are again, Gil Blas in full blast! You use Fane and his not very interesting physical infatuation to intro-duce us to scene after scene into which without his fatuous intervention we could never penetrate. Quite right, but frankly picaresque; and please hesitate before you do it again. I have a million more things I want to say. Do write and tell me that you are not offended with my frankness—yourself and your work interest me so deeply that I must be sincere with you.

Ever truly yrs.,

Edmund Gosse

FERSEN had brought back with him from Siam a pair of cats from the royal palace. The male had died during the voyage and the female, deprived of love, had an affair with a ginger Tom in the garden of Fersen's villa. Two tortoiseshell kittens were born and Fersen, finding that their mews disturbed his opium dreams, gave them to us before they were weaned and we had quite a time for a week or two to feed them. We were successful and they were brought up to the studio where they lived in a covered basket called Plasher's Mead, which Brooks gave us. In fact Guy was as much of a girl as Pauline, and as they were both tortoiseshells we should have known this; these two kittens were my constant joy all that winter and spring.

A fortnight after starting *Guy and Pauline* I was laid out by an attack and when recovering I must have written to Henry James:

> 21 Carlyle Mansions
> Cheyne Walk, S.W.
> *January 23rd, 1915*

My dear Monty,

I am acknowledging your so interesting letter at once; because I find that under the effect of all our conditions here I can't answer for any postal fluency, however reduced in quality or quantity, at an indefinite future time. My fluency of the moment even, such as it is, has to take the present mechanic form; but here goes, at any rate, to the extent of my having rejoiced to hear from you, not of much brightness though your news may be. I tenderly condole and participate with you on your having been again flung into bed. Truly the haul on your courage has to keep on being enormous—and I applaud to the echo the wonderful way that virtue in you appears to meet it. You strike me as leading verily the heroic life at a pitch nowhere and by nobody surpassed—even though our whole scene bristles all over with such grand examples of it. Since you are up and at work again may that at least go bravely on—while I marvel again, according to my wont, at your still finding it possible in conditions that I fear would be for me dismally "inhibitive". I bless your new book even if you didn't in our last talk leave me with much grasp of what it is to be "about". In presence of any suchlike intention I find I want a subject to be able quite definitely to state and declare itself—as a subject; and when the thing is communicated to me (in advance) in the form of So-and-So's doing this, that or the other or Something-else's "happening" and so on, I kind of yearn for the inexpressible idea or motive, what the thing is to be done for, *to have been presented to me: which you may say perhaps is asking a good deal. I don't think so, if any cognisance at all is vouchsafed one; it is the only thing I in the least care to ask. What the author shall do with his idea I am quite ready to wait for, but am meanwhile in no relation to the work at all unless that basis has been provided. Console yourself, however: dear great George Meredith once began to express to me what a novel he had just started ("One of Our Conquerors") was to be about by no other art than simply naming to me the half-dozen occurrences, such as they were, that occupied the pages he had already written; so that I remained, I felt, quite without an answer to my respectful inquiry—which he had all the time the very attitude of kindly encouraging and rewarding!*

But why do I make these restrictive and invidious observations? I bless your book, and the author's fine hand and brain, whatever it may consist of; and I bend with interest over your remarks about poor speculating and squirming old Italy's desperate dilemma. The infusion of that further horror of local devastation and anguish is too sickening for words—I have been able only to avert my face from it; as, if I were nearer, I fear I should but wrap my head in my mantle and give up altogether. The truth is however that the Italian case affects me as on the whole rather ugly—failing to see, as one does, their casus belli, and having to see, as one also does, that they must hunt up one to give them any sort of countenance at all. I should—

January 25th.

I had to break off two days ago, having been at that very moment flung into bed, as I am occasionally liable to, somewhat like yourself; though happily not in the prolonged way. I am up this morning again—though still in rather semi-sickly fashion; but trying to collect my wits afresh as to what I was going to say about Italy. However, I had perhaps better not say it—as I take, I rather fear, a more detached view of her attitude than I see that, on the spot, you can easily do. By which I mean that I don't much make out how, as regards the two nations with whom her alliance (originally so unnatural, alas, in the matter of Austria!) she can act in a fashion, any fashion, regardable as straight. I always hated her patching up a friendly relation with Austria, and thereby with Germany as against France and this country; and now what she publishes is that it was good enough for her so long as there was nothing to be got otherwise. If there's anything to be got (by any other alliance) she will go in for that; but she thus gives herself away, as to all her recent past, a bit painfully, doesn't one feel?—and will do so especially if what she has in mind is to cut in on Turkey and so get ahead, for benefit or booty or whatever, of her very own allies. However, I mustn't speak as if we and ours shouldn't be glad of her help, whatever that help is susceptible of amounting to. The situation is one for not looking a gift-horse in the mouth—which only proves, alas, how many hideous and horrible such situations have. [sic] Personally I don't see how she can make up her mind not, in

*spite of all temptations, to remain as still as a mouse. Isn't it rather luridly borne
in upon her that the Germans have only to make up their minds ruthlessly to
violate Switzerland in order, as they say, "to be at Milan, by the Simplon, the
St Gotthard or whatever, in just ten hours"? Ugh!—let me not talk of such
abominations: I don't know why I pretend to it or attempt it! I too am trying
(I don't know whether I told you) to bury my nose in the doing of something
daily; and am finding that, however little I manage on any given occasion, even
that little sustains and inflames and rewards me. I lose myself thus in the mystery
of what "art" can do for one, even with every blest thing against it. And why it
should and how it does and what it means—that is "the funny thing"! However, as I just said, one mustn't look a gift-horse etc. So don't yourself so scruti-
nise this poor animal, but believe me yours all faithfully*

Henry James

In the middle of January there was a violent earthquake in Italy in
which the town of Avezzano was destroyed and much damage was
done in Rome itself. The only intimation of it we had in Capri was
the quiver of hanging perches in birdcages. In the middle of February
a battalion of Welsh Guards was raised and mounted guard at
Buckingham Palace on St David's Day. I had invented the Welsh
Guards in *Sinister Street* and to this day I get an occasional letter asking
me whether I had not been mistaken in making the Welsh Guards
serve in South Africa; was it not the Irish Guards who fought there?

Some time in that spring I had an opportunity to buy for £400 the
whole of the southern face of Monte Solaro—some sixty acres rising
from the sea up to 2,000 feet, including a promontory under which
was the magical Green Grotto. It was a piece of land which must have
looked just the same when Tiberius built his twelve villas on Capri—a
sanctuary of birds and flowers, of lentisk, myrtle and rosemary. The
rocky beach along the sea's edge could only be reached by boat from
the Piccola Marina round the jutting cliff of Monte Solaro. Mimi
Ruggiero and I planned to set a hunchbacked *contadino* to work making
a long winding path from the beach to the summit, which we anticipated would take at least two years to accomplish.

The price of Ventrosa, as the Solaro property was called, would be
10,000 liras or £400. I had the money from royalties on *Sinister Street*;
Mimi was busy getting the various owners to agree when a man arrived
at Casa Solitaria with seventeen carpets to sell. There was one large
silk Persian carpet, two smaller silk Persian rugs, and fourteen large
Persian, Bokhara and Samarkand carpets and rugs. I felt that somehow or other he must have stolen these carpets and was sure he had
when he offered them to me for 10,000 liras. Should I buy Ventrosa, or

should I buy the carpets? It must be one or the other. In the end I decided that Ventrosa would give me more pleasure, and I refused the carpets. From an economic point of view I made a stupid mistake, for those carpets would be worth at the very least £5,000 to-day. However, Ventrosa would give me such delight, as I shall tell in my next Octave, that although after the second war I should sell it for £1,000 I have never regretted the choice I made.

On the fourth of April, when I had written 270 pages of *Guy and Pauline* and still had 125 pages to do, a letter from my old friend Orlo Williams reached me.

> On board the Cunard
> R.M.S. *Franconia*
> *March 23rd* 1915
>
> *I don't know when this will get to you, but I am writing to you by order of Sir Ian Hamilton, Commander-in-Chief of the Mediterranean Expeditionary Force. I'm cipher officer on his Staff with the rank of Captain, having left London at twenty-eight hours' notice. Well, I noticed a day or two ago that he had bought Vol. II of* Sinister Street *to read. So when I was in conversation with him I told him I knew you, etc., and that you had tried for a commission in Egypt. So he said at once, "Write to him and tell him to get into communication with Eddie Marsh[1] and get sent out to me as a Marine or anything, and I will find him a job of some kind, sub-cipher officer or something like that." He says that if I write to you, he will write to Marsh. So there you are. He told me to write to you again to-day, so I am doing it. Our mail went the day before yesterday and when the next will go I can't say. But if you take the opportunity and feel up to it do come. The General Staff are a charming lot of people, and the possibilities of this show are romantic to a degree.*

I sent a telegram to Eddie Marsh, who was Winston Churchill's private secretary, the draft of which was scrawled on the back of some notes for the construction of the last third of the book, and hoped to hear of my commission in about a fortnight. I had not counted on the vigilance of Italian neutrality. On the very next day I was informed by the Naples post-office that my telegram addressed Marsh, Admiralty, London, had been stopped by the censorship. However, on April 14th this telegram arrived:

> *Lieutenant Marines await instructions from Hamilton.*
> *Marsh.*

---

[1] The late Sir Edward Marsh.

Q

And some days afterwards this welcome reply to an excited letter of mine reached Capri:

Admiralty
Whitehall
April 14th, '15.

I hope you will have got my telegram. Your letter came to-day, and I got you made a Lt. R.M. in record time! Sir Ian had written to me about you. I thought the only possible plan was to telegraph to him to send you instructions, and to you to await them, as I didn't know where to tell you to report yourself. As for uniform, God knows where you will get one, but I suppose you can scratch up something that will do when you get there.

I hope you will have started before this arrives, so I won't write a long letter, but I must say how much I enjoyed your 2nd volume of Sinister Street.

Yours,
E. Marsh

What between trying to finish the book and grow a military moustache, suffering agonies from neuritis, and imagining all the various obstacles that might prevent my helping to force the Dardanelles (our intention to do which was by now a topic of the Italian papers) I wonder I did not go permanently off my head. I was half-delirious with pain for the whole of a night and a day and, being under the impression that the Turks had landed and attacked Ventrosa I was with difficulty restrained by Faith and Brooks from sallying forth in my pyjamas to deal with them.

I was duly gazetted on the auspicious date of April 23rd; no orders came. It was just as well; I was finishing *Guy and Pauline* in bed, and if I had set out then, as I certainly should, I might never have got nearer to Gallipoli than Naples. To add to my agony of mind and body came the news of the landing. I can see the headlines in the *Mattino* now. GALLIPOLI SAREBBE GIÀ OCCUPATO? "Good heavens!" I groaned, "we shall be in Constantinople before I leave Capri."

Faith wrote to my mother:

I've never spent such a heartrending day. I was dreading all the time that a wire would come calling him up. He couldn't possibly have gone. He was half-delirious all day, talking of regiments and Turks. I suppose I oughtn't to harrow you with all this but I want you to know how hard it is being for him. The commission came so easily, it seemed as though everything falls into his lap—but now all this luck is counter-balanced by his tragic suffering. He must go. I think he will die if he doesn't, and I am dreading losing him. In his worst agony this morning his heavy boots arrived from the shoemaker studded with nails for active service!

In answer to another despairing telegram from me, Eddie Marsh replied:

Advise waiting have wired Hamilton.

I learnt afterwards that Sir Ian Hamilton had made every effort to get me sent out in time to sail with him to Mudros; my unimportant self was as hard to extract out of the authorities as those precious munitions, of which he was in such urgent need.

The problem of a uniform and equipment which had seemed to Eddie Marsh insoluble except by God was solved by what to my then overheated fancy did appear to be a Divine intervention. Roger Onslow, a delightful Cornish baronet, with his equally delightful wife Muriel had come to Capri a fortnight before, after he was invalided out of one of Kitchener's battalions of the Duke of Cornwall's Light Infantry. He had brought with him a Wolseley valise with Jaeger sleeping-blanket and waterproof sheet, a Webley pistol and fifty cartridges, six khaki shirts, a pair of puttees, and a pair of Bedford-cord breeches. He was hoping to get back into the Army after some months in the south, but he sympathetically sold me what was left of his kit; my adventure seemed a little nearer of attainment.

I finished *Guy and Pauline* on the last day of April, and next day went over to Sorrento, where I had heard of a small yacht for sale belonging to a German and likely to go very cheap. I was right, and I was able to buy it, renaming it the *Fede*.

We had a dinner party on the fourth of May to celebrate the finishing of *Guy and Pauline*; for me there was a faint hope that it might be a farewell party.

It is difficult in the light of later knowledge not to invest such an occasion with an undue significance, not to fancy that the mind misgave some consequence yet hanging in the stars and really did bitterly begin his fearful date with that night's revels.

Yet I could not honestly claim that, when the guests bade me good-bye that night, I had the least premonition they were saying good-bye to somebody whom they would never see again. Looking back at that party now, I can recognize that it marked the end of a period in my life; at the time it seemed to be just the end of another jolly evening.

Our friends in Capri might have been excused for beginning to think that my commission in the Marines was a fiction, my departure to the

Dardanelles a dream; I was almost beginning to think so myself. On the very next morning the longed-for telegram arrived. I was to proceed immediately to Alexandria and there report to the Base Commandant for orders. We telephoned to Naples to find out when there would be a steamer to Alexandria. An hour or so later came a message to say that the steamer *Roma* was leaving for Alexandria on the following afternoon. That meant I should have to be away from Casa Solitaria by four o'clock next morning to catch the boat to Naples.

That white house among fantastic limestone crags half-way up an almost sheer cliff might seem a magical abode to the passer-by even upon a day of drenching *scirocco*; how magical it seemed to me upon that azurous May dawn I could never hope to tell. Drifts of snow-white cistus in the hollows of that stupendous cliff; wreaths of snow-white cloud round Monte Sant' Angelo on the mainland opposite, snow-white at first, but gradually assuming the carnation of living flesh; towering wraiths of the remote Apennine miles away across the Salernian Gulf; the spurge on the slopes above that narrow path cut along the side of the precipice, already dying in dolphin hues at the first hint of the summer sun; no sign of humanity except the white house and those empty columned terraces against the pale blue sea of the morning, and framed in one of those windows, Faith waving to me as I limped round the corner and reached the comparative sophistication of the Via Tragara . . . but this is all incommunicable as sleep.

On the Piazza, though it was not yet five o'clock, there was a good deal of kissing of my hand and cheeks by Capresi friends of every age and station, some of whom had walked all the way down from Anacapri to wish me *"Buon viaggio e presto ritorno!"* Being mercifully free from the least embarrassment under such demonstrations of Southern kindliness, I was able to disappear into the funicular with the bouquets I had been given by those dear people as coolly as a prima donna into the wings.

Mimi Ruggiero came with me to Naples. I wish everyone could have a companion like him at such moments in their lives. Intelligence beamed from his eyes; sympathy flowed from the tips of his expressive fingers. With the manners of a diplomat, the appearance of a genial brigand in an opera, and the gestures of an orator, he used to manage carnations as less gifted gardeners might be able to manage dandelions. He was a raconteur of the first order; he was as good a judge of character as he was of plants; he could cook a plate of *maccherone* with anybody.

Mimi had one adverb of emphasis I never heard anybody else use. From the *"ermeticamente sigillato"* (hermetically sealed) on a tin of paint or whatnot he used *"ermeticamente"* to stress any confident prophecy or positive assertion. As we went into the funicular that morning he turned to me *"Siete sicuro, signore mio, vio ermeticamente tornerete a Capri. Io so—ermeticamente."* (Be sure, sir, you will hermetically come back to Capri. I know—hermetically.) To-day Mimi's son Gigi maintains the tradition of his father; he married Gelsomina, the daughter of our beloved Carolina, and no doubt one of his family will sustain the great Ruggiero tradition started by his grandfather.

We found when we reached Naples that the steamer for Alexandria was to leave at five o'clock the following afternoon, which allowed me plenty of time for limping round the shops to buy the various things I fancied might be useful adjuncts to the siege of Constantinople. I have a note that the fare to Alexandria was 266 liras, or about ten guineas, and another note that when I sailed from Naples there were only 637 liras left in my account at the Credito Italiano; it was a good job I had managed to finish *Guy and Pauline.*

Among other tasks I had to perform during these two sweltering days was getting photographed for my passport. The result was ghastly, and the self-consciousness I began to feel at the prospect of appearing before General Headquarters of the Mediterranean Expeditionary Force became painful. My little Capri barber's attempt to cut my hair to a shortness that might propitiate the natural prejudice of the military against writing fellows had merely produced a capital imitation of a German tourist on his Capri honeymoon; the moustache, which had been grown as a kind of earnest of that uniform whose whereabouts, according to Eddie Marsh, only God had known, was obviously the moustache of one who had never had any previous experience of moustaches.

"Do I really look like this?" I asked Sidney Churchill, our Consul-General, who himself looked like an ancient Assyrian. He, who was not prone to respect appearances, even he shook his head doubtfully. Poor Sidney Churchill! The Anglo-Neapolitan bourgeoisie succeeded in persuading the Foreign Office to transfer him to Lisbon a year or two later and thus separate him from the young woman his affair with whom was considered a scandal; there, after losing his eyesight, he died of a broken heart. When I heard about this I wished the British old maids (alas, a Scottish one was the most poisonous of the lot) whose gossip ruined his end such an ignominious poverty as would match their own mean imaginations.

Churchill was a man who did not suffer fools with the gladness that was expected of a British Consul; he despised too evidently the disloyalty and envy of some of his subordinates. It was Norman Douglas who introduced me to him as he introduced me to many of the good things of this world; Churchill was like a savoury dish such as you only get in countries where the sun is really hot.

The *Roma* was sailing on a Friday; Mimi discovered some compensation for the bad omen in the fact that it was the feast of Our Lady of Pompeii. He secured two of her medals, hung them on fine silver chains, gave me one for an amulet, and took the other back to Faith. He also brought on board a large bunch of deep crimson carnations which he divided into half. *"Per voi e per la signora,"* he told me. He had to leave Naples at half-past three in the hope of reaching Casa Solitaria in time to see the steamer go through the *bocca*—the three miles of sea, that is, which divide Capri from the Sorrentine peninsula. In case Mimi should not arrive in time I sent a telegram to say that the *Roma* would pass about half-past six o'clock and that she would be recognized by her black, blue and white funnel.

However, Mimi had been watching up on the terrace of Casa Solitaria for a long time before the *Roma* did actually pass. It was already dusk when after crossing the Bay of Naples in a scarlet sunset we sailed between the Cape of Campanella and the thousand-feet cliffs of Capri; although it was already too dark to distinguish the figures that were waving from the terrace, I could see the flag. No doubt that old flag was committing a breach of etiquette by flying after sundown, but I was glad to see the Lion Rampant on his field of gold glimmering against the empty egg-shell whiteness of the house. Yes, I know that properly we should have been flying the St Andrew's Cross; no matter, Lyon King was not around to rebuke our presumption.

I went forward and waved my hat to the moth-dim figures on the terrace, but the light was dying as swiftly as the *Roma* was gliding past; Casa Solitaria faded like a ghost upon the battlements of Elsinore. The lamps in the clustered houses on the south side of Capri came into view, with the island soaring in jagged pinnacle on pinnacle against the last embers of the sunset. Nobody who has not approached Capri from the south can have the least idea of the island's architectural magnificence; the view of it from the Bay of Naples is comparatively tame. I sat on a coil of rope in the bows and watched that great Gothic shape turn to a dark cloud along the horizon.

The *faro* on the point of Campanella shone out across the calm sea. I was remembering that sunny March day—how the March sun felt like May!—over a year ago when Faith and I had first explored that promontory, and the wild sweet-peas we gathered there, and the little votive head of Minerva in terra cotta I found among the rubbish of centuries. I was wondering how the great temple of Minerva had looked to sailors coming with the corn-ships from Alexandria to feed Rome, and how I would look on the way to Constantinople unless I was delayed long enough in Alexandria to be able to get hold of some kind of uniform instead of this blue flannel jacket with the Bedford-cord breeches.

A twinge in the sciatic nerve reminded me that the last place I ought to be sitting, if I wanted to be cured of my limp before I landed, was on a coil of rope in the bows of a steamer an hour after sunset. So I went below and studied my fellow-passengers in the saloon.

For the last half-dozen pages I have used most of what I wrote at the beginning of my book *Gallipoli Memories*[1] in 1929. After I have written about an experience I let the details pass from my memory. Without referring to what I wrote thirty-five years ago I should not have been able to recapture these hours which when I look back at them mark like a deep gorge the end of a period of my life.

[1] Paper-back edition published by Panther in 1965.

APPENDIX A

LIFE AND DEATH ON CHELSEA BRIDGE

To H.W.H. ("Dick" Hewlett)

What whisper of Love's wings in sudden flight?
What chord struck on the scattered notes of Chance
Brought you and me upon this bridge to-night?

You say it was the shaft of Circumstance,
But metaphors will not illuminate
The bleak unknown—see how the shore-lamps dance

And quiver in the silent water—straight
Ahead a barge comes creaking through the gloom.
Such things we notice though we see our fate

Suspended plainly from the savage loom,
The shears held ready to destroy or spare
And the three Sisters heedless of our doom.

God knows, my love, I would not have you stare
Too fixedly: you will not hold the seam:
The Sisters use sharp scissors, O beware!

How furtive flows the black untroubled stream
Where many men have leapt intent to try
To solve all riddles—how the shore-lamps gleam—

Strange in such wise to cheat perplexity!
What if the meaning slept for aye unknown
And Hell were one eternal sobbing Why?

How warm that hand of yours in mine has grown—
Ah! let me hold it—is it yours or mine?
The roar of London lessens. Time has flown,

And we are left to seek that anodyne,
That sense, which night and water sometimes give,
Of sleeping drowsed by fumes of ancient wine.

This hour is not like others fugitive,
And yet it has no niche in time or space,
This hour when you and I alone can live.

Ah! let your hair blow all about my face:
It brings a memory of April dawns,
And grasses waving in a windy place.

I hear again the laugh of hidden Fauns,
The thud of Centaurs sweeping o'er the down,
Pan crying on the dewy upland lawns.

You do not understand this wish to drown?
Why, nor do I in reasoned words, and yet
Many with less have won a martyr's crown.

That hansom rattles like a castanet:
Haply within two lovers kiss, as I'd
Kiss you if this bridge were an oubliette.

You start, nay, think no more of suicide,
I thought of love's remorse, remembering
How *she* once said that you were like a bride.

We sit perched on a feather from the wing
Of the immeasurable Night that broods
Upon the earth: sometimes we seem to swing

Right out above a black abyss, where floods
Of elemental passions seethe and boil—
Yet are these passions more than Passion's moods?

I ask you this—we ought not to despoil
Love's garden of its multitudinous flowers,
And on one sterile weed waste fruitful soil.

Is this an empty paradise of ours,
Raised by enchantment, fading all too soon,
And leaving but a tale of ruined hours?

Look, love, behind us where the waning moon
Rides ominous and red o'er Westminster!
The very wind comes with a baleful tune.

I never saw the moon so sinister,
Or feared a planet's influence before;
But then, I had not yet been false to *her*,

I had not stabbed her true love to the core.
Put your cool arms around me utterly,
Close, hold me closer, and I doubt no more.

You say you are in love with Love, not me,
But there's the fire in which you blindly trod
And you will be consumed like Semele,

Unless you steel your heart against the god,,
And are content to glorify the man.
('Twas rash of Psyche to suppose a clod.)

Miranda, had she seen but Caliban
Might well have made a hero of a brute,
And in such adoration grown as wan

As any love-sick maid of poet's lute.
Then sudden Ferdinand was in the world
To set her lips afire, who found them mute.

How like a violin your hand has curled
Itself in mine, our fingers interwove—
See that long barge's smoke by lamps empearled.

We must take heed that skeletons of Love
Haunt not his house, nor ever let Remorse
And Bitter Memories like Gorgons move

With vile intent along his corridors,
So that the God of Love becomes a bust
Carved out of stone, to glorify a corse.

The wind is rising—that was a keen gust!
Along the embankment, quite deserted now,
There blows a moon-parched whirling cloud of dust.

Your hand waits resting on the fateful plough:
So look not back, your furrow lies ahead,
Nor ask in querulous accents why or how.

Tread you the grapes within the winepress, tread,
Nor ask what far-off gardener grew the tree;
That knowledge will not make the juice more red.

A fatalist? yes, if you leave will free;
If not, you say the world's an ill-timed jest.
I think things happen for the good, and we

Work on them till we make them for the best.
It's simple, this philosophy of mine
And solves some riddles, even the crookedest.

Indeed it's foolish for us to repine;
Poets fall into greatness, ignorant,
Yet still can worship the immortal Nine.

Let's clear the air of sentiment and cant.
I heard your heart beat, and you caught my eyes—
A man, a maid: what cause to gasp or rant?

Fata Morgana is a hollow prize
And leaves her dupe exhausted, torn by briars,
To beat upon the gates of Paradise.

Idealists are sentimental liars
Who build an iridescent dome of glass,
And people it with impotent Desires.

But you and I will never cry Alas,
Like penitents who, though absolved from sin,
Lack still the courage to approach the Mass.

I've talked enough—we'll let the Sisters spin
Their threads and jig about their puppet-show.
They've tangled ours; but still—the threads are thin,

And we can cut them in the river's flow:
Our souls would jig for ever in the stream
Among the dancing shore-lamps down below.

We'd spoil the high Gods' laughter, wreck the scheme
Made for their mirth;—but Hamlet sheathed his sword
Before an unimaginable dream.

What if we acted still and spoke no word
Upon the phantom stage of death, flung hence
To jig for ever from a ghostly cord,

No more to merry gods as audience,
But each to his own body's soulless flesh,
That blinks at him without intelligence?

Will any man dare to cut through the mesh
Which—as he thinks—is wound about his will,
And wade reliant through his vice's plesh,

Reliant on himself and some mute Jill,
Who, patient follower, is fain to trust
Her viewless soul for him to cure or kill?

See how the water flickers to the gust,
Laps the dark pier and ripples up the beach!
Shall we fling obligations to the dust,

And spurning fools go blindly forward, each
Kept to the firm track by the other's hand
Held out?—somewhere in Heaven there is a breach!

God send we find it! why, the gulf is spanned
Already, sweet; did you not hear me pray?
That was confiding faith, you understand.

That's victory for God, not me; half-way
To Paradise you'll find a praying-stool;
If once you kneel, 'tis sure that you obey.

So on we chatter while the deepest pool
Waits gaping for us there below—why not?
One leap, one cry! and then the water cool,

Swirling around us like a widening blot
Of ink; a momentary lightning-flash
Will cleave the past, and Life will be forgot,

For aye forgot and ended! is it rash
So to approach Death, the late lingerer,
Upon his road? ah! grey as a young ash.

In frost, did you not see a figure stir
In the pale lamplight? is it Death? ah no!
While we demurred some soul brooked no demur,

And, leaping from the parapet below,
Smiled to meet Death. Ah God! I saw her face,
White, ghastly white upon the river's flow!
And see, the dawn is creeping up apace!

Home! home! there's horror in the morning air!

APPENDIX B

It is with a consciousness of deep humility that I take up my pen to write these words about Belgium. When others have pleaded her case so much more worthily than I can ever hope to plead it and when I have seen even the most passionate eloquence turn to an idiot's tale signifying nothing in its attempt to express a nation's crucifixion, I ask myself by what right I dare intrude with these poor words of mine.

The cities of Belgium are razed and her people are crying out for bread. Louvain is become a heap of rubbish about which women scratch aimlessly: Brussels that once was a gay princess has been debased to the similitude of a starving drab: in Charleroi and Dendermonde, in Maestricht and Blankenberghe the children are whimpering for food: in Antwerp the children have clawed their victuals from the hands of the German soldiers: in the windows of Malines, windows that now are as empty as the eye-sockets of a skull, little ghosts are peering, not the ghosts of the happier dead, but the ghosts made by that hunger which is Death-in-Life.

The world has read of the destruction of cathedrals and shuddered for the loss of great monuments of art: the world has uttered paeans for the heroism of a nation that esteemed honour above gain and laid down her life for an ideal: it is not too much to say that the world has actually been baptized again in the blood of Belgium. Now comes a paler story and one that is horrible with all that despair can bring of horror. Women stand shivering in the winter slush as they wait for as much bread as once upon a time they would have seen thrown away without a second glance. Women are driven back at the point of the bayonet, as they fight even for salt. Children are kneeling to gnaw at the sodden roots of the fields. Rich and poor must see themselves degraded from their humanity to lead the lives of rats. Nothing that misfortune can give of uncleanliness and indignity, of age and youth humiliated, of pain and hunger has been spared to Belgium. Yet with all that they have endured, and with all that, whatever the world's compassion, they must still endure, seven million Belgians are still alive in the husk of what was once a country. They may be trampled upon by the march of the conqueror: they may be denied all news of their devoted army: they may be taxed and fined and paid for their labour with bits of paper: they may be rained upon and snowed upon and frozen and thawed and frozen again: the very foundations of their shorn houses may be lost like the foundations of Babylon and Troy: the future may be more black than the blackened shells of their churches: they may have lost mothers and sisters and daughters in that vile fog which follows in the wake of war: they may have lost fathers and sons and brothers, some gloriously on the field of battle, some with bandaged eyes shot against the doors of their own cottages not less gloriously: and yet seven million Belgians are alive in Belgium.

But—and if ever that conjunction was fraught with a heavy alternative, it is fraught with it now—these people will not be alive much longer unless the sum of five million dollars is found every month to pay for food and for the transport of food to Belgium. I wish that "but" could be printed in letters of blood—in letters of blood, did I say? Nay, rather in letters of imperishable fire that would burn the alternative into the eyesight of our humanity fed so full with horrors as scarcely to be able any more to heed their reiteration. The fate of these seven million people is the world's responsibility. This is not the moment to try to say who is guilty of their state: the wrangling of diplomats and the clash of armies will not drown the moans of seven millions starving for bread. We have read before 1914 of earthquakes, of pestilence and shipwrecks, of railway accidents and mining disasters; and yet if all the lives lost in fifty years by sudden visitation of calamity were added together, they would not nearly equal the sum of these poeple who are at this moment actually dependent for the breath of life upon five million dollars a month. It is costing the powers of Europe more than fifty million dollars a day and ten thousand lives a day to determine the future of the country; let us at least three hundred times as cheaply preserve seven million lives for that country. We read now (such a shuttlecock have we made of human life) in a small paragraph of losses that a year ago would have occupied a journal for days with their harrowing narration. Yet even this dreadful induration of our senses must be softened by the prospect of seven millions starving slowly to death. How for ever it haunts one to meet in the swirl of some great city's tide of humanity the eyes of a starving man; but at least in a city that wretched creature, could he conquer his pride or his scruples, might obtain food by breaking the window of a baker's shop. These seven millions cannot do that. Their land is empty of nourishment. When the last scraggy cabbage-stalk is devoured, when the last hen has starved, when the last rind of cheese had been raked out of the darkest corner of the desolate house, unless they can nourish themselves upon the earth of the land to protect the violation of which they have martyred themselves, these seven millions must die. And when they die, Belgium is dead. What will peace bring to the world then? To what shall we ever look forward again? If these people are allowed to die while there is food on the earth, it were better that the earth should die like the moon and humanity itself become not even a name among the spheres of the universe.

For the fact that these seven million Belgians are still alive we owe an unparagoned debt of gratitude to the American Commission for Relief: and because of the amazing difficulties which that commission has already surmounted, one is tempted to place an even greater, an even more strenuously exacting faith for the future in the American people. This commission was organized by American citizens living in London. Amid the blood and tears of Europe a few gentlemen resolved that the ultimate reproach of a people's starvation should not be levelled against this merciless time of ours: it was Mr Brand Whitlock, that fine Mayor of Toledo and now the American Minister in Brussels, who made the first appeal. He saw the starvation and caring nothing for the pettiness of diplomatic restraint he appealed for help through the American Ambassador in London. Dr Nelson Page upon his own initiative appointed a committee of American citizens resident in London in order that they might apply themselves to organize the feeding of a nation. Consider how fantastic and improbable that scheme must have looked and think of the stupendous quixotry of it. War which is resorted to for the solution of political problems offers no solution for the misery it entails upon humanity. War with its myriad tentacles squeezing the life out of Europe and squirting forth a murky and loathsome juice to poison the tide of pity, was nevertheless impotent against the determination of these men. They were armed with the conviction that their countrymen at home would support them and with a serene faith that has already been magnificently justified they brushed aside the objections of the chancelleries and walked over the prejudices of generals. Nor would they listen to the croaking of financiers who spoke of the cost, and their resolution prevailed even against the uncertainty of shippers who pointed out the restriction upon the export and import of foodstuffs. Finally they allayed the doubts of the Allies when they procured from the Germans an assurance that the relief would be allowed and be distributed: indeed they did more: they persuaded the Germans to facilitate the distribution.

The organizer and chairman of the Commission was Mr H. C. Hoover, a Californian and probably the greatest mining expert in the world. This gentleman had already presided over the American Relief

Committee which financed over 10,000 Americans and sent them back to America in the early weeks of the war. Night and day for a month Mr Hoover, Colonel Hussiker, Captain Lucey, Mr John B. White, Mr Edgar Richard, Mr Millard Slater and other well-known Americans living in London devoted the whole of their time to the colossal task of proving to the warring governments of Europe the feasibleness, more the positive success of their scheme for the relief of Belgium. They assimilated into one perfect organization known as the Commission for Relief in Belgium, the Belgians' own central committee at Brussels and the various charitable activities of Italy and Spain. They did not appeal to the people of England, but they got without asking thousands of dollars: and from America they have received millions already. Thirty-eight steamers with an aggregate tonnage of 150,000 are speeding at full steam across the Atlantic bringing 128,000 tons of food valued at over eight million dollars and costing in collection, shipping and delivery another two millions. But more is wanted. Five million dollars every month is wanted to keep seven million Belgians from dying of hunger amid the ruins of their houses and churches.

The opportunity of America at this moment is one that has surely never been offered to any nation before in the history of the world. The task of preserving from the lingering death of hunger seven million human beings demands self-sacrifice, determination and magnanimity. Great victories on the field of battle have been won by these virtues, but every victory in war carries with it also the horror and the misery of war. A victory is offered to the American people that will not cloud a star or smirch a stripe upon her banner. A victory is offered that will indeed add to her banner a star which may seem more bright than any star there posited. There is no one in that mighty republic who can afford not to give: there is no one who can afford to know that a nickel given now will keep a child alive for two days. This is not an appeal which calls for money about the spending of which efficaciously there can be any doubt or delay. The need is instant. Merely a cent given now is to save a child drowning in shallow water before your eyes. No one would allow that to happen without calling himself a coward for the rest of his life: surely no one will think a nickel too much to give.

But I do not write these words because I have the least doubt that America will give again and again as generously as she has already given. The thought is to me unimaginable. These words of mine are intended to try however inadequately to bring before the notice of an immense and charitable people the violent need for haste in giving.

R

People are dying now who can be saved: those who have been kept alive have been only kept alive by America in defiance of the inexorable results of war.

When the history of this time is written to the last red streak, when the last bugle has sounded and the last widow is left to her mourning: when the heroes of all the warring nations have fought their last fight, and Europe turns to regard the bloody work she has accomplished, you, O great republic, must say, "We took not one life. We robbed not one mother of her son nor any woman of her lover. We saved seven millions from a slow inglorious death."

They are grateful already in Belgium. A well-known New York lawyer, who was travelling by special permission from the German authorities in order that he might see personally the work that was being done by the American Commission for Relief, speaks of many instances of appreciation accorded to him by a forlorn people. Amongst others he tells how in one village a woman with a child on one arm and a loaf of the Commission's bread on the other came up to his car and touched with her lips the little flag of the stars and stripes fluttering upon the bonnet. "For the love I bear your flag," she said. "It has saved our lives."

Whoever in America whether he be in New York or Illinois, in Iowa or Texas or California, Louisiana or Michigan, in Virginia or Tennessee, in Montana or Ohio or Arizona, gives at this moment a nickel, offers a loaf to a starving woman and the flag of his country to be saluted by the admiration and affection of the civilized world.

INDEX

OCTAVE THREE AND FOUR

R*